D1809908

COLOUR FOR TEXTILES: A USER'S HANDBOOK

Copyright © 1993 Society of Dyers and Colourists. All rights reserved. No part of this publication may be reproduced, stored in a retrieval system or transmitted in any form or by any means without the prior permission of the copyright owners.

Published by the Society of Dyers and Colourists, PO Box 244, Perkin House, 82 Grattan Road, Bradford, West Yorkshire BD1 2JB, England, on behalf of the Dyers' Company Publications Trust.

This book was produced under the auspices of the Dyers' Company Publications Trust. The Trust was instituted by the Worshipful Company of Dyers of the City of London in 1971 to encourage the publication of textbooks and other aids to learning in the science and technology of colour and coloration and related fields. The Society of Dyers and Colourists acts as trustee to the fund, its Textbooks Committee being the Trust's technical subcommittee.

Typeset by the Society of Dyers and Colourists and printed by Staples Printers Rochester Ltd and Steffprint Ltd, Keighley.

ISBN 0 901956 56 2

Colour for textiles
A user's handbook

Wilfred Ingamells PhD MSc CText FTI CCol FSDC

School of Home Economics and Institutional Management, University of Wales, Cardiff, UK

1993

Society of Dyers and Colourists

Preface

For many years the Society of Dyers and Colourists has been aware of the need for a book covering the basic science and technology of textile coloration for the benefit of readers without a detailed scientific background. In the mid-1980s the late Dr Frank Jones of the University of Leeds started to write such a book, but sadly he died before he could complete this worthwhile task. The torch was then passed to me, with the brief to prepare a work for those who probably lack science qualifications at A-level but who nevertheless need to become familiar to some extent with the work of the professional colourist. The target readership included people working in nontechnical capacities in industry, and students of home economics, textile design and management. The aim is to introduce such readers to the relevant technological background and the basic principles of coloration, and show how colour is assessed objectively in modern industry.

I am grateful to several people for their assistance, including Paul Dinsdale (the Society's editor), Jean Macqueen, for her expert editorial work on the manuscript and index, and Carol Davies, for painstaking typesetting and layout. I also acknowledge the Textile Institute, Manchester, for permission to reproduce Figures 4.12, 4.13, 6.7, 6.9, 6.10 and 6.12, and Miss B Lomas of the Textile Technology Department, UMIST, Manchester, for permission to reproduce Figures 4.1 and 4.2, and for kindly providing suitable copies.

WILFRED INGAMELLS

Contents

CHAPTER ONE

Introduction and the role of testing

Introduction

The pleasure derived from imparting colour to clothing has existed since the time of the earliest civilisations; a world of fashion without colour is impossible to imagine. Coloration processes produce the most visible results of all the finishing operations carried out during the preparation of textile goods. As such they reveal both the care taken with the coloration and the degree of control exercised during other stages of the manufacturing process.

Dye uptake is dependent on many factors. The result of unplanned variations in the conditions of operation during any step of the manufacturing chain may not become apparent until the fabric is dyed. Variations in temperature during the texturising of synthetic fibres, or irregular changes of tension during weaving, can lead to the development of either darker or lighter stripes after dyeing, wherever the affected yarns are incorporated into the fabric. Freedom from manufacturing faults and adequate resistance to the various treatments likely to be received by the goods during use are important to a consumer. Intensive efforts are therefore made to ensure that the coloration of fabric and yarn conforms to well-defined specifications. Commercial success in the modern coloration industry depends upon technical efficiency at all levels of activity, and this requires an appreciation of the properties of dyes and fibres, the way in which both behave during use and the objective manner in which the results of coloration processes are represented.

Origins of textile dyeing

The origins of dyeing are uncertain, but it is believed that coloured fabrics found in the ancient tombs of Egypt were in existence before 2500 BC. It is likely that the ancient art of dyeing originally spread westwards from India, and it may well have been accidental staining from berries and fruit juices that initially stimulated its development.

The use of colouring materials from plants (using roots, stems, leaves, flowers, fruit, seeds and lichens) and from the animal kingdom (using insects and shellfish) continued until the latter part of the nineteenth century. During the Middle Ages relatively few dyes were available, and European dyers imported their dyes from the Middle and Far East. During the fifteenth and sixteenth centuries their sources extended to the Americas with the discovery there of previously unknown natural dyes. It was during this period, when Spain and Portugal became prominent in the art of dyeing, that the Portuguese discovered a tree in South America from which a very desirable red dye could be extracted. In fact the tree was also known to the inhabitants of the Anderman Islands in the thirteenth century as 'sappan', but in its South American location it was called 'brazil'. For this reason the Portuguese called the area in which it was found Terra de Brazil, and thus the name of the country was derived from the dye rather than the other way around.

The colour range of the natural dyes could be expanded to a limited extent by treating the fabric or yarn with metal salts (mordanting). Some of the results obtained on wool are illustrated in Plate 1 [1]. Even so the only blue dye of the time was indigo, extracted either from the indigo plant (*Indigofera* sp.) or from woad (a different species of plant which gave a colour of less satisfactory performance), and greatly valued because of its excellent fastness to light.

Some form of quality appraisal existed even in ancient times. For example, the use of the dye Tyrian purple, with its high resistance to daylight, was restricted to the garments of those in authority. Tyrian purple was extracted from shellfish in the eastern Mediterranean, and was the most highly prized and expensive dye of classical times, being used for the robes of the kings of Medea and the royal houses of Persia, Babylon and Syria, as well as for the togas of Roman emperors. It ranked alongside indigo as one of the few natural dyes with resistance to fading. The high cost of this dye in ancient times is indicated by the quantity of sea snails required to provide sufficient extract for the purposes of dyeing. The efforts of Friedlander may be quoted as an example. During his elucidation of the chemical structure of the colour, he needed 12 000 of the creatures to obtain just 1.4 g of the dye!

Nowadays, when care of the environment is a major issue, it is tempting to assume that the use of natural colours is an environmentally friendly alternative to present-day practice. Unfortunately such assumptions change to doubts after the imagination has been stimulated by the details in Figure 1.1, which shows a description of the application of the once widely used Turkey red dye, obtained from the roots of the madder plant.

Indigo was the only natural dye to yield blue shades; its fastness to light was outstanding when compared with other natural dyes. As a result it achieved particular importance. Even so, the bacterial fermentation process used for its extraction from either *Indigofera* or woad plants was highly unpleasant and prompted Queen Elizabeth I to order the curtailment of the production of woad.

Compared with the extensive lists of dyes in today's *Colour Index*, the colorants in use up to the nineteenth century were few in number. The more important ones are listed in Table 1.1. The last natural dye to be used commercially was logwood, which remained in use until the 1940s.

Mordanting
Treat the cloth with sour olive oil, pearl ash, sheep's dung and water. Dry in warm air. Repeat seven or eight times.

Tanning
Treat in a decoction of nut-galls. Dry. Treat with neutralised alum. Age for three to four days. Treat with warm water containing ground chalk.

Dyeing
Treat with extract of madder root.

Cleaning
Treat two or three times with salt solution.

Figure 1.1 *Recipe for the application of Turkey red*

Synthetic dyes

The most significant event in the recent history of coloration was the discovery by W H Perkin in 1856 of the first dye to be obtained by synthesis rather than by tedious extraction from natural products, which he named mauveine. Thousands of dyes have since been made by synthesis, and dye manufacture has become a significant part of the chemical industry. Natural dyes have now been superseded, along with the need for extensive pretreatments with mordants. Colorants with chemical and physical properties better suited to contemporary demands have been synthesised, sometimes aiding the development and extension of the use of particular products. For example, the development of synthetic fibres such as polyester and cellulose triacetate would have been severely hindered without the design and synthesis of dyes with appropriate properties. These fibres do not absorb water to any marked extent and therefore the water-soluble dyes available at the time of their discovery could not be used. Dyes and pigments can now be synthesised for almost any purpose, and consumers can be assured of satisfaction with the

Table 1.1 Colours of some natural dyes

Dye	Colour
Alkanet	Violet-grey
Annatto	Red
Barwood	Red-brown
Brazilwood	Red-brown
Camwood	Red-brown
Cochineal	Scarlet
Fustic	Yellow
Indigo	Blue
Lac	Scarlet
Logwood	Purple-black
Madder	Red
Orchil	Purple
Persian berries	Yellow
Quercitron	Yellow
Saffron	Orange
Sanderswood	Red
Turmeric	Yellow
Weld	Yellow

properties of coloured fabric during use. The initial sign of confidence came from Sir James Morton, the first member of the textile trade to offer a replacement of the fabric if its resistance to fading in light and ordinary washing was not sustained during the product's lifetime.

The present-day consumer can now assume that purchased goods will be fit for their purpose because the industry is able to provide assurances of product quality by working to voluntarily agreed standards. It has taken time for the concept of providing consumer reassurance to develop. The mechanisms now adopted started to evolve during the industrial revolution through cooperation between producers of basic products and the manufacturing industry. Although it was some time later that they were adopted and rigorously applied in the textile industry, the efforts made at that time were the forerunners of current quality assurance schemes.

Development of standards

The advantages of working to standards first became established during the development of the railways. Easier transportation of goods from one place to another removed the need to obtain components locally, but small variations in the dimensions and quality of goods made in different locations caused difficulties in that the buyer could not know exactly what to expect. This was an inconvenient source of the mismatch of components in construction work. For instance, variations in the cross-sectional shape of steel girders and in the screw threads of nuts and bolts highlighted the advantages of standardisation – the reason why the familiar Whitworth screw thread was adopted as a standard during this period.

The need to manufacture goods in different parts of the country during the two world wars intensified efforts to bring uniformity in production through the use of voluntary standards and specifications. The British Standards Institution (BSI) took up this responsibility and an illuminating account of the origin, development and introduction of standards has been published [2].

During World War 2 various standard specifications were produced for textile goods, in particular for blackout material. It was at this time that the BSI began to formulate standards relevant to consumer goods. The best use had to be made of very scarce resources, and by working to specified standards manufacturers supported the 'Utility' scheme operated at the time by providing clothing and household textiles of predictable quality. The domestic consumer derived further help from the specifications for the sizes of a wide range of children's clothing; nowadays, however, articles of clothing are no longer labelled with garment measurements but according to a system based on body size.

After the war the Utility scheme was eventually abandoned in favour of informative labelling. This was due in part to a survey carried out by the Consumer Advisory Council, which revealed a strong desire among the public to receive more safety information about textile goods. Children's clothing, blankets, furnishing fabrics and carpets featured high on their list of priorities. Some time later various tragic accidents involving burning textiles directed attention to the development of standards for flame-resistant fabrics and the fillings of mattresses and pillows.

At the time of World War 2 the natural fibres cotton, linen, silk and wool and the synthetic fibres viscose, secondary acetate and cuprammonium rayon were the only ones available. Subsequently, with the intensive development of synthetic fibres and production methods, modern fabrics have become so multifarious that neither the sales person nor the purchaser can be expected to predict the performance of textile products using only personal experience. The mixing of natural with synthetic fibres to give blends with some of the characteristics of each component, and the development of finishes that impart to the synthetics characteristics previously associated with natural fibres, have contributed to the complexity of the situation. Consequently the use of informative labels has become a most appropriate way of providing a measure of quality assurance. The use of hallmarks on gold and silver jewellery by craftsmen to assure their customers of the quality of their goods can be traced back to the Middle Ages, but the origin of labelling schemes for textile goods is a concept of modern times.

There was considerable consumer dissatisfaction with synthetic dyes produced during the first 50 years of their existence [3]. Their convenience of application was counteracted by poor resistance to both daylight and washing. This stimulated the continuing search for dyes with improved resistance to a variety of destructive agencies, and as progress was made manufacturers began to approve various labels with colour fastness implications. The Sundour label of Sir James Morton was probably the first example; many other manufacturers' brand-name labels, however, did not indicate the quality of the dyes used. Some dye manufacturers attempted to help the consumer by approving labels for fabric dyed with particular dyes selected for their high standard of fastness. Similarly fibre manufacturers imposed the requirement for the fibre content of the fabric to appear on the label, whilst other labels have been promoted by dyers and printers, manufacturers of detergents or appliances, retail organisations and consumer-oriented magazines. At the present time an overview of the International Care Labelling Scheme, discussed in Chapter 2, is maintained by the Home Laundering Consultative Committee.

The familiar Kitemark now attached to a wide range of goods to indicate quality assurance was first introduced in the 1950s. Its presence on an article is a visible means of assurance, denoting conformance to relevant standards developed through the BSI.

The initial standards for textiles were concerned mainly with constructional details. But the continuing development of domestic appliances and of new materials has led to the provision of labels containing more detailed information relevant to the performance of manufactured textile goods during use. For the consumer, quality assurance is now indicated through labels that show both fibre content and information on aftercare. In addition the manufacturers benefit from the efforts of their suppliers in ensuring that the raw materials and the products of intermediate stages of manufacture will also match agreed standards.

The fastness of dyes to various agencies is of particular relevance to the subject matter of this book, and voluntary coordinated activity in this sphere began in 1927 with the Fastness Tests Committee of the Society of Dyers and Colourists. Since that time the committee has been responsible for the development and continuous review of a wide range of appropriate fastness tests for dyed materials, of which full accounts are to be found in other publications [4,5].

The International Organisation for Standardisation (ISO) was formed in 1947 and a technical committee, the Colour Fastness Subcommittee, became responsible for bringing uniformity to the various systems adopted in different parts of the world. The internationally agreed standard test procedures recommended by that committee are now automatically adopted as British Standards.

The concept of quality assurance is now well documented and embraces all facets of production, services and management, with British Standards having been developed for every aspect of related activity, most of which are covered in appropriate publications [6].

Requirements for the adoption of standard quality procedures appropriate to both large and small organisations are detailed in a far-reaching British Standard, BS 5750. It covers the organisation, management and documentation of quality control procedures from the initial purchase of raw materials to the appraisal and delivery of the goods or service, including matters relevant to process design and staff training. Like many other industrialists, textile manufacturers are increasingly following the principles laid down in BS 5750.

Significance of quality in relation to coloured goods

Quality as defined by the BSI is 'the totality of features or characteristics of a product or service that bear on its ability to satisfy a given need' [6]. From the point of view of the retailer this also involves the *value* of a product as represented by the relationship: value = quality/price [7].

The implication of this relationship to a company concerned with providing quality and value is that price and quality are balanced. Clearly there is no point in providing perfection of quality if the added cost is so high that the value of the goods falls to a level too low for the purpose which the customer has in mind.

Perception of quality varies from one person to another, depending upon his or her immediate needs. Thus to a commercial buyer price, delivery date, colour and style may be more important than technical quality. To an interior decorator the fastness to light of curtains for the stage of a cinema or theatre is less important than their aesthetic properties. On the other hand, the same person would regard fastness to light as of prime importance if asked to provide curtains for a south-facing window of a seaside hotel. Similarly a wedding dress does not require the same fastness specifications as a child's anorak. Many highly fashionable and expensive goods bearing brand names have a low quality in objective terms, and the simple relationship cannot always be valid when choice is made entirely on subjective grounds. The final judgement of the consumer with regard to quality and value is influenced by his or her perception of both subjective and objective factors. This book, however, deals with only the objective factors involved with coloration. Accordingly the first consideration will be the principles of some of the underlying testing procedures used by manufacturers in establishing consistency and quality during the preparation and use of their products.

Standards related to coloration

The development of standards has been of great value to the colourist in both the provision of objective assessments and the transmission of relevant information between dye manufacturer and dye users. The general groupings of British Standards cover a wide range, including the following:

(a)   glossaries, which provide agreed definitions of terminology in specialist fields of activity

(b)   dimensional standards, which provide for interchangeability of manufactured components from different sources

(c)   performance standards for the specification of expected performance

(d)   standard methods of test with precise and detailed specification of operation that are of particular use in setting up quality assurance schemes

(e)   codes of practice for the design, installation, maintenance and servicing of equipment or services.

These are not the only source of standard definitions, however, and readers may also find other references to be of equal value when becoming acquainted with terms used in the technology of the coloration of textiles [8,9]. The subject matter of this area of study falls into the fourth category of British Standards, i.e. standard methods of test.

Results from the standard methods of test are widely used for the objective appraisal of the behaviour of dyes under an extensive range of circumstances [10]. Once the commercial decisions about an appropriate level of fastness have been taken, a performance specification may be formulated and dyes selected for the purpose in hand.

Principles of colour fastness testing

Appraisal of the performance of a dye begins at the time of its synthesis and ends with tests designed to indicate the level of performance during its use. Obviously, consumer goods must have satisfactory resistance to domestic cleaning treatments and a reasonable resistance to fading under the action of daylight, but many other factors also need to be considered if the requirements of the textile finisher and dyer are to be met. In some cases a very high level of fastness is provided for the consumer because the dyes used are expected to withstand processing conditions that are far more severe than any likely to be encountered during normal use. In other cases special efforts are made to find new dyes that will withstand particularly intensive conditions associated with the use of a new product.

The wide-ranging end uses associated with coloured textiles are accommodated by the development of realistic test methods for the fastness to wet treatments. These often involve the formulation of appropriate variations in the severity of the testing conditions. The objective assessment of the effects obtained are usually made on the basis of visual comparison of the intensity of any change in the appearance of the sample with calibrated standard *grey scales*. The fastness of the coloured textile is then rated numerically according to the contrast step in the scale that matches the intensity of the observed change. The test is twofold: changes in both the depth of the dyeing and the staining of previously undyed fabric in the presence of the test pattern are examined, although different scales are used for the assessment. These are shown in Figure 1.2.

After the dyed material has been subjected to the test conditions, the extent of staining is assessed by placing a sample of the unstained material alongside the stained material. A judgement of the degree of contrast between the two is then made by comparison with the relevant steps in the grey scale under the recommended conditions of illumination. The scale used for staining (BS 1006:A03:1978) covers five full steps arranged in geometrical progression.

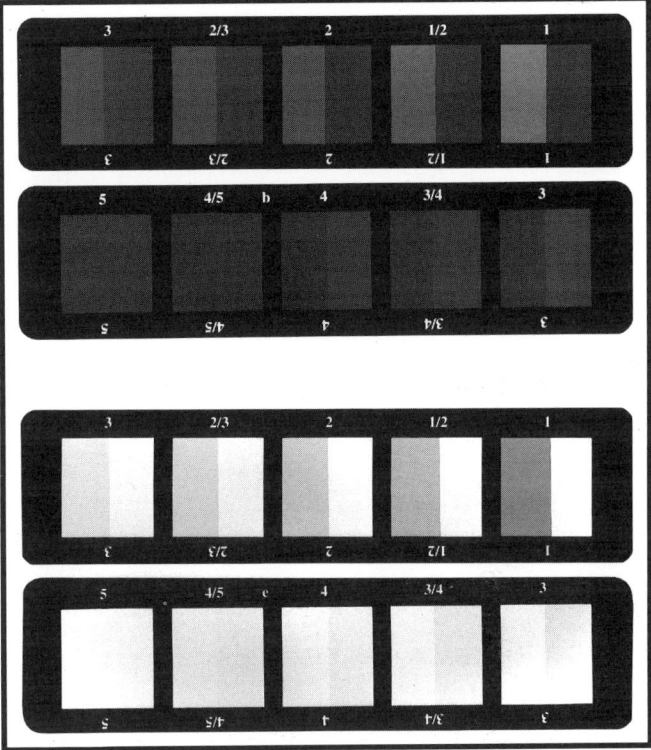

Figure 1.2 Grey scales: (top) the scale used for the assessment of colour change in the sample, (bottom) the scale used to assess staining

When no staining occurs a rating of 5 is appropriate but the numerical rating decreases as the staining worsens. Half-steps in the grey scale are provided to increase the precision of the assessment.

The scale for assessing the change in colour is used in a similar manner to compare the treated and the untreated dyed fabrics, but in this case the rating may be supplemented by letters to indicate an accompanying change of hue or brightness [11]. For example, the change may be indicated by a number alone to indicate a loss in depth only, but the number followed by a letter indicates other changes; for example 3 W, Bl, D signifies that a loss in depth (weaker) corresponding to grade 3 of the grey scale is accompanied by a change in hue towards blue and that the pattern has become duller. According to convention the qualifiers are always placed in order of magnitude. The terms used for this purpose are shown in Table 1.2 overleaf, and are discussed further in Chapter 7 (page 140).

Fastness to light is assessed using a different set of standards, which enable account to be taken of the variability in the quality of both natural and artificial light sources and in the ambient

Table 1.2 Terms used for the qualitative description of colour changes

Redder (R)	Weaker (W)	Duller (D)
Yellower (Y)	Stronger (Str)	Brighter (Br)
Bluer (Bl)		
Greener (G)		

conditions of weathering. The standards recommended by ISO for this purpose consist of eight blue dyeings on wool, of which No. 1 provides the lowest rating and No. 8 the highest. Each successive standard requires twice the exposure time of the one below in the series to cause the same degree of fading (Plate 2). As with other standard tests, the conditions of exposure are rigorously specified and include exposure to standardised sources of artificial light as well as to daylight.

Standard depths of shade

In addition to the inherent resistance of a particular dye–fibre combination to the agency in question, the assessment is also dependent upon the depth of the colour. Obviously a deeper dyeing of poor fastness to wet treatments will release more dye into the water than will a paler dyeing, and thus both the degree of staining and the visual effect on the coloured pattern itself will be affected. The results from individual fastness tests are therefore characterised by reference to one of a series of standard depths of shades. The ISO has recommended the use of 20 reference colours, for which a series of six standard depths are displayed. These are known as 2/1, 1/1, 1/3, 1/6, 1/12 and 1/25 standard depths respectively [12]. They are produced on a matt wool gabardine cloth and on a lustrous bright viscose fabric; whenever tests are carried out the standard depth of the shade closest to the pattern under test is quoted.

Resistance of coloured fabric to harmful agencies

The visual effects observed as a result of fastness testing may be caused either by a chemical breakdown of the dye or by removal of dye from the fabric, or by both. Whether or not the adjacent uncoloured material will be stained by dye removed from the pattern will depend on the attraction of the textile for that particular dye under the testing conditions. The dye may also decompose for any of a variety of reasons (such as chemical instability to the action of light or to the oxidising reagents contained in detergent powders, or even the presence of foreign substances in the textile), and the colour of the products of degradation of the dye may be different from that of the dye itself. Dyebath additives necessary for the dyeing of polyester fibres may influence the fastness to light of dyes on the fibre if residues are left after the washing process. Crease-resist finishes or dye-fixing agents applied to some cotton dyeings also adversely affect the fastness to light of some dyes.

In the production of man-made fibres, titanium dioxide pigment is often incorporated into the polymer mass to render the resulting fibres opaque (dull fibres) and this can reduce their fastness to light as compared with the corresponding unpigmented material (bright fibres). The significant influence of moisture content on the fastness to light is also well recognised.

Fastness assessments are also affected by the fineness of the fibres, simply because a given amount of dye on a fine fibre is spread over a larger surface area than is the same amount on the same mass of a coarser fibre. The compactness of the fibre structure can also have a bearing on how easily the dye fades or can be removed during washing treatments. The nature of the fibre itself can also markedly affect fastness to light: the fastness to light of basic dyes, for example, is very poor on cotton and wool, but high on acrylic fibres.

Further influences originate from the state of the dye in the fibre. Insoluble pigments trapped mechanically inside the fibre, or dyes that have formed a strong chemical linkage with the fibre, will obviously be more resistant to removal by wet treatments than dyes that are more loosely attached. Yet another factor is the yellowing of fibres with age, which is impossible to prevent. Also fluorescent brightening agents in household detergents may be left on the fibre after washing, and these superimpose an additional effect on the change in the appearance of the colour.

Washing fastness tests (ISO C01–C06)

Domestic and commercial washing conditions are covered by six ISO wash tests, which are directed towards simulation of the conditions likely to be encountered in normal use (Table 1.3). If possible, colour changes should be assessed using the grey scales. If these are not available the staining of different white fabrics

Table 1.3 Differences in severity of ISO washing fastness tests

ISO test	Composition of wash liquor	Temperature (°C)	Duration (hours)
1	Soap 5 g/l	40	0.5
2	Soap 5 g/l	50	0.5
3	Soap 5 g/l + soda 2 g/l	60	0.5
4	Soap 5 g/l + soda 2 g/l	95	0.5
5	Soap 5 g/l + soda 2 g/l	95	4.0

tested alongside the pattern may still be compared, through the use of either a multifibre strip (page 162) or a piece of undyed fabric of identical size stitched to the pattern on one side and a piece of

Table 1.4 Standard 'adjacent fabrics' for use in fastness testing

Specimen fabric	First adjacent fabric	Second adjacent fabric
Cotton	Cotton	Wool
Wool	Wool	Cotton
Silk	Silk	Cotton
Linen	Linen	Wool
Viscose	Viscose	Wool
Acetate/triacetate	Acetate/triacetate	Viscose
Polyamide (nylon)	Polyamide (nylon)	Wool or cotton
Polyester	Polyester	Wool or cotton
Acrylic	Acrylic	Wool or cotton

specified but different undyed fabric on the other. The standard 'adjacent fabrics' are listed in Table 1.4.

The composite specimen is agitated in a solution with a defined concentration of soap and, where appropriate, other prescribed additives. Controlled agitation is maintained at the temperature required by the test conditions and the ratio of liquid volume to mass of fabric is also defined. At the end of the testing the sample is removed and rinsed, and the components separated and allowed to dry. A visual assessment is then made.

The nature of the detergent to be used is stipulated in the standard, together with the concentration of sodium carbonate (soda ash) needed to make the solution alkaline in reaction. Tests 4 and 5 are of greater severity than the others. The mechanical action is intensified by the inclusion of ten non-corrodable steel balls together with the composite sample in the container, while the detergent has been modified so as to allow for the effects of the various components of the different brands of washing powder used in commercial and domestic laundering. The detergent composition is based on a mixture of synthetic detergents and natural soap, a phosphate, a silicate, an inorganic salt (Glauber's salt) and a compound that inhibits soil redeposition when used for cleaning off particulate matter. The specially formulated detergent is used in the additional test proposed for colour fastness to domestic and commercial laundering, which provides for a greater rubbing action through the use of up to 100 steel balls.

Determination of light fastness

The influence of light on the fading of dyes is a complex phenomenon influenced by many variables, and accordingly predictive tests for fastness to light are amongst the most difficult to establish. The depth of colour, the presence of unwanted additives, humidity, air temperature, the surface temperature of the sample, the presence of atmospheric impurities and the spectral quality and intensity of the light source all have a bearing on the end result.

When using daylight the samples are exposed behind glass alongside the blue wool standards, taking care to place the samples at an angle equal to the latitude of the location of the testing station, facing due south in the northern hemisphere and due north in the southern hemisphere. Adequate ventilation is essential. The rate at which the samples fade is determined by partially covering both standard and pattern with an opaque card and inspecting both fading standards and sample periodically. The specimen is faded to the equivalent effect on the pattern of a grade 3 contrast on the grey scales. At this stage the degree of contrast between the exposed and unexposed pattern is compared with that for the standards, and the rating given is the number of the standard that exhibits the same degree of contrast.

The time taken for daylight testing can be inconveniently long, however; furthermore, the conditions are variable from one geographical location to another. Consequently it would be useful to be able to carry out the tests using artificial light sources. For many years various light sources were used to imitate the spectral distribution of daylight, all of which have been subjected to close scrutiny. Although the light of a xenon arc is currently favoured as the best substitute for daylight, the matter is constantly under review.

There are other factors to be taken into account when designing the equipment for carrying out fading tests. A means has to be found for maintaining the humidity at the surface of the patterns to prevent them drying out. The variations that occur between the results from different light sources and from operating the same light source under different conditions are mainly due to differences between the spectral composition of the lights, their intensity and the effective humidity at the surface of the pattern. The effective humidity represents a combination of air temperature, the temperature of the surface of the pattern and relative humidity, which governs the moisture content of the fabric. The conditions of operation are therefore specified very carefully in the standard tests, and control of the effective humidity is recommended through the use of a humidity test control in the form of a fabric coloured with a particular red pigment. The relationship between the fastness to light of this fabric and the operating humidity is known with reasonable precision. Preliminary tests are then carried out to check if the humidity test control fades to the correct blue standard, and adjustments in the operating conditions made if required. Once the correct conditions have been established the testing is carried out in the normal manner.

Photochromism

Sometimes the colour of a dyeing changes on exposure to light, but reverts to its original state after the sample is kept in the dark. In such a case an additional test is carried out to indicate the extent of the change (as well as the fastness rating test). The extent of this *photochromism* is expressed as a grey scale assessment given alongside the rating for fastness to light.

Other fastness properties

Tests have been designed to establish the resistance to a wide range of aqueous agencies, including distilled water, sea-water, chlorinated water and perspiration, and to spotting in cold and hot water, acid and alkaline solutions, and various other agencies relevant to different end uses of the goods.

The resistance to bleaches of different types, atmospheric contaminants and a variety of other agencies are all covered by tests described with full details in the appropriate manual [10]. The situation with regard to the development of tests is never static; they are perpetually under review as conditions and products change. Very often intensive effort is required to ensure reproducible results by establishing conditions that simulate those encountered by the material. There is also a dominant need for speed with accuracy in executing the tests because they may form part of an independent certification scheme that must be completed before further steps in manufacture, marketing or purchasing can proceed. A comprehensive bibliography concerning the development of the various testing methods has been compiled [4], and their application to coloration practice is described in various sections of this book.

References

1.   S Grierson, *The colour cauldron* (Tibbermore, Perth: Mill Books, 1986).
2.   C D Woodward, *The story of standards* (London: British Standards Institution, 1972).
3.   K McLaren, *J.S.D.C.*, **81** (1965) 522.
4.   M Langton, *Rev. Prog. Coloration*, **14** (1984) 176.
5.   *The dyeing of synthetic-polymer and acetate fibres*, Ed. D M Nunn (Bradford: Dyers' Company Publications Trust, 1979).
6.   *Quality assurance*, BSI handbook 22 (London: British Standards Institution).
7.   I Levy in *Quality, design and the purchaser* (Manchester: Textile Institute, 1983) 1.
8.   *Colour terms and definitions*, 2nd Edn (Bradford: SDC, 1988).
9.   *Textile terms and definitions*, 8th Edn (Manchester: Textile Institute, 1988).
10.   *Standard methods for the determination of the colour fastness of textiles and leather*, 5th Edn (BS 1006 and ISO 105) (Bradford: SDC, 1990).
11.   BS 1006:A02 (1978).
12.   BS 2661:SDM and SDG.

CHAPTER TWO

The colourist and colour quality

Concerns of the textile colourist

The aesthetic appeal of the colour of a manufactured article is often the first factor to arouse the interest of the consumer. Consequently it is important that initial expectations of standards of colour performance during use are satisfied. The colourist is therefore responsible for building in the quality of the colour by ensuring appropriate selection and application of colorants that will withstand any likely aftercare treatments. Such matters are important for any manufactured coloured product such as plastics, printing inks, paints and textiles. In this book attention is devoted to the extensive topic of textile coloration, but equal weight could also be given to any other specified technology involving the use of colorants.

Thousands of new coloured compounds have appeared on the market since W H Perkin discovered the first viable synthetic route for producing a commercial dye. Of these, relatively few have become commercially significant. Even so, the dyer is confronted by a bewildering array of dyes when attempting to satisfy a customer's expectations for resistance to the destructive agencies the goods are likely to meet in use. Unless the correct choice of dyes is made, even the best-quality fabric will be perceived as substandard if the colour fades badly or washes out easily the first time the goods are cleaned.

Usually those dyes with the highest resistance to agencies such as sunlight or repeated washing are also more expensive to make, and if the use of the end product does not warrant a high price the choice of dyes is further restricted. Consequently the minimum level of fastness required is judged in accordance with the intended end use of the fabric. For some articles such as dusters or wrapping paper, or cinema curtains which will be dry-cleaned and rarely be exposed to daylight, fastness to light or wet treatments is not particularly important. At the other end of the scale goods such as furnishing materials, carpets and curtains are expected to last for many years, and resistance to light and cleaning become of paramount importance. Other articles may be required to withstand a particular treatment associated with their use; swimwear, for instance, needs to resist the effects of chlorinated water and sea-water, while children's wear must be able to stand up to repeated washing.

Matching the fastness properties to the end use also requires a careful choice of dyeing method, because the level of wet fastness provided by a dye is inescapably linked to the ease with which a uniform dyeing can be achieved.

The general aims of the textile colourist reach well beyond the selection of appropriate colours to match the latest fashion shades. In addition to the shade strength and fastness properties of the colour, the issues of the productivity of the work force and capital costs have to be tackled on the route to the final product. These in turn are often dictated by the equipment available, the amount of material to be dyed and the energy consumption of the chosen process. Sometimes a repeat dyeing may be required years after the product was first dyed, by which time some of the original dyes may have vanished from the market; it is then necessary to reformulate the dye recipe to a price using different dyes, and possibly fabric of a different specification.

An awareness of the likely effects of processing on the fabric is also essential, since modification during processing of properties such as strength, elasticity, abrasion resistance and dimensional stability needs to be kept within prescribed limits. Clearly, the success of the dyer is dependent upon a comprehensive understanding of the user properties of fibres, yarns, fabrics and dyes as well as their expected behaviour during finishing processes.

Choosing dyes of suitable substantivity

Coloration is a stepwise process that involves attraction of the dye from the liquid or print paste to the fibre surface, from where it diffuses into the fibre. Within the fibre the dye molecules move from one point of attachment to another. Unless they become chemically bonded to the fibre or converted to an insoluble pigment, this process continues for as long as the fibres remain in the dyebath. Both the speed with which the dye molecules move into the fibre and the ease with which they can move about (*migrate*) from site to site depend upon the strength of the attraction between dye and fibre. The *substantivity* of the dye is a measure of the strength of this attraction. Within any one class of dye are dyes with a range of substantivities, and this is of significance both in practical application and in the fastness to wet treatments of the end product.

As a general rule of thumb, dyes with high substantivity have poor migration properties, since the strong interaction works against release of dye from the initial point of attachment. Such dyes are more difficult to distribute evenly – they are said to have poor *levelling* properties. But with high substantivity is associated the fastest exhaustion from the dyebath and the greatest resistance to washing off in clean water. Of course the converse is also true: dyes with lower substantivity exhaust more slowly, have better migration properties and are good levelling dyes. The penalty in this case is poor wet fastness properties, since the weaker dye–fibre linkages allow easier reversal of the dyeing process.

Dyers are therefore obliged to strike a balance between these properties when fitting the choice of dyes to the intended use of the product. Dyeing methods are thus governed as much by application criteria for level dyeing as they are by the chemical nature of the dye and the fibre. Consequently the logical way to aid dye selection is by sorting dyes into groups according to their best method of application. In this way dyes that are suited to protein fibres such as wool are separated from those appropriate for cellulosic fibres such as cotton, whilst those for synthetic fibres form yet another category. This aspect of fibre finishing is dealt with in Chapter 4.

Expanding activities of the colourist

Synthetic dyes for natural fibres

The first synthetic dyes were used alongside natural dyes, but gradually the latter were displaced completely by the broadening range of more easily applied colours. Dyers' understanding of the coloration process began to deepen as the quest for improved products continued, and the physical chemistry of the dyeing process came into focus in an attempt to address such questions as why dyes are attracted to fibres, how they are held, why some are less resistant to washing than others and why a distinction can be made between dyes suited to fibres of different chemical origin, as shown in Table 2.1.

Table 2.1 Main dye classes and fibre types with which they are used

Dye class	Fibre type
Acid[a]	Protein[b], nylon
Mordant (chrome)	Protein, nylon
Reactive	Cellulosic[c], protein
Direct	Cellulosic
Sulphur	Cellulosic
Vat	Cellulosic
Basic	Acrylic
Disperse	Polyester, nylon, acrylic cellulose acetates

a   Including metal-complex acid
b   Wool, silk, etc.
c   Cotton and regenerated cellulose

Once ideas of the nature of the dye–fibre attachment began to develop, it became clear that the ultimate bonding between a dye and a fibre would be through a link formed by a chemical reaction, but it was not until 1956 that this goal was first realised by I D Rattee and W E Stephen. Even then, the dyes in question were under examination as potential reactive dyes for wool rather than for the cellulosic fibres for which they first became commercially available.

In the laboratories of the time, experimental samples were numbered by attaching short loops of thin string with the relevant number of knots tied in the loose ends. Rattee noticed that at the end of the dyeing the string (made of cellulosic fibres) also became coloured, and realised that the dyes were reacting with cellulose. From then onwards intensive research led to the creation of the new class of *reactive dyes* for cellulose. Novel methods of application were devised, and since ICI's introduction of the first commercial range of reactive dyes (the Procion dyes), many other ranges have appeared, all notable for their good wet fastness and their bright shades.

Investigations like this are often regarded as esoteric in the early stages, because no one can know with certainty how the work may aid the design or application of dyes with improved performance. Very often the development work that follows leads to unexpected and difficult problems, an elegant solution of which may well appear to the outsider, with the benefit of hindsight, as an obvious answer.

Synthetic dyes for synthetic fibres

The rapid development of synthetic fibres provided further motivation for research, which was stimulated into fresh activity when cellulose acetate first appeared on the market. Until that time the only textile fibres available were *hydrophilic* (i.e. water-attracting) and could be dyed using water-soluble dyes or the soluble precursors of insoluble pigments. Acetate fibres, however, are *hydrophobic* (i.e. water-repellent) and consequently they would not accept the conventional dyes of the time. Fibres that cannot be dyed are limited in their outlets, and this defect was a serious threat to progress. But the eventual solution came with the use of insoluble or sparingly soluble pigments dispersed in water using specially formulated surface-active agents. The stability of the dispersions enabled the pigments to 'dissolve' in the fibre and give a uniform distribution of colour throughout the dyed goods.

These were the first *disperse dyes*, a class of dyes that is now always used for the coloration of certain synthetic fibres. They are very different from water-soluble dyes, particularly in their response to heat. This difference is their ability to pass into the vapour phase without melting, a process referred to as *sublimation*. It soon became apparent that some disperse dyes will sublime from the dyed synthetic fabric when stored against a current of warm air, to leave irregular pale markings on the fabric, and dyes with improved fastness to sublimation were therefore developed.

But with the appearance of other synthetic fibres, particularly polyester, the propensity of disperse dyes to sublime became an advantage that has been exploited in two ways: firstly, in the printing of knitted goods and, secondly, in the dyeing of polyester/cellulosic fibre blends.

Knitted goods are difficult to print because the fabric is easily distorted during the application of the print paste, which is carried out under pressure. This difficulty can now be overcome using a two-stage process. The pattern is first printed on paper, using a disperse dye paste. Later the patterned paper is placed face down on the fabric and held firmly in close contact with it without distorting it, whilst the secured combination passes into a heating chamber. The dye vaporises and moves to the fabric, where it is absorbed in the well-defined localised areas of the pattern by the hot thermoplastic polyester fibres. Thus printing takes place without the printing paste touching the fabric, which is ready for use without further washing-off treatments immediately it has passed from the heaters.

Transfer of dye through the vapour phase is also useful in dyeing blends of polyester and cellulosic fibres. The requirements of polyester and cellulose for dyeing are completely different: polyester needs the disperse dyes whilst cellulose requires water-soluble dyes. One way of colouring the combination is to carry out one dyeing for the cellulose and another for the polyester, thus doubling the effort. It is possible, however, to apply to the fabric a mixture of both classes of dye. In the drying stage most of the dye is absorbed by the hydrophilic component but on subsequent heating the disperse dye transfers through the vapour phase to the polyester.

The continuing pressure to conserve water and energy is now providing a further stimulus to the development of methods and equipment. The need to eliminate toxic substances from dyehouse effluent is leading to fresh innovations, including the removal of chromium and other metals from the bath before the liquor is discharged.

Efficient colour matching

Over recent decades improvements have been concerned mainly with improving speed and economy in meeting customer requests. Progress here began with work carried out around the early 1960s. Until that time the only recognised way of matching customer shades and fastness requirements involved lengthy laboratory trials and visual assessment of the results. The process was repeated until successive corrections eventually provided the desired end result. Further adjustments were then needed to transfer the laboratory results to the equipment in use.

The introduction at this time of a pioneering instrumental match-prediction system offered the possibility of matching a shade from suitable instrumental measurements of the customer's fabric and stored knowledge of the spectra of the available dyes. This work was the forerunner of present-day practice, but in these early stages many people perceived the work as an example of impractical theoretical concepts. The intervention of the microprocessor has left the value of the work unchallenged, however, and modern dyehouses and dye manufacturers now depend on instrumentation for the prediction of recipes. In this way the necessary quality is achieved, with dyes selected from a minimal number of stock colours. Furthermore, the required precision of dyebath and textile preparation has encouraged a marked improvement in the standards of accuracy provided by the operatives. Thus subjective judgement of colour has been superseded, along with the old routine trial-and-error methods.

Transmission of information on colour quality

Over the years each manufacturer has produced ranges of dyes suited to particular fibres under their own brand names. Consequently there are often different brand names for the same class of dye, and even chemically identical dyes may be sold under different brand names. In this situation there is a need for comparison of the qualities of the differently named products.

Provision of product information for the colourist

A dyer cannot assess from the label on the container alone whether a sample of dye from one manufacturer is equivalent to an apparently similar sample from another maker. It is impractical to carry out a full range of exploratory fastness tests on each dye of potential interest, but since the primary concern is with the quality of the end product, a comparison of fastness properties will be of more interest than a determination of the chemical structure. If the dyes have identical fastness properties then the choice can be made on the basis of cost; otherwise the merits of one chemical structure over another may become a consideration. The selection process is aided by the dye makers, who provide extensive information with regard to shade, fastness to light and washing, and recommended dyeing methods. This is usually presented in the form of pattern cards, as shown in Plate 3. The dyes chosen as the example are intended for wool and the fastness ratings to standard tests are shown alongside samples of wool coloured with the appropriate dye.

The *Colour Index*

The manufacturer's brand name generally bears no obvious relationship to either the chemical or the application class of the dye. But the merit of this apparently random approach is that the colorant may be readily recognised without the need for specialised chemical knowledge. Moreover, the chemical names of dyes are often cumbersome and lengthy; for example, the full chemical name of the dye with structure *2.1* is *N*-[(2-methylbenzene-4-sulphonic acid)-2-azo-1-naphthol-3-sulphonic acid]-*N'*-[(2-methoxybenzene)-2-azo-1-naphthol-3-sulphonic acid-6-]urea sodium salt: it is sold under the name Chlorazol Fast Scarlet 4BA, however. Little imagination is needed to realise the practical difficulties that could ensue, even for a chemist, if dye containers were labelled with the correct chemical name instead of the commercial one.

Nevertheless, the need for some systematic indexing of the many synthetic dyes and pigments is clear, and this is

2.1

available in the form of a publication called the *Colour Index*, in which dyes are referred to by an unambiguous *Colour Index* number [1]. The *Colour Index* serves as a reference source for both the chemical structure and technical properties of dyes. It is divided into three parts.

Part 1 consists of three volumes that classify dyes and pigments according to their usage, as in Table 2.1 (page 17). There is a further subdivision of the dye classes into two groupings, which serves to indicate whether the absorption of dye is reversible or irreversible. Those dyes for which the absorption is easily reversed in clean water will have the lowest resistance to washing, and the loose dye will cause staining of any undyed fabric present. The dyes of the remaining classes are irreversibly absorbed by the fibre, either through the formation of a chemical bond, as with reactive dyes, or through the deposition of a water-insoluble pigment, as with sulphur and vat dyes and azoic components. Thus the general dyeing behaviour and fastness properties are reflected by the way in which the dye classes are set out in the *Colour Index*.

Dyes in each of the divisions are grouped according to their colour and each is given its own five-figure CI number, which serves as an unambiguous reference. Thus the yellow dyes of the acid type are classified as CI Acid Yellow 1, CI Acid Yellow 2 . . . through acid oranges, reds and so on, ending with blacks. These are the CI *generic names* of dyes. For example, the generic name of Chlorazol Fast Scarlet 4BA, mentioned above, is CI Direct Red 24 and its reference number is 29185.

Part 2 is a single volume in which dyes and pigments are classified according to chemical constitution, and important intermediate products used in the manufacture of colorants are also included. Every dye in Part 1 appears also in Part 2, provided its formula is known. Formulae are grouped in order of chemical classes, such as those of monoazo, disazo, trisazo, polyazo, anthraquinone and natural dyes. The list finishes with inorganic pigments.

Part 3 includes a list of all the commercial names notified to the publishers in alphabetical order together with the appropriate CI constitution numbers and generic names. There is also a listing of these commercial products in CI generic name order.

Commercial names of dyes and pigments

The relative simplicity of commercial names has already been mentioned. Another advantage of their use is that with time a given name becomes associated with defined standards of manufacture so that the user can anticipate reliability on repeating an order. The colourist is also aided by the broadly systematic approach to the commercial naming of dyes that is now in use. The convention used is represented in Figure 2.1.

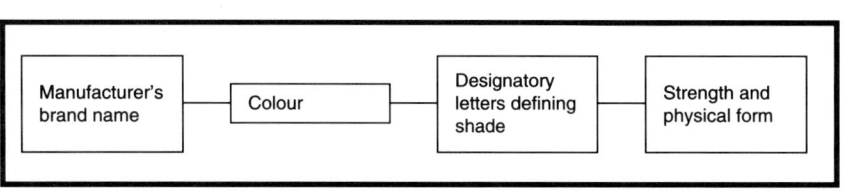

Figure 2.1 *The convention for the naming of dyes*

Manufacturer's brand name

The brand name of a particular class of dye distinguishes between those originating from different manufacturers. For example, Chlorazol and Durazol are the ranges of direct dyes produced by ICI, while Ciba-Geigy have chosen the names Cuprophenyl and Solophenyl for their equivalent dyes. The brand name therefore communicates to the dyer as much about the dye as names like Granada, Cavalier and Golf do to the motor car enthusiast. For example, the name Chlorazol Red makes it clear that the dye is a red direct dye manufactured by ICI.

Designatory letters

These letters are used because not all dyes of the same basic colour are exactly the same shade. Colours with a yellowish tint, such as a yellowish-red, bear the letter G (German *gelb* = yellow). Similarly those with a reddish tinge will be identified by R (*rot* = red) and those with a blue tinge by B (*blau* = blue). The designatory letters are sometimes preceded by a number which indicates the intensity of the deviation from the main colour. Plate 3 shows some examples of nomenclature.

Strength and physical form

The dye powders sold by the manufacturer may contain only about 30% colouring matter. They would be prohibitively expensive if they were prepared in pure form. Consequently each new batch of dye has to be standardised to ensure a defined physical strength when used for dyeing. A proportion of a second or even a third colour component may be added to ensure the shade matches other batches of the same dye. Sometimes, for reasons of economy in transportation, dyes are required with a strength greater than standard. When a dye is prepared in different strengths this is indicated by an S at the end of the name, and strengths greater than standard are followed by numbers showing the strength relative to the standard: for example, 'Dispersol Fast Yellow A 300' means that this dye preparation is 3 times the standard strength. The standardisation is usually done by mixing dye powder with neutral electrolytes; in some cases (vat or disperse dyes) dispersing agents may be incorporated.

Dyes may be packaged in the form of fine powders, grains or pastes, and the physical form is indicated on the package labelling – for instance, 'Dispersol Fast Orange Brown RN 150 powder fine' or 'Duranol Blue G grains'. The different forms are prepared for the convenience of handling. The use of readily dispersed grains eliminates the problems arising with some dyes in powder form which 'fly' into the atmosphere and cause contamination, whilst a colorant presented in a paste form is more readily mixed evenly into a printing paste.

Informing the consumer about colour quality

Whilst the detailed information available to the colourist is helpful for choosing dyes with appropriate properties, such information is not easily available to the consumer at the point of sale. Even if it were, it is unlikely that the presentation of technical data on fastness properties would be readily understood. Nevertheless, the area of colour fastness is a dominant factor in the difficulties encountered with the quality of coloured textile goods. There is therefore a real need for clear, simple and informative recommendations relating to the appropriate aftercare for purchased goods.

The restoration of worn textiles to a clean and presentable state for re-use is an everyday affair, and a wide variety of possible procedures may be used. These include washing using proprietary detergents (some of which may contain bleach), drying, tumble drying, dry or steam ironing, dry cleaning and other special methods depending on the nature of the article. Generally smaller articles are more conveniently cleaned in a washing machine, whilst wool suits and more bulky items like curtains are usually dry cleaned. Apart from convenience, however, the properties inherent in both the dye and the fabric are of equal importance in relation to the cleaning conditions.

Mechanical action such as wringing, spin drying or tumble drying can have a detrimental effect on some fabrics. For example, if woollen goods are washed at too high a temperature or with severe agitation, the result will be an unacceptable shrinkage. Acrylic fabrics may stretch as a result of the degradation of their physical properties during unsatisfactory washing, whilst the use of dry cleaning solvents can have a harmful effect on some synthetic fibres. For tightly woven acetate fabrics dry cleaning is preferable to washing, because when such fabrics become wet and crumpled they may crease badly or even crack. If the melting of synthetic fibres or damage to the aftertreatments on natural fibres is to be avoided, careful attention must also be given to the temperature of ironing.

Obviously the formulation of realistic conditions for the aftercare of textile goods involves many factors. This is complicated further by the wide-ranging combinations of temperature, time, degree of agitation and spinning speeds encountered with domestic washing machines. A further complicating factor is the range of different fibres that may be used together in blends, together with their associated differences in ironing conditions. It is therefore difficult to provide simple foolproof aftercare recommendations. Until the middle 1960s some manufacturers provided aftercare recommendations as a fixed form of words. Unfortunately the confusion was exacerbated, because manufacturers tended to use different forms of words to mean the same thing. The subsequent efforts made to provide a more consistent and informative system of aftercare labelling led to the provision of sewn-in information labels.

There were two views about the form in which the information should appear on the labels. One favoured clear, compact and precise statements, whilst the other preferred the use of descriptive symbols. Ultimately agreement was reached to use symbols and a few informative words that encompassed the temperature of the washing water, suitable methods of water extraction and drying, and recommendations for ironing. Development of the currently used International Care Labelling Code was carried out by the Home Laundering Consultative Council (HLCC), constituent representative members of which included individuals from industries concerned with the production of textile goods.

The basic care labelling symbols in current use are presented in Figure 2.2. They convey details of washing processes (wash-tub), the ironing temperature (iron), and suitability for chlorine bleaching (triangle) and dry cleaning (circle). The HLCC in cooperation with Ginetex (the European care labelling body) have covered most eventualities by categorising the various possibilities into

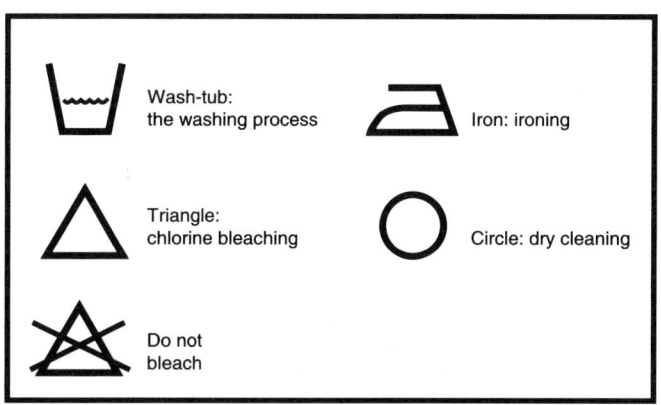

Figure 2.2 Care labelling symbols

nine groups, which are now recognised by most washing machine manufacturers. The current International Care Labelling Code together with examples of its application is shown in Figures 2.3 and 2.4.

Examples of application	Examples of application
95 — White cotton and linen articles without special finishes	40 — Acrylics, acetate and triacetate, including mixtures with wool; polyester/wool blends
60 — Cotton, linen or viscose articles without special finishes where colours are fast at 60 °C	40 — Wool, wool mixed with other fibres; silk
50 — Nylon; polyester/cotton mixtures; polyester, cotton and viscose articles with special finishes; cotton/acrylic mixtures	Handwash (Do not machine wash)
40 — Cotton, linen or viscose articles, where colours are fast at 40 °C but not at 60 °C	Do not wash

Figure 2.3 The International Care Labelling Code

25

Figure 2.4 *The International Care Labelling Code*

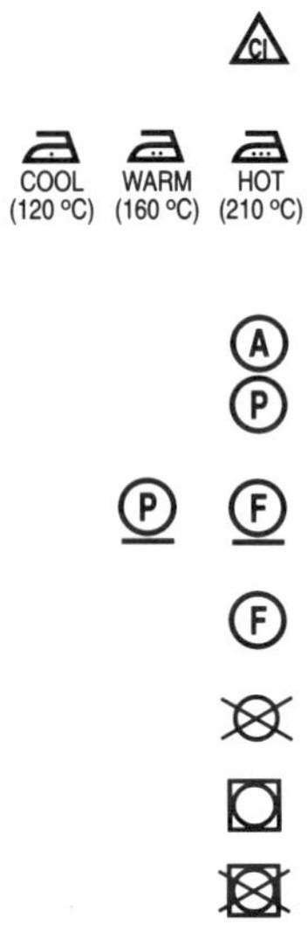

The labels are self-explanatory and take into account localised variations in common laundry practice. A recent additional symbol has been adopted: a bar below the wash tub indicates reduced action and a short spin to reduce the danger of creasing certain fabrics. The broken bar indicates reduced action but with normal rinse and spin, whilst the absence of a bar is used for normal washing machine action together with the words 'wash as cotton'. The symbol for hand washing is reserved for those articles that are particularly delicate or for which the wet fastness properties of heavily dyed shades may result in the staining of other materials.

Reference

1.   *Colour Index International*, 3rd Edn, 8 vols. (Bradford: SDC, 1971 *et seq.*).

Further reading

D G Duff and R S Sinclair, *Giles's laboratory course in dyeing*, 4th Edn (Bradford: SDC, 1990), 3–6, 148–51.
The dyeing of synthetic-polymer and acetate fibres, Ed. D M Nunn (Bradford: Dyers' Company Publications Trust, 1979), Chapter 1.
W R Beath, *Textiles*, **8** (1979) 42.
J E Ford, *Textiles*, **16** (1987) 37.
J E Ford, *Textiles*, **17** (1988) 32.

CHAPTER THREE

The chemical principles of coloration

Introduction

Although dyeing is a chemical operation, most of the simpler processes may be carried out on the small scale by sensible people who have very little chemical knowledge. Nevertheless, following a set of instructions in ignorance of the reasons behind their formulation is unlikely to lead to the deeper understanding of textile coloration that is needed by professional people in the coloration industry. Consequently this chapter has been included for the benefit of those with little working knowledge of chemistry. It contains a brief description of some of the chemical principles involved in coloration processes, as a supplement to more rigorous chemical studies that may be pursued elsewhere.

Modern chemistry is based on the belief that all matter is built from a combination of exceedingly minute particles (*atoms*) of the various chemical elements. Many different elements are found in nature, each possessing characteristic properties; the atoms of any one element are all chemically identical. Atoms combine together to form *molecules* of chemical compounds.

A single atom consists of a central core or *nucleus*, which contains numbers of positively charged particles (*protons*) and uncharged particles (*neutrons*), together accounting for almost all the mass of the atom. Numbers of very small negatively charged particles or *electrons* circulate around the nucleus in fixed orbits or 'shells', each corresponding to a certain level of energy of the electrons it holds. The number of electrons in an atom is equal to the number of protons in its nucleus, so that the atom is electrically neutral. The total number of electrons within a given atom is a characteristic of the element from which it originates.

The ways in which atoms of different elements combine to give molecules determine both the physical properties of the molecule and its chemical reactions with other molecules. These facts are as significant for the reaction of a dye molecule with a fibre molecule as they are for any other reaction. Dyeing reactions are also influenced by additives used in a dyebath and therefore some preliminary explanations of their chemical nature will be relevant for the later chapters of this book.

Electrolytes

An *electrolyte* is a substance that, because of its chemical nature, conducts electricity in solution. The addition of electrolyte to the dyebath is frequently recommended in textile coloration, common salt being the most often used; its function is discussed below.

The chemical name for common salt is sodium chloride, to signify that it is made up of sodium atoms and chlorine atoms. The reaction of a sodium atom with a chlorine atom is shown in Figure 3.1. In both atoms the shell (i.e. the energy level) closest to the nucleus contains only two electrons: this is the maximum number of electrons that can be accommodated in that orbit. (Hydrogen and helium atoms, the two smallest atoms, have only a single shell, and are never associated with more than two electrons each.) The next is filled by eight electrons. Although strictly speaking an oversimplification, it is convenient to assume from now on that eight electrons is the maximum number that can be accommodated in an outer shell. The significant feature that governs the way in which different atoms combine is the number of electrons in the outermost shell.

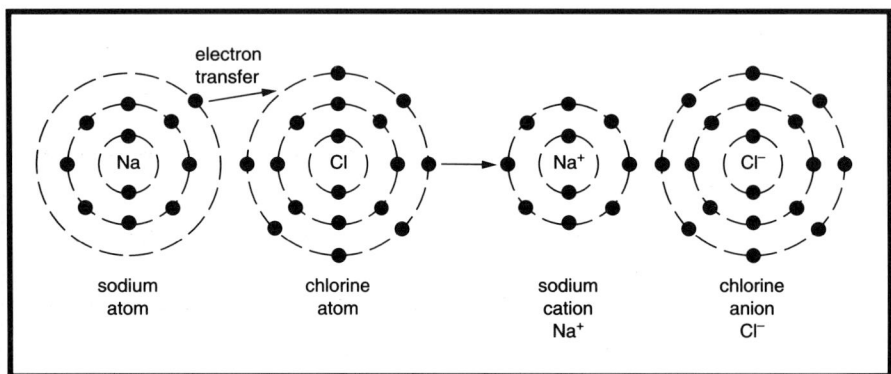

Figure 3.1 *The reaction between sodium and chlorine atoms*

The sodium atom has a single electron in the outermost shell, while the chlorine atom has seven. In the reaction between the two, one electron is transferred from the sodium atom (leaving the outermost shell with a complete octet of electrons) to the chlorine atom (making up an octet in its outermost shell). Since the atoms started out electrically neutral, the loss of one electron by sodium leaves the atom positively charged (it is now a positive *ion*, or *cation*) and the gain of one electron leaves the chlorine atom negatively charged (a negative ion or *anion*). The sodium chloride crystal is thus made up of equal numbers of sodium ions and chloride ions. Since opposite charges attract each other, there is a strong electrostatic attraction between the two kinds of ion, which makes sodium chloride a very stable compound.

Electrolytes are compounds made up of ions, and are often referred to as ionic compounds. When simple electrolytes of this kind dissolve in water they split up (*dissociate*) into separate ions. It is for this reason that they will allow an electric current to pass through the water (an electric current may be regarded as a flow of negatively charged particles round a circuit). There are many simple electrolytes and the two most commonly used in coloration are sodium chloride ($NaCl$) and sodium sulphate (Na_2SO_4), the latter being known as Glauber's salt.

Water-soluble dyes are also electrolytes, but in this case the coloured part of the molecule is very large and usually an anion, whilst the cation, usually a sodium ion, is very small by comparison. In fact water-soluble dye molecules are all synthesised to contain at least one group of atoms known to confer water solubility on the dye molecule through the formation of ions. Very often this is the sulphonic acid group, —SO_3H, or the carboxylic acid group, —COOH, both of which form sodium salts which dissociate in water; Scheme 3.1, in which D represents the coloured part of the dye molecule, illustrates the dissociation of a sulphonate.

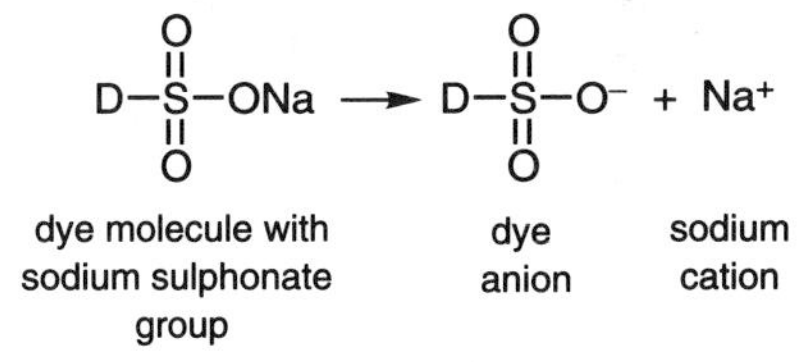

$$D-\overset{\overset{O}{\|}}{\underset{\underset{O}{\|}}{S}}-ONa \longrightarrow D-\overset{\overset{O}{\|}}{\underset{\underset{O}{\|}}{S}}-O^- + Na^+$$

dye molecule with sodium sulphonate group

dye anion

sodium cation

Scheme 3.1

Role of electrolyte in the dyebath

When a fibre is immersed in water, a negative electrostatic charge develops on its surface. This charge repels any dye anions present in the solution, so that the fibre cannot be dyed satisfactorily. If, however, the dyebath also contains an electrolyte such as sodium chloride or sodium sulphate, a diffuse layer of positive sodium ions forms at the fibre surface, neutralising its charge. The dye ions are then able to approach sufficiently closely to the fibre for the inherent attractive forces between the dye and the fibre to operate.

The covalent bond

A covalent bond differs from the bonding in a crystal of an ionic compound in that there is no transfer of electrons from one atom to another. Instead two atoms share two electrons, each atom providing one electron of the pair. Figure 3.2 represents the covalent bond in the simple inorganic molecule of chlorine (Cl_2) as an example. (In this diagram some of the electrons are represented by black circles and some by white. You should not be misled by this convention, which is introduced in the interests of comprehensibility: all electrons are alike, irrespective of the associated nucleus.)

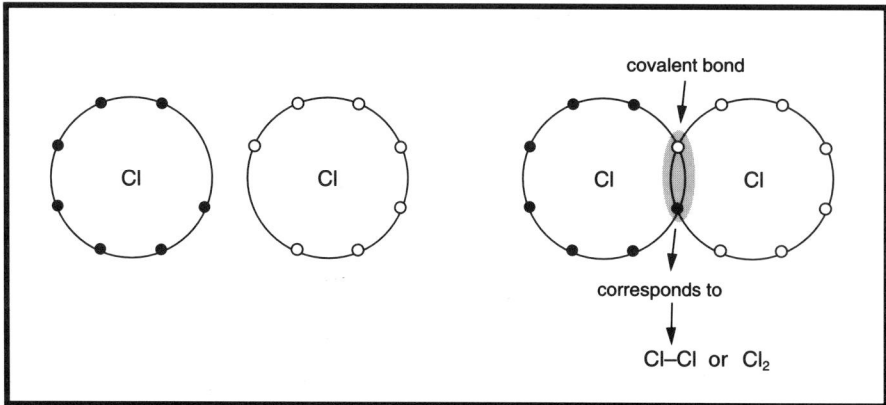

Figure 3.2 *The formation of the chlorine molecule*

The covalent bond is the most stable chemical linkage to operate between a dye and a fibre molecule, because the co-valently bound dye is an actual part of the fibre molecule.

In effect the combination of the dye and fibre through a covalent bond is equivalent to forming a coloured derivative of the fibre molecule.

The structures of all organic molecules, including dye molecules, are based on carbon atoms linked by covalent bonds. The structure of carbon atoms acts as a scaffolding upon which other groups of atoms may be placed to provide the molecule with particular proper-ties, which in the case of a dye may be a group of atoms that produce or modify the colour.

The simplest organic compound is methane, CH_4 (Figure 3.3). In methane there are four covalent bonds from the carbon atom, one to each hydrogen atom, arranged in the form of a symmetrical tetrahedron with the carbon atom in the middle (Figure 3.4). The carbon atom thus has eight electrons in the outer shell and each hydrogen atom two. The electronic requirements of

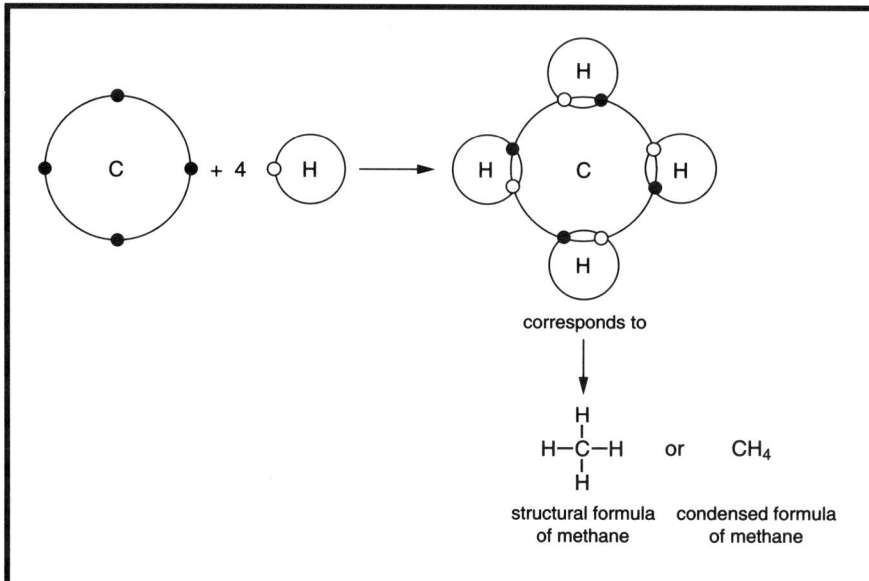

Figure 3.3 *The formation of methane (outer electron shells only are shown);* ● *electron from carbon,* ○ *electron from hydrogen*

both carbon and hydrogen atoms are thus satisfied and the compound is very stable. Such bonds do not dissociate in water, and most covalent compounds are insoluble in water and do not conduct electricity. Covalent bonds are the most stable of all chemical bonds and they cannot be broken easily. The discovery

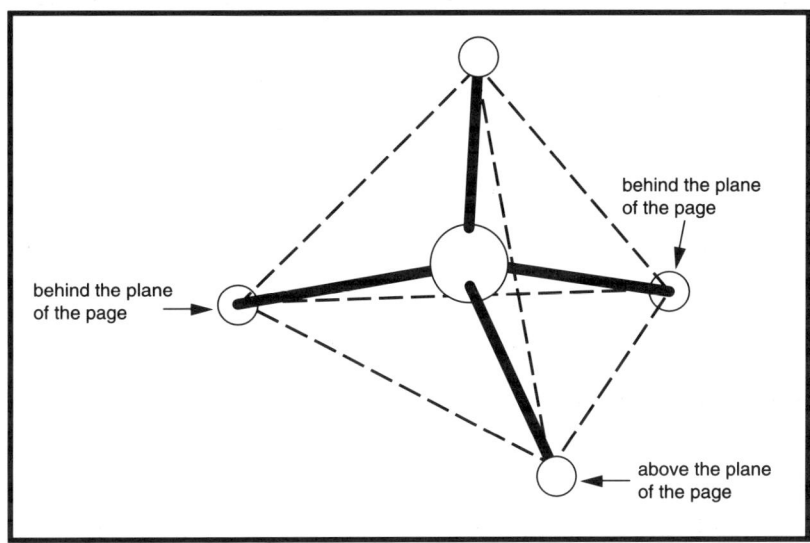

behind the plane of the page

behind the plane of the page

above the plane of the page

Figure 3.4 The tetrahedral molecule of methane, CH$_4$

of dyes that form covalent linkages with cellulosic fibres is the most recent major discovery in the field of textile dyes.

Most organic molecules are more complicated than methane. For example, there are long chains of covalently linked carbon atoms in the molecules of the surface-active agents used as detergents for washing-off fabric or as dispersing agents for dispersing the sparingly soluble colorants in the dyeing of synthetic fibres; *3.1* and *3.2* are typical structures. They are good examples of how the properties of compounds may be modified by the introduction of specific chemical groups. The ionic group in the detergent molecule imparts water solubility to an otherwise insoluble chain of carbon atoms.

H$_3$C CH$_2$ CH$_2$ CH$_2$ CH$_2$ SO$_3^-$Na$^+$
CH$_2$ CH$_2$ CH$_2$ CH$_2$ CH$_2$ anionic
3.1

H$_3$C CH$_2$ CH$_2$ CH$_2$ CH$_2$ $\overset{+}{N}$—CH$_3$ Br$^-$
CH$_2$ CH$_2$ CH$_2$ CH$_2$ CH$_2$ CH$_3$ cationic
3.2

Carbon chains are often represented in the zig-zag fashion shown in Figure 3.5 (overleaf), which is a two-dimensional representation of the tetrahedral arrangement of the four bonds of the carbon atoms in space (Figure 3.4). Because the angles between the single bonds of a carbon atom are fixed, a chain of carbon atoms cannot lie flat in a straight line. Instead it is forced into a zig-zag arrangement. The arrangement of carbon atoms in space is important because it governs the three-

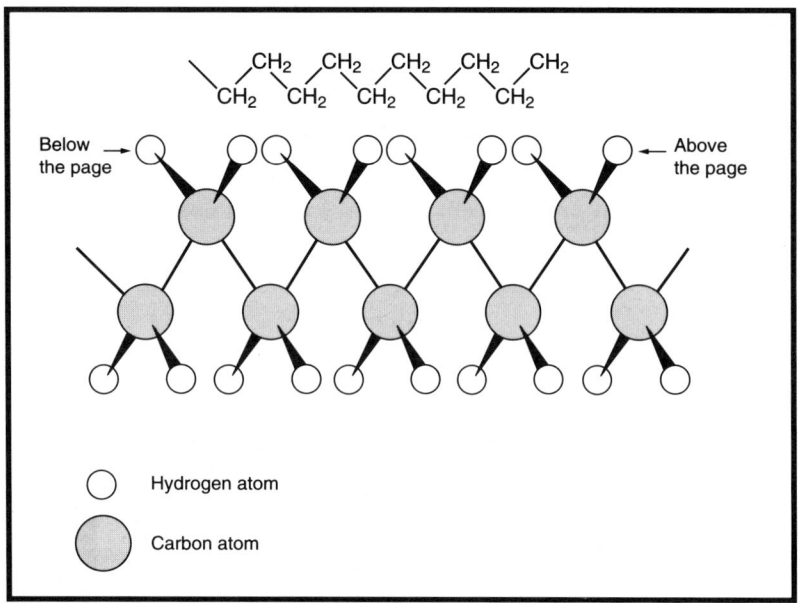

Below → the page

Above ← the page

CH₂ CH₂ CH₂ CH₂ CH₂
CH₂ CH₂ CH₂ CH₂ CH₂

Hydrogen atom

Carbon atom

Figure 3.5 *The zig-zag conformation of a hydrocarbon chain*

dimensional shapes of organic molecules, which may in part determine their physical and chemical properties.

Fibres contain long chains of carbon atoms linked by single covalent bonds; each atom is able to rotate relative to its neighbour and this imparts great flexibility to the chain, a factor which is particularly relevant to the design of synthetic fibres (Chapter 4). For example, it can lead to the formation of long straight chains, as in polypropylene, or of chains with a helical configuration, like the keratin molecules of wool. With other more chunky molecules such as those of glucose or dyes, the configuration of the bonds of the constituent atoms gives a more bulky three-dimensional shape to the molecule.

Molecules containing only carbon and hydrogen atoms (*hydrocarbons*) are chemically unreactive and insoluble in water, but when ionic groups are added to large hydrocarbon molecules in order to make them soluble in the manner indicated above they may form a special kind of solution called a *colloidal electrolyte*. Like other ionic compounds, such a molecule dissociates in water, but the large ions do not remain separate. They cluster together to form special loosely knit spherical structures called *micelles*, in which the insoluble hydrocarbon chains (the 'tails') tend to associate together and form a hydrophobic (water-repelling) environment with the ionic 'heads' on the outer surface, keeping the micelle dissolved. Water-insoluble matter such as oil may dissolve within the micelle, suspended in the solution. This is the principle upon which detergents act. Similarly the micelles can engulf small colorant particles and keep them in a stable form of dispersion (Figure 3.6).

Methane is the simplest of a series of compounds called *alkanes*. They all have similar chemical properties, and differ only in the number and arrangement of the carbon atoms joined together by covalent bonds. After methane, the next member of the group is ethane, with two carbon atoms (*3.3*, overleaf), then propane with three (*3.4*). A series of compounds built up in this way is referred to as a *homologous series*. There are many such compounds in the alkane series, all with the general formula C_nH_{2n+2}, where *n* is the number of carbon atoms in the molecule. All the atoms of the compounds in this series are joined by single covalent bonds, and they are referred to as *saturated* compounds.

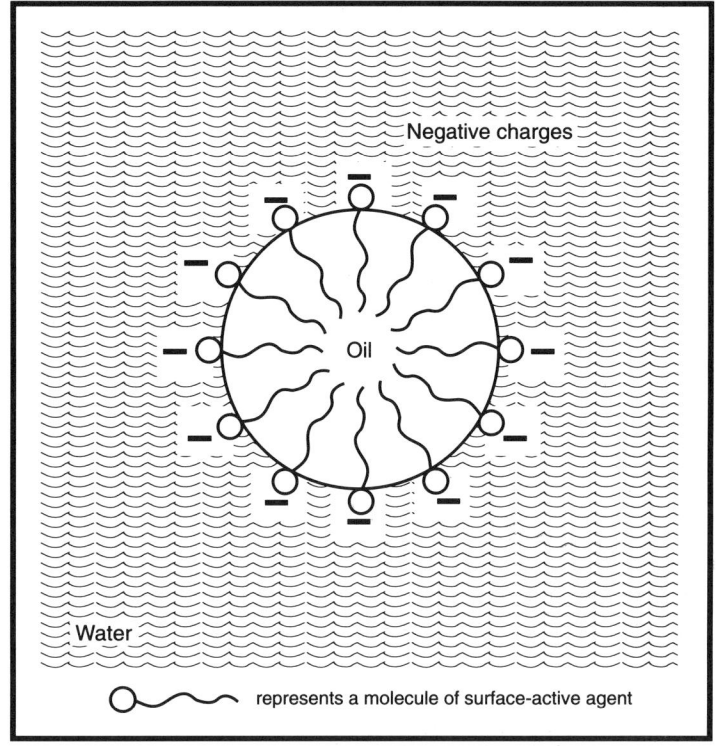

Figure 3.6 *Micelle formation by an anionic surface-active agent*

This distinguishes them from similar compounds in which some double bonds exist between the constituent atoms. Such compounds are known as *unsaturated* compounds, and their properties are different from those of saturated compounds because of the presence of the double bonds.

The double bond

A single covalent bond is formed by two atoms sharing a pair of electrons. The *double bond* is formed by two atoms sharing two pairs of electrons. The simplest homologous series of unsaturated hydrocarbons is the *alkenes*, of which the simplest is ethene (*3.5*, known as ethylene in the past), with two carbon atoms linked by a double bond.

The presence of a double bond does not double the strength of the bonding between the two carbon atoms. The second bond is much less chemically stable that the first, that is, it is more reactive. The first bond has true covalent character with one shared electron from each atom forming the bond. It is termed a σ (sigma) bond. The two electrons involved in the second bond are also shared but they are much less securely bound, and as a result are easily influenced by external

H₂C–C₂H (structure)

3.3

structure *3.4*

structure *3.5*

agencies. The second bond is referred to as a π (pi) bond, and it is this reactive bond that is responsible for the characteristic chemical reactions of double-bonded hydrocarbon compounds. The reactions of these unsaturated compounds include the polymerisation reactions used in the formation of synthetic fibres (Chapter 4) and the dye–fibre reactions of certain dyes.

Aliphatic and aromatic compounds

Organic compounds based on hydrocarbon chains are classed as *aliphatic* compounds. In aliphatic compounds the chains of carbon atoms are linked together by single or double covalent bonds, and may be straight, branched or even linked into rings. Dyes, however, belong to a different group of compounds referred to as *aromatic* compounds.

cyclohexane
(aliphatic)
3.6

benzene (aromatic)
also represented as

3.7

The molecules of aromatic compounds contain ring structures of a special kind. The structural formulae of aromatic rings may be drawn as if alternating single and double bonds existed between adjacent carbon atoms. Compare, for example, the six-carbon aliphatic cyclic compound cyclohexane (*3.6*) and the six-carbon aromatic compound benzene (*3.7*). An arrangement of alternating single and double bonds is called a *conjugated system* and it is very important in the molecular structure of dyes.

The bonds in the benzene ring are of a very special kind, however, and do not form a conjugated system. All six bonds in the ring are exactly alike, and none of them undergo the characteristic reactions of the double bonds in, say, alkenes; they are in fact much more stable (unreactive) than double bonds. The π electrons are distributed above and below the ring, forming diffuse clouds of negative charge: they are said to be *delocalised,* and the phenomenon is known as *resonance.* The delocalising of electrons makes aromatic compounds different from aliphatic compounds. In recognition of the nature of the benzene ring, its structural formula is often

34

represented as a hexagon with a central circle rather than with alternating single and double bonds. Furthermore, for simplicity's sake the benzene ring is drawn without showing the individual carbon and hydrogen atoms, their presence being implied by the notation.

All dye molecules contain aromatic ring structures. The reactions of functional groups such as the carboxyl group or the amino group are noticeably different when they are linked to an aromatic ring and when they form part of an aliphatic molecule. For example, one particularly important reaction

Scheme 3.2

in dye synthesis is that carried out using the amino (–NH_2) group attached to a benzene ring in phenylamine (aniline), a primary aromatic amine. Scheme 3.2 shows this *diazotisation* reaction in which a colourless aromatic base (amine) is diazotised with nitrous acid to form a *diazonium* salt (no diazonium salt is formed if an aliphatic amine is used). These salts will react readily with an appropriate *coupling agent* to form a dye molecule.

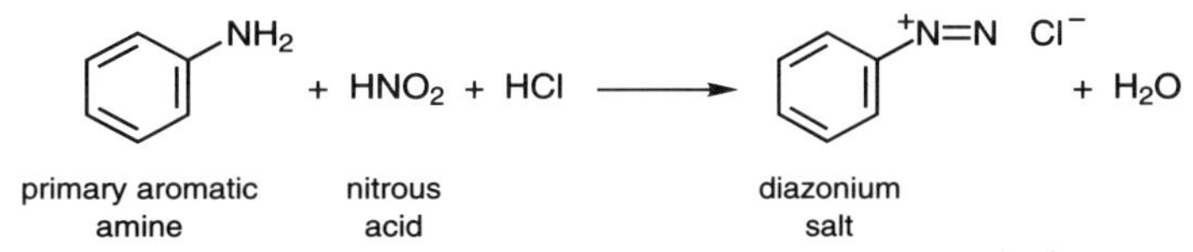

It is more usual in dye molecules to find fused rings, such as naphthalene (*3.8*), or rings joined through other groups, as in anthraquinone (*3.9*), on which many vat and disperse dyes are based.

There are many possibilities for building dye molecules using such structures as a scaffolding to which functional groups of atoms may be joined to impart particular properties, and the fundamental features that allow this to be carried out systematically are outlined below.

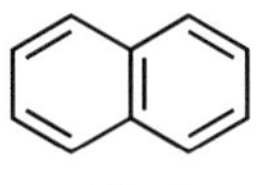

naphthalene
3.8

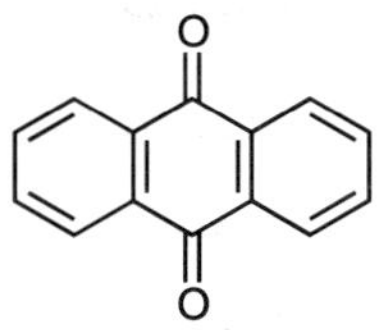

anthracene-9,10-dione
(anthraquinone)
3.9

Colour of dyes

The physiological sensation of colour arises when an object does not reflect all the incident white light falling on it. Some of the light energy is absorbed and the remainder is reflected and perceived as colour.

The absorption of light energy by an organic dye or inorganic pigment causes an electron to 'jump' into a higher energy level, thus bringing the dye molecule into an 'excited' state. It is easier for an electron to jump into an excited state from a double bond, where it exists as a π electron. Less energy still is required for the transition if alternate single and double bonds (i.e. conjugated double bonds) exist in the same molecule. Consequently, as the excitation of an electron becomes easier, the required spectral energy moves from the invisible ultraviolet into the longer wavelengths of the visible spectrum. For example, in structure *3.10* there are eight alternating single and double bonds. This compound absorbs violet light and as a result it is perceived as yellow in colour. Conjugated double bonds are present in the molecules of all dyes and many other coloured organic compounds.

3.10

Extended conjugated systems occur in several natural colouring matters, including carotene in carrots and fruit juices, and crocin which is found in saffron. Such compounds are not very substantive to fibres, however, and are unsuitable as starting points for dye synthesis. Structures containing benzene or naphthalene rings are of more use to dye chemists. Moreover, in aromatic rings the excitation of an electron is further aided by the enhanced delocalisation of the π electrons. Examples of such dyes and other dyes based on different chromophores (see below) of general commercial interest are given in Appendix 1.

One of the most widespread functional groups in coloured organic compounds is the azo group (—N=N—) mentioned earlier. It will react with other aromatic molecules to form the azo compounds that are widely distributed in several different classes of dye.

phenylazobenzene
3.11

The simplest azo molecule is phenylazobenzene (azobenzene), which has a weak yellow colour (*3.11*). Phenylazobenzene is called the *chromophore* (colour-bearing) group of azo dyes, and the colour of the molecule may be modified and increased in intensity of colour by introducing a variety of smaller groups into the molecule, examples of which are shown in Table 3.1. Such groups are called *auxochromes*. In addition, other groups can be added that have no influence on the colour, but change the insoluble molecule to a water-soluble dye. Thus compounds may be synthesised to produce all colours of the visible spectrum by suitable choice of auxochrome.

Approximately 50% of the available commercial dyes contain at least one azo chromophoric group.

Another important chromophore in dye chemistry is anthraquinone (*3.9*). Anthraquinone itself contains two carbonyl ($>$ C=O) groups in a conjugated system; it absorbs ultraviolet light weakly and appears cream in colour, but replacement of hydrogen atoms in the outer rings by suitable auxochrome groups based on nitrogen, oxygen or sulphur brings about the development of strong colours. Such compounds are the basis of many vat and disperse dyes

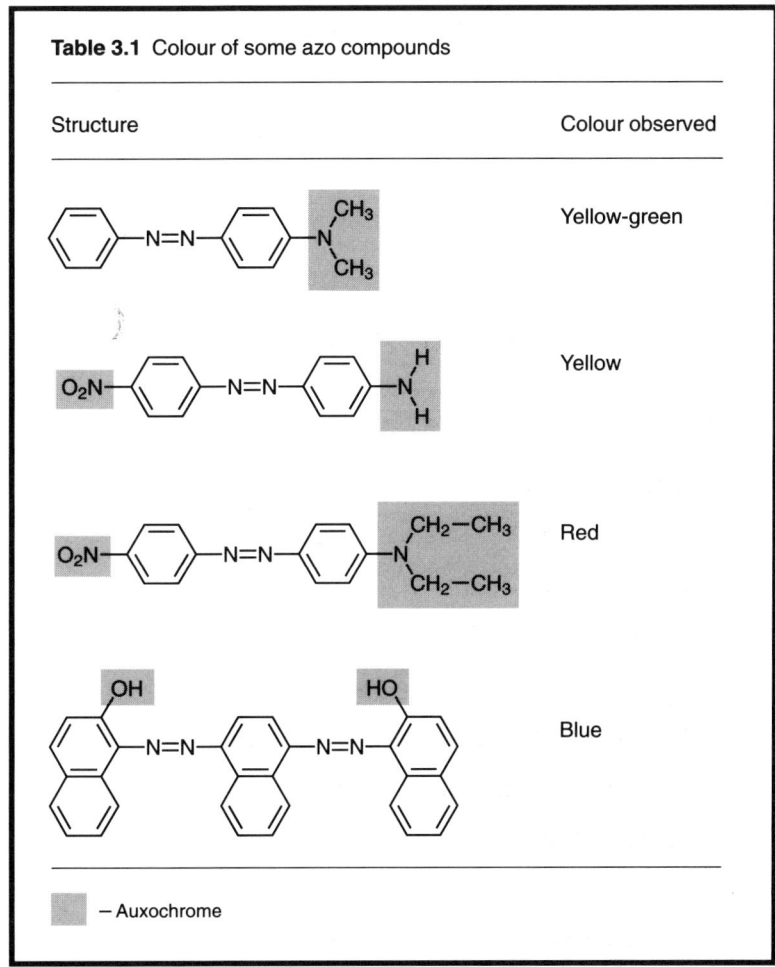

Table 3.1 Colour of some azo compounds

Structure	Colour observed
	Yellow-green
	Yellow
	Red
	Blue

☐ – Auxochrome

(Appendix 1) whilst other ranges of vat dyes are based on indigo (*3.12*; CI Vat Blue 1).

The first chromophore to be synthesised for commercial use was Perkin's mauveine, but since that time many others have been produced. Unlike most water-soluble dyes, which are anionic, mauveine is cationic and is referred to as a basic dye. Other well-known examples of basic dyes are based on triphenylmethane, such as crystal violet (CI Basic Blue 11) (Appendix 1, examples 18–21). By modern standards their fastness is poor and they are of limited use on fibres other than acrylics.

One further chromophore deserves mention because of its high chemical stability and unique turquoise shades. This is copper phthalocyanine (*3.13*), which with appropriate auxochrome groups incorporated is used in several dye classes.

3.12   indigo

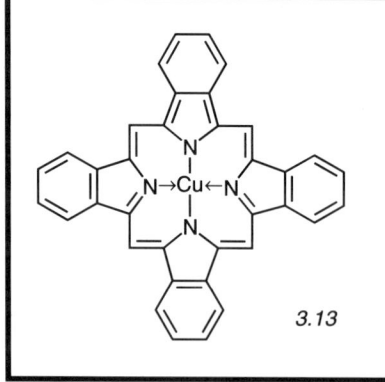

3.13

Role of intermolecular forces in coloration

Various attractive forces have the potential of binding dyes to fibres, and often more than one type of chemical bonding can operate with the same dye–fibre combination. In any dye–fibre system the dominant force depends on the chemical character of the fibre and the chemical groups in the dye molecule. The relative strengths of different bonds is given in Table 3.2.

Table 3.2 Comparison of bond strengths

Bond type	Relative strength
Van der Waals	1.0
Hydrogen	3.0
Salt link	7.0
Covalent	30.0

Van der Waals forces and hydrophobic bonding

The large size of dye molecules contributes to the general attractive forces that they exert on surrounding molecules. The forces in question are called *van der Waals forces* after their discoverer. They are individually weak and are present in all organic compounds, but their collective effect in large organic molecules is considerable. They originate as weak interactions between the nuclei of the constituent atoms of one molecule with the electrons of another. They operate only when dye and fibre molecules are in close proximity to each other, when they can become the dominant force of attraction.

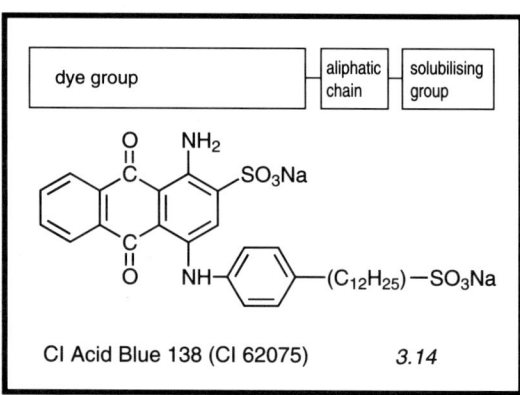

CI Acid Blue 138 (CI 62075) 3.14

Sometimes the term 'hydrophobic bonding' is used to describe a situation in which hydrophobic groups in molecules tend to associate together and escape from an aqueous environment, i.e. from a dyebath to a fibre. For instance, the attraction of the molecules of simple acid dyes for wool fibres is greatly enhanced by the incorporation of a hydrocarbon chain in the molecule (*3.14*). This converts them to milling acid dyes (discussed in Chapter 5).

Hydrogen bonds

Hydrogen bonds are a further source of attraction between molecules, somewhat similar to van der Waals forces. The hydrogen atom is the smallest of all the atoms; in organic compounds it normally forms a single covalent bond only. Often, however, a neighbouring atom may have a higher affinity for electrons than does the hydrogen atom, causing a drift of the electrons shared by the hydrogen towards the larger atom. This leaves a slight positive charge on the hydrogen atom, which in turn encourages bond formation between it and nearby atoms such as nitrogen or oxygen (*3.15*). Such bonds are

$$\text{cellulose}-\overset{\delta^-}{O}\ \overset{\delta^+}{H}\text{- -}NH_2$$
$$\overset{|}{\text{dye}}$$

3.15

readily broken and re-formed and they are one of the factors involved when substances are dissolved by water. Most dye and fibre molecules possess groups with hydrogen-bonding capability. Consequently hydrogen bonds are often involved in dye–fibre attractions. One of the features of direct dyes that contributes to their attraction for cellulosic fibres is that their molecules are long and flat, and so can align themselves in close contact with the cellulose molecule, making it easy for hydrogen bonds to form.

Dye aggregation

Individual dye molecules are also attracted to each other through van der Waals forces and hydrogen bonds, with the result that many dyes exist in solution as large molecular clusters called dye *aggregates*, which are colloidal electrolytes (page 32).

The large size of the dye aggregates can lead to a drastic reduction in the rate of fibre penetration, or in some cases to the precipitation (separation) of a dye from solution after prolonged storage. The addition of electrolyte to a dyebath can increase the degree of aggregation, but fortunately the aggregation process is reversible and may be decreased by a rise in temperature. A certain degree of aggregation can be beneficial since it tends to increase the attraction of the dye for the fibre (this is discussed further in Chapter 4). Adding salt and raising the temperature of the dyebath are both often used in the control of dyeing processes.

3.16 cyanuric chloride

Covalent bonding

Covalent bonding between dye and cellulosic fibres is achieved nowadays by the incorporation in the dye molecule of special *reactive groups*, linked to the rest of the molecule through a *bridging group*. Many such groups can be used, but the first reactive dyes were based on cyanuric chloride (*3.16*, *3.17*).

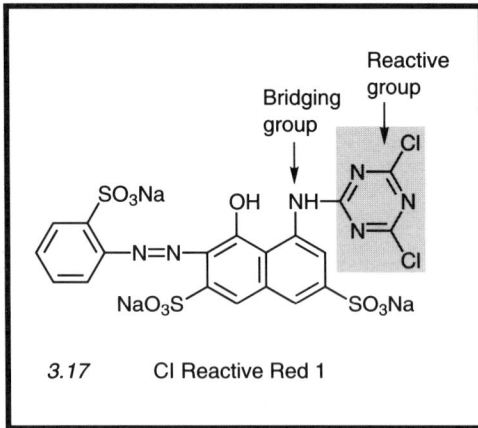

3.17   CI Reactive Red 1

$$HCl \longrightarrow H^+ + Cl^-$$
cation   anion

Scheme 3.3

$$D{-}SO_3H + NaOH \longrightarrow D{-}SO_3Na + H_2O$$

Scheme 3.4

Acid and basic groups in dyes and fibres

Reference is frequently made to acidic and basic groups when discussing coloration processes because in some dye–fibre systems they react together to form *salt links* (i.e. electrostatic links). For the purposes of understanding dye–fibre interactions, an *acid* may be regarded as a compound that will dissociate in solution to liberate hydrogen ions, H^+. For example, hydrogen ions are formed when hydrogen chloride dissolves in water, forming hydrochloric acid (Scheme 3.3).

An acidic group in a dye molecule will dissociate similarly, and will react with a basic compound. For example, the sulphonic acid group in a dye molecule will react with sodium hydroxide to form the sodium salt of the dye, already mentioned (Scheme 3.4).

Likewise, a basic group in a large molecule, such as a fibre molecule, will react with an acidic group and form a salt. Once the basic group has been liberated from combination with other acidic groups in the fibre (for instance, by the addition of a simple acid such as hydrochloric acid), it can react with an acidic dye molecule to form a salt linkage between the dye and the fibre, as shown in Figure 3.7.

pH values

The *pH scale* is a convenient way of expressing the strength of solutions of acids or bases. It distinguishes between strongly acidic and strongly basic compounds, which are completely – or almost completely – dissociated in solution, and between weak acids and weak bases which dissociate only slightly. A solution with a pH of 7 is neutral; pH values of less than 7 represent acidity and values greater than 7 alkalinity (basicity), the full scale ranging from 0 to 14.

These figures are not arbitrary. They are derived from the concentration of hydrogen ions in the solution, written $[H^+]$. Consider first the case of water, H_2O. Even liquid water undergoes dissociation to some extent: about one water molecule in every 10 million molecules dissociates. Those molecules that dissociate do so according to Scheme 3.5. Each positively charged hydrogen ion is accompanied by a negative hydroxide ion, OH⁻, so that the number of positive and negative charges in the solution are balanced.

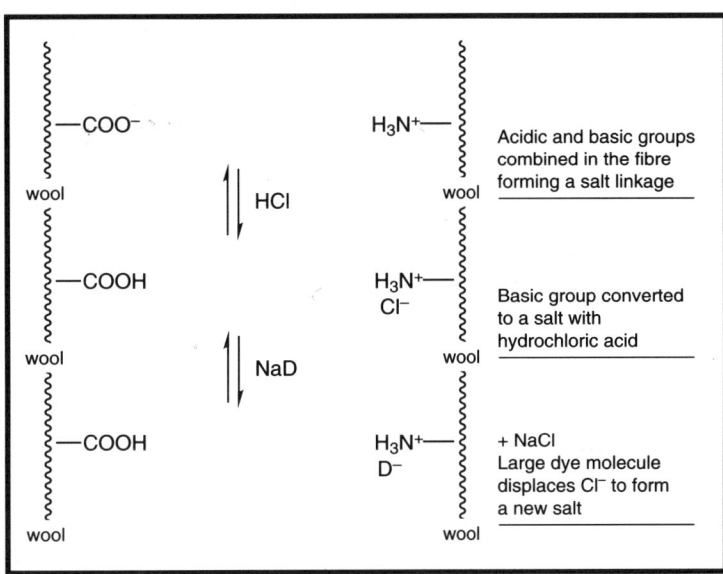

Figure 3.7 *The formation of salt linkages between a dye and a wool fibre: NaD represents the sodium salt of a large dye molecule*

A solution containing an excess of hydrogen ions, however, is acidic. Sulphuric acid, H_2SO_4, is an example of a *strong acid*, that is, one in which the acid is completely dissociated (Scheme 3.6).

Other acids, such as ethanoic acid (acetic acid, CH_3COOH), only partially dissociate in water and therefore are said to be *weak acids*. Even in weak acids, however, the number of hydrogen ions is very large, so the hydrogen ion concentration is more conveniently expressed on a logarithmic scale (Equation 3.1):

$$H_2O \longrightarrow H^+ + OH^-$$

Scheme 3.5

$$H_2SO_4 \longrightarrow 2H^+ + SO_4^{2-}$$

| sulphuric acid | 2 protons (2 electrons lost) | / | sulphate ion (2 electrons gained) |

Scheme 3.6

$$pH = -\log(H^+ \text{ concentration}) \qquad (3.1)$$

For pure water the pH = $-\log(1/10\ 000\ 000)$, i.e. $-\log(10^{-7}) = 7$. As the acidity increases the pH value diminishes, as shown in Table 3.3, overleaf.

In solutions where the pH is greater than 7, the concentration of hydrogen ions is less than in neutral water. In order that the numbers of positive and negative ions should be equal, the concentration of hydroxide ions (OH⁻) has to be higher than in water. Such solutions are *alkaline* solutions. An example of a strong alkali is sodium hydroxide (caustic soda), which dissociates according to Scheme 3.7, overleaf.

Table 3.3 Description of acidity in terms of pH

H⁺ concentration (moles per litre)	pH units	Condition of solution
10^7	7.0	Neutral
10^5	5.0	Weakly acidic
10^3	3.0	Strongly acidic
10^2	2.0	Very strongly acidic
10^1	1.0	Highest acidity

The pH of a solution can be monitored using special instruments called pH meters, or more simply (and less precisely) by putting a drop of the solution on an appropriate indicator paper. Indicator papers take on different colours at different pH values.

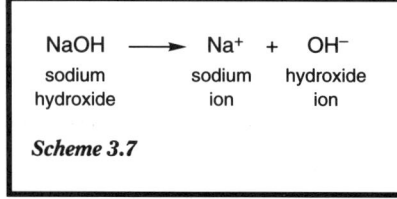

$$NaOH \longrightarrow Na^+ + OH^-$$
sodium hydroxide   sodium ion   hydroxide ion

Scheme 3.7

Redox reactions

Oxidation–reduction reactions (*redox reactions*) are important in textile coloration because they are an essential part of the process of the application of vat and sulphur dyes. In rather oversimplified terms, when a compound is *oxidised* it gains oxygen; when something is *reduced* it loses oxygen. Reduction of a substance can also be thought of as gaining hydrogen atoms, and oxidation as losing hydrogen atoms. For example, when hydrogen reacts with oxygen to form water the hydrogen becomes oxidised and the oxygen is reduced. In a redox reaction there is always a compound acting as a *reducing agent* (hydrogen in this example). The reducing agent becomes oxidised during the reaction by the compound that is being reduced, which is acting as an *oxidising agent* (in this case oxygen).

In the water molecule, each hydrogen atom shares the only electron it possesses by pairing with one of the six electrons of the oxygen atom, to form a covalent bond. Thus the hydrogen atom has lost one electron to become oxidised and the oxygen atom is reduced by gaining electrons. This is a more general way of expressing the phenomena of oxidation and reduction:

–   Oxidation – entails the loss of electrons by the oxidised compound and

–   Reduction – entails a net gain of electrons by the reduced compound.

Vat dyes such as indigo and compounds derived from anthraquinone are applied after the temporary reduction of two carbonyl groups ($>C=O$) in a conjugated chain; this converts the dye into a colourless water-soluble form. The conversion is carried out using a strong reducing agent, and in the reaction the two oxygen atoms become reduced to $-O^-$ and the two hydrogen atoms are oxidised to H⁺ (Scheme 3.8). The reduced (soluble) form is called the *leuco vat acid*, and is applied from an alkaline solution. Once on the fibre it can be re-oxidised back to the insoluble carbonyl form by air or by the use of an oxidising agent (that is, the redox reaction is reversed).

Sulphur dyes are also applied using a redox re-action mechanism, in which sodium sulphide is used as the reducing agent (Scheme 3.9).

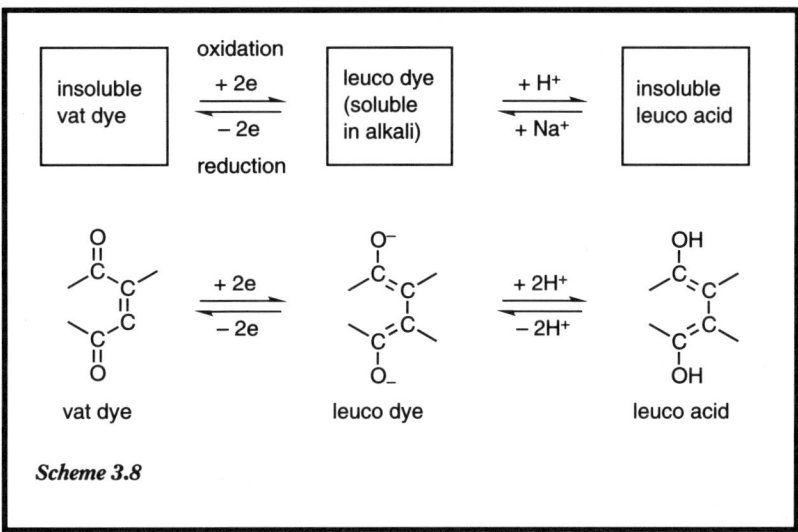

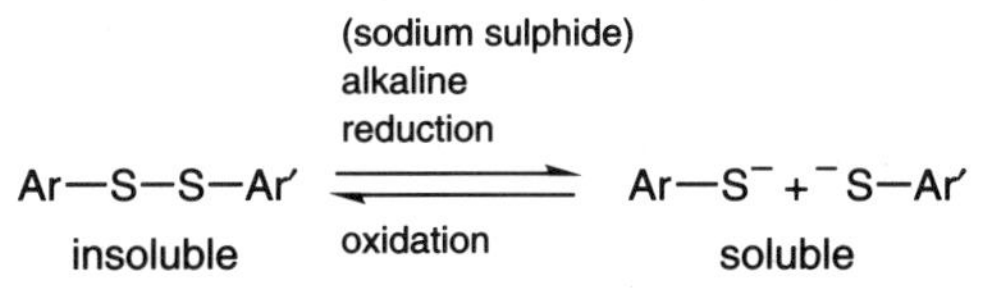

Scheme 3.8

Further reading

R Gallagher and P Ingram, *Chemistry made clear. GCSE edition* (Oxford: Oxford University Press, 1990).
R Hart, *Chemistry matters. GCSE edition* (Oxford: Oxford University Press, 1988).
E P G Gohl and L D Vilensky, *Textile science* (Harlow: Longman, 1990).

$$\text{Ar—S—S—Ar'} \underset{\text{oxidation}}{\overset{\substack{\text{(sodium sulphide)} \\ \text{alkaline} \\ \text{reduction}}}{\rightleftharpoons}} \text{Ar—S}^- + {}^-\text{S—Ar'}$$

insoluble   soluble

Scheme 3.9

CHAPTER FOUR

The attributes of fibres

Introduction

For thousands of years, humans have exploited the attributes of fibres for the provision of clothing. Sources of natural fibres are wide ranging, but fall into two main categories: cellulosic fibres (chiefly cotton) and protein fibres, which provide the hairy coating of many animals. Wool was used in primitive textiles, and linen-type fabrics were made in North Africa from stem fibres 7000 years ago. Until the advent of synthetic fibres, however, flax, cotton, wool and silk were the only four fibres chosen from all those available.

The chemical and physical properties of natural textile fibres have been thoroughly studied, and the information obtained has been put to good use in many spheres of activity. The studies provided insight into the fibres' long thread-like molecules, in which many relatively simple units are joined together as a chain, and the ways in which the physical properties of a fibre are related to the arrangement of the molecules within it. Using such knowledge, chemists have been able to synthesise materials with properties appropriate for use in almost any conditions, such as heat-resistant materials, glass substitutes, synthetic rubbers, adhesives, and aircraft and rocket components, as well as dozens of different kinds of synthetic fibre.

The total annual world production of fibres today is approximately 30 million tonnes; cotton is the most important in terms of quantity produced. Over 50% of production consists of cellulosic fibres, of which one-fifth is the regenerated cellulose fibre viscose, while cotton accounts for the bulk of the remainder. Wool, although significant in commercial terms, claims a 5% share of world fibre production only, whilst the synthetic fibres make up around 40%, of which polyester fibres account for almost half.

In this chapter we shall look at the properties of fibres in general before examining those of different classes of fibre and outlining the processes of manufacture of synthetic fibres.

Physical properties of fibres

Fibre length

The length of natural fibres varies considerably. The length (*staple*) of cotton fibres is of the order of 12 to 36 mm, depending on the source, whilst wool fibres are from 50 to 400 mm long. There is a minimum useful length of about 10 mm, however, below which the fibres are too short to be spun together into yarn. Furthermore, the characteristics of the yarns depend on the fibre length. A fluffy, spongy yarn with a soft feel is obtained from shorter fibres where many loose ends remain disoriented in the yarn. Longer fibres give smoother, finer yarns with a higher lustre.

A yarn is only as strong as its weakest point, so uniformity of yarn strength is important. To this end a minimum number of around 100 fibres is needed in the cross-section of yarns derived from short-staple fibres, and the finer the fibres the more uniform will be the strength. As the length of the fibres is increased, the degree of twist needed to hold the fibres together and develop a satisfactory strength becomes less and the yarns are correspondingly softer.

Synthetic fibres are produced in the form of continuous filaments, the advantage of which is that they can be either cut into predetermined lengths to suit the type of yarn needed or kept as continuous filaments. Natural and synthetic fibres are often blended together to combine the advantages of both in one yarn. In such cases the length of the synthetic filament may be cut to match that of the natural fibre, thus making it possible to use the same spinning machinery for both fibres.

Fibre fineness

Fibres from different sources show distinctive variations in their cross-sectional shape, but the measured width of a fibre can be taken as the fibre diameter. The theoretical relationship between the diameter and stiffness of a rod can then be invoked to explain the significance of fibre diameter in relation to the practical applications. For example, the stiffness of a fibre is proportional to the fourth power of the diameter, which means that doubling the diameter increases the resistance to bending sixteen-fold! Other factors being equal, this increase will sharply reduce the ability of the fabric to drape over shapes or to hang elegantly.

Fibres with a diameter of more than 40 microns (1 micron (μm) = one thousandth of a millimetre) tend to scratch and stick into the skin because they do not deflect easily. This diameter is

45

about that of coarse wool fibres from cross-bred sheep. Usually such fibres are used for the pile in carpets, where more resilient fibres are needed. Other wool fibres range in diameter from 15 to 40 µm, depending on the breed of animal and the position on the fleece on which it grew. Merino sheep produce the finest fibres, with a diameter of 17–25 µm. By comparison, horse hair is of the order of 100–200 µm in diameter, cow hair is coarser still at around 200 µm, whilst hairs from 180 to 250 µm in diameter are stiff enough to be referred to as bristles. (Fibres derived from animals other than the sheep are usually referred to as hairs to distinguish them from sheep's wool; few have proved suitable for specialist textile uses, but more information is available elsewhere [1]. Even though the shorter, softer fibres from different parts of various animals are often also called wool, the description should always be qualified by adding the name of the animal source – for example, cashmere wool.)

Fibres for clothing need to be soft and pliable, that is, their diameter must be small. But if the diameter is halved, the corresponding increase in softness is accompanied by a four-fold reduction in breaking strength. Consequently there are also lower limits needed for the fibre diameter if damage is to be avoided during processing. The minimum practical strength for natural fibres is associated with a diameter of 10 µm, which is found with the finer Sea Island cottons and with Canton and Japanese silks.

Fibre diameter also has a significant influence on the dyeing properties of the fibre, because the surface area of a given mass of fibres is higher for finer fibres. This relative difference between the surface areas of fine and coarse fibres allows the finer fibres to take up dye more rapidly. Fibre diameter can also affect the depth of colour of the dyed goods in relation to the amount of dye applied. For example, fibres with a diameter of 25 µm must absorb about twice as much dye per unit mass as fibres of 44 µm diameter to appear the same depth, because the colour is spread over a larger surface area with the finer fibres.

Fabric lustre

Several factors contribute to fabric lustre, including the fibre diameter and cross-sectional shape (page 66). Such factors influence the way in which light is reflected from the surface of the fabric. The alignment of the fibres in the yarn and the structure of the fabric also have an influence. A harsh shine is associated with large smooth filaments arranged in parallel, whilst finer fibres with a less uniform surface in a yarn with a lower degree of fibre orientation produce multiple reflections and a correspondingly subdued lustre. For example, the ribbon-like structure of unmercerised cotton fibres gives a low-lustre fabric. The wavy nature (i.e. the crimp) of wool from some breeds of sheep has the same effect on the sheen of wool fabrics, whilst coarser, straighter wool fibres give a lustre limited by their rough, scaly surface (see page 48). The smoothness of silk filaments is also associated with a characteristic sheen.

Morphological features of fibres

Cotton

Other characteristics of fibres become evident on more detailed study. The intricate structure of cotton fibres only becomes apparent when viewed under the optical or electron microscopes. The cotton fibre is a single-cell structure taken from the cotton plant as a seed hair which develops its characteristic appearance under the microscope as it dries out. As used, it appears as a flat ribbon-like structure with occasional convolutions along its length (Figure 4.1). These prevent parallel

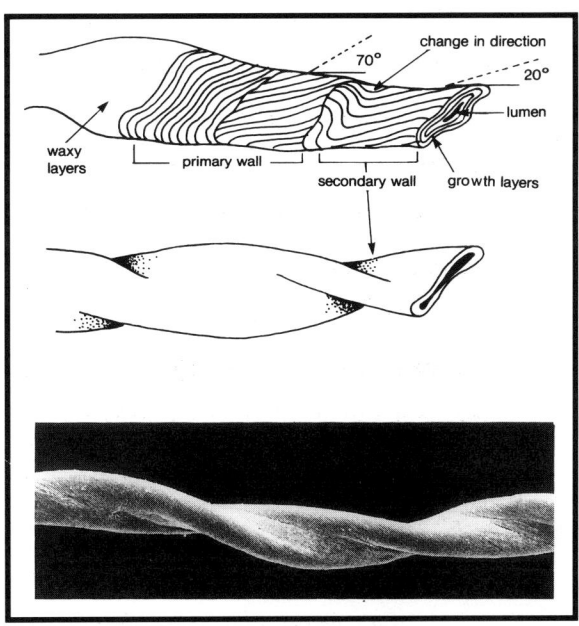

Figure 4.1 *The structure of a cotton fibre, seen (above) diagrammatically and (below) in a photomicrograph*

fibres from slipping past each other, thus contributing to the strength of the yarns when they are twisted together during spinning. The greater magnification possible with an electron microscope has enabled various morphological components of the fibre to be identified.

The outermost layer of the fibre is the thin waxy cuticle, which protects the fibre from its environment. Before cotton can be used as a textile fibre this layer has to be removed by scouring, otherwise the absorption of water-soluble dyes and other reagents is hindered during processing. Beneath this layer is the primary wall of the fibre cell, which is composed of fine threads of cellulose laid down during growth and spiralling round the longitudinal fibre axis at an angle of about 70° (just visible in Figure 4.1). Most of the fibre mass is present as the secondary wall. This also consists of spiralling fibrils, in this case with an inclination to the main fibre axis that varies from 20–30° near the primary wall to around 40° near to the central air-filled channel (the *lumen*). The direction of this spiral changes periodically along the fibre length, corresponding to the position of the convolutions mentioned above.

Wool

The appearance of wool fibres is very distinctive, with overlapping scales oriented in the direction of the tip of the fibre (Figure 4.2). The scale structure gives the fibre surface its characteristic roughness, which creates the friction between fibres in a yarn, thus contributing to its strength. Because of the orientation of the scales, however, the friction is greater in the direction of tip to root than from root to tip. This may be readily detected by lightly gripping a long hair or a wool fibre between the nails of the thumb and forefinger and pulling the fibre through the grip, first one way and then the other: the greater resistance to movement in the tip-to-root direction is evident. This directional friction effect has important technical consequences because, as the fibres are mechanically agitated in the hot wet conditions of processing, they migrate preferentially in the direction of least resistance, i.e. towards the tip of adjacent fibres. If the movement is allowed to go too far, individual fibres begin to form loops and become entangled, and the fabric or yarn structure becomes compacted. The effect can be technically desirable if controlled (as in milling or the manufacture of non-woven felt materials), but serious when it is responsible for the excessive shrinkage of a wool garment during laundering.

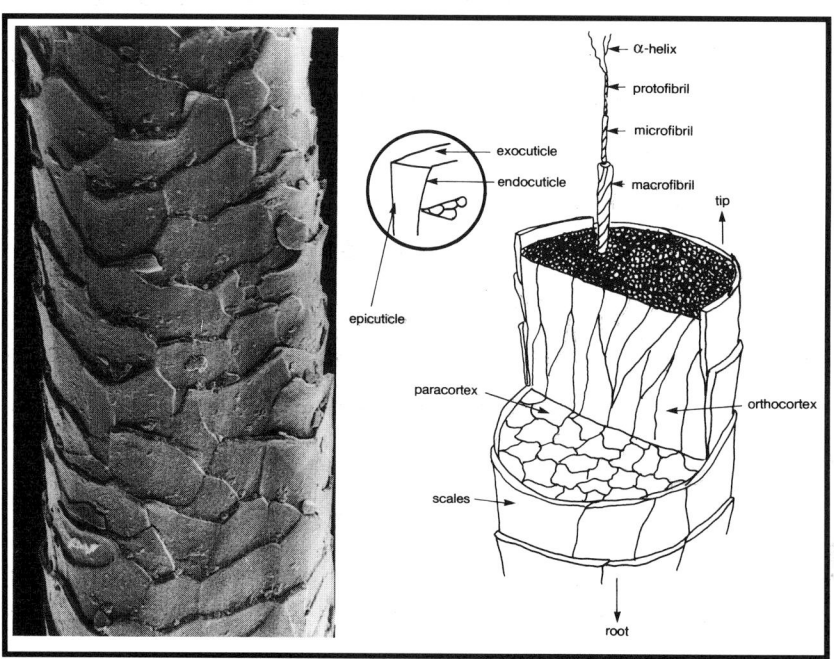

Figure 4.2 *The structure of a wool fibre*

The outer scale cells are thin structures that form the main component of the wool fibre cuticle. This surrounds the bulk of the fibre material, which is contained in the cellular cortex beneath. The cortex is a complex structure, illustrated diagrammatically in Figure 4.2, which also shows the two components of the scale cells (the exocuticle and the endocuticle).

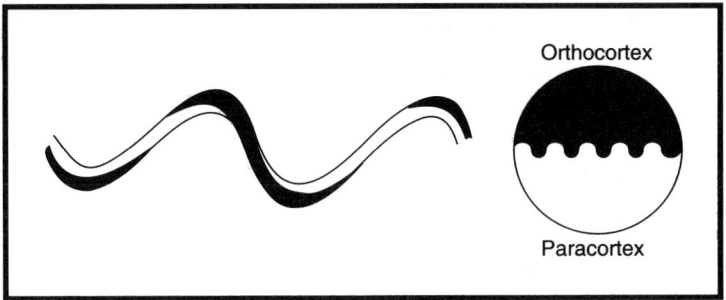

Figure 4.3 *The distribution of the orthocortex and the paracortex in a wool fibre*

The cortex cells are tapering spindle-shaped structures, constructed from component macrofibrils in which the successively smaller microfibrils, protofibrils and finally the helical structure of the protein molecule may be detected. The cortex is heterogeneous and is divided into two regions along the length of the fibre, known as the orthocortex and paracortex. The two halves spiral along the main axis of the fibre, with the more extensible orthocortex always lying on the outer curvature of the fibre (Figure 4.3). They differ slightly in their chemical composition, and the difference is responsible for a difference in their elasticity; this endows the fibres with a characteristic crimp. Other animal fibres are also cellular in structure, but both the scale structure and the crimp frequency vary from one type of animal fibre to another.

The whole fibre is held together by a series of membranes surrounding the cell structure, the outermost of which is the epicuticle.

Silk

Silk, which is also a protein fibre, is produced as a cocoon by the larva of the silk moth *Bombyx mori*. The protein is extruded from two spinnerets, one on each side of the head of the caterpillar, as a pair of continuous filaments between 3000 and 4000 m in length, joined together by a gum called serecin. The gum is removed during processing to release the individual filaments, which have a triangular cross-section and a smooth surface.

General characteristics of cotton and wool fibres

Comfortable clothing can be made using either cotton or wool fibres; both have the capacity to keep the body comfortable by conducting water from the skin to the atmosphere. Both are hydrophilic (water-attracting) fibres, because they possess functional groups that are capable of hydrogen bonding with water molecules. In cellulose they are mostly hydroxyl (OH) groups, but there are several different kinds of hydrophilic group in wool molecules.

In most other respects their chemical and morphological dissimilarities make the attributes of cotton and wool very different. For example, cotton can be safely sterilised in boiling water or by ironing at around 200 °C. Wool, by contrast, becomes harsh and scorched under a hot iron and weak when wet, with detrimental chemical changes taking place at higher washing temperatures. On the other hand, cotton creases very easily, whereas the higher resiliency of wool allows fabric to recover from creasing and retain its shape. Cotton fibres are easier to store because wool protein is palatable to the larvae of certain moths and beetles.

The crimp of wool fibres prevents their close packing in a yarn. Consequently a good deal of the volume of the yarn is air, which makes for a lofty (bulky) warm yarn, the warmth being due to the insulating properties of the static air inside the yarn. Once external pressure is applied (for example, on a windy day), the air begins to flow through the fabric and the warmth of the garments is reduced. In contrast, the flat straight shape of cotton fibres allows them to pack together into a closely structured high-density yarn, which when tightly woven produces a wind-resistant fabric.

The biggest drawback of cellulosic materials, however, is the ease with which they ignite and burn. In this respect wool is superior because it does not readily support combustion, showing only a tendency to become badly singed, due in part to the high nitrogen content of the fibre.

Molecular structure of fibres

In Chapter 3 the formation of molecules was discussed, without considering their size. In general, of course, the more atoms there are in a molecule, the larger it will be. The size of the molecules of most familiar chemical compounds may be deduced precisely from their chemical formulae. But many of the molecules forming the structural material of naturally occurring substances are so immense that simple chemical analysis is no longer an adequate guide to their true structure or shape. Such molecules are referred to as *macromolecules*.

The general concept of structure upon which modern macromolecular chemistry is based was first proposed by Staudinger, who envisaged such molecules as exceptionally long chains of repeating identical units. Each unit is a single simple molecule, but within the chain many such units are chemically linked in a head-to-tail arrangement, like the carriages on a train (Figure 4.4).

His views have since been adequately confirmed, particularly by the work of Carothers, who was the first person to take simple compounds, synthesise a polymer and adapt its chemical structure to obtain a material with specified physical properties. The resulting nylon fibres soon became appreciated by the public through the hosiery trade during the time of World War 2, when the traditional silk filaments were unobtainable.

The molecule used as the building block in the construction of the long-chain molecule is referred to as the *monomer* and the long molecules themselves are *polymer* molecules, the word polymer being derived from the Greek *poly* (many) and *meros* (parts or segments). The chemical properties of the polymer chains are therefore governed by the monomer, so that a monomer with hydrophilic groups will produce a hydrophilic polymer and a hydrophobic monomer a hydrophobic polymer. Wool and cellulose, for example, are both constructed from hydrophilic monomers, and accordingly the fibres are hydrophilic in character.

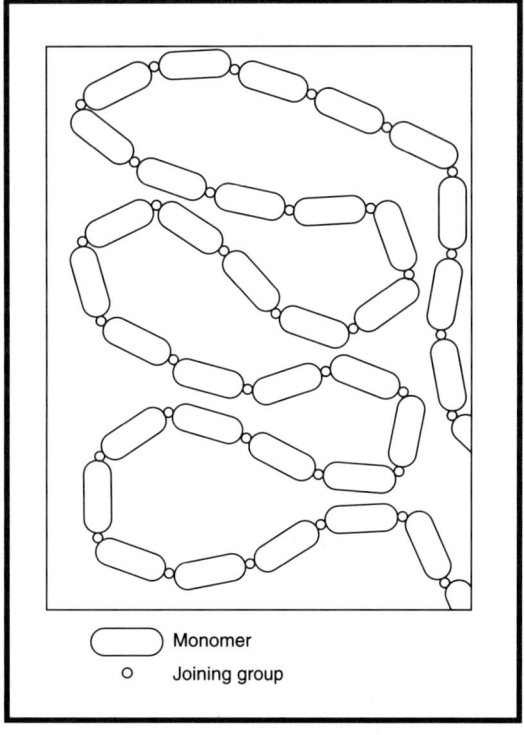

Figure 4.4 Representation of a step-growth polymer chain

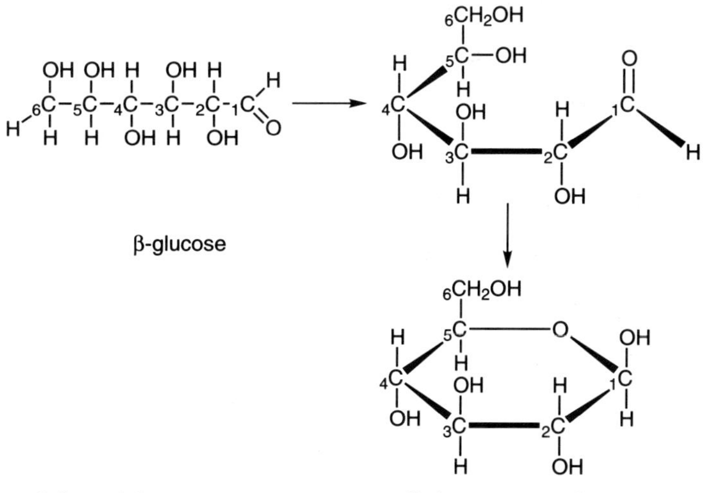

Scheme 4.1

β-glucose

β-glucopyranose ring

Structure of the cellulose molecule

The cellulose molecule is closely related to the simple sugar glucose. Glucose forms a ring structure comprising five carbon atoms and one oxygen atom (Scheme 4.1). In this conformational formula

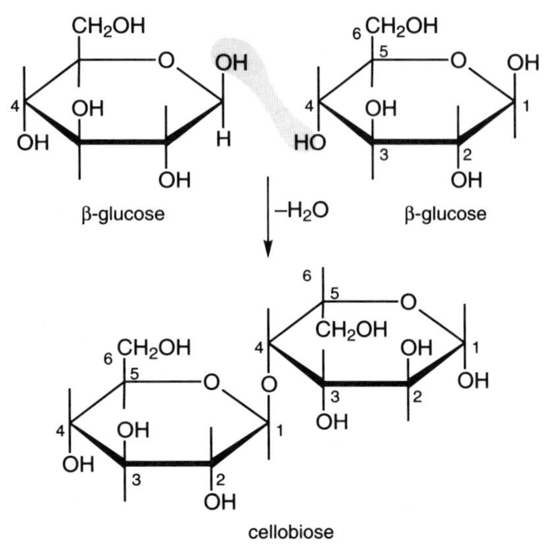

Scheme 4.2

the thick bonds are taken as being in front of the plane of the paper and the thin bonds behind the plane of the paper, while the tapered bonds indicate the relative dispositions of the adjoining atoms. Glucose is the monomer unit of the cellulose polymer, whilst the repeat unit is cellobiose, a sugar formed by the joining of two glucose units at the terminal hydroxyl groups attached to carbon atoms 1 and 4 with the loss of a molecule of water (Scheme 4.2, in which the hydrogen and carbon atoms incorporated in the ring are omitted for clarity; notice the inversion of the second glucose unit in cellobiose).

Structure *4.1* represents the structure of the cellulose chain; the repeat unit is shown in brackets and marked with a subscript n, to indicate that there are many such units in the chain. For cellulose this number, often called the *degree of polymerisation*, depends on the origin of the sample: for isolated cellulose n is of the order of 3000 (that is, 6000 glucose units) but for cellulose in fibres it may be twice this value, or even more.

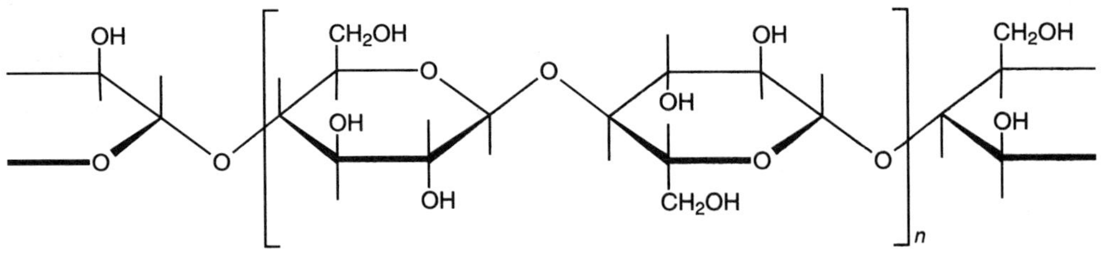

4.1   cellobiose

Each glucose ring in the chain contains three hydroxyl groups and it is their presence that allows cotton to absorb moisture and form hydrogen bonds, in particular with certain direct dyes (*4.2*). The formation of hydrogen bonds between adjacent cellulose chains has a particularly important effect, for without them a water molecule would become attached to each hydroxyl group in the cellulose chains and the fibre would dissolve. Cellulose will not dissolve in water, however, and in fact is insoluble in all but a few organic solvents. Furthermore, the interaction between the polymer chains is so strong that cellulose does not melt on heating; the chains break down and degrade before the temperature rises to a level at which they could be torn apart to form a liquid.

4.2   cellulose chain

Structure of the wool molecule

Wool is a protein, and all protein material is composed of polymer

4.3

chains containing many different *amino acids* as monomer units. The differences between the various proteins lie in the proportions of each acid they contain, and the sequence in which they appear along the length of the polymer chain. All amino acids contain carbon, hydrogen, nitrogen and oxygen, and some contain sulphur too. Some proteins have globular molecules, and these are soluble in water. Others, the fibrous proteins that form the structural material of animal life, are insoluble. Wool is one of the *keratin* group of fibrous proteins, which includes other animal hairs, horn and nails.

Each amino acid contains a carboxylic acid group (—COOH) and a basic amino group (—NH_2). This pattern is common to all the amino acids, the simplest of which is *glycine*; structure *4.3* shows the generalised formula. The middle carbon atom in glycine is linked to a carboxylic acid group, an amino group and two hydrogen atoms. One of the hydrogen atoms can be replaced by another group to form a different amino acid and thus a whole series of such acids can be obtained, each containing a different side-group.

Growth of a protein chain requires the amino group of one acid to react with the carboxylic

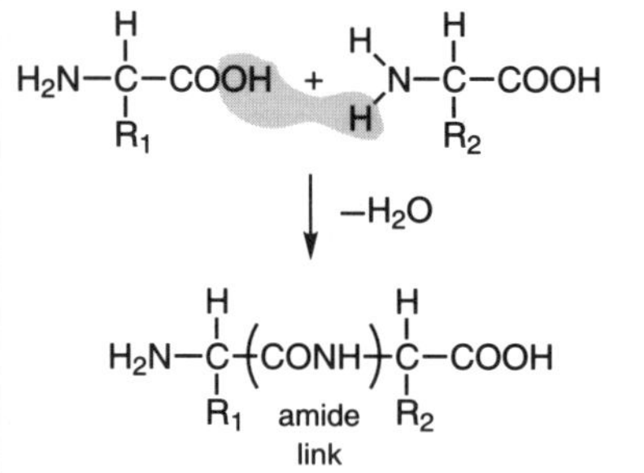

Scheme 4.3

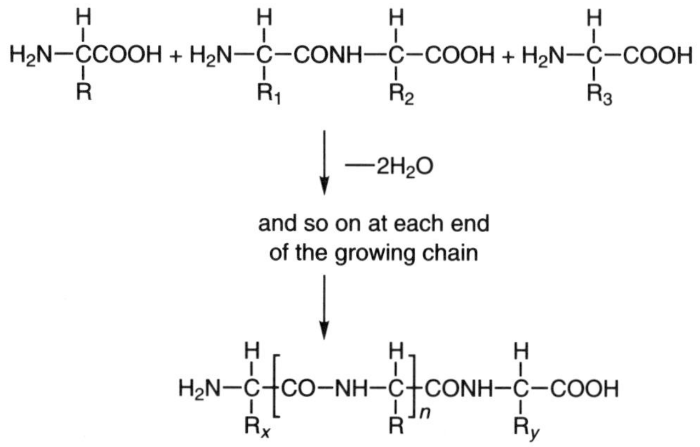

$$H_2N-\underset{\underset{R_1}{|}}{\overset{\overset{H}{|}}{C}}-COOH \; + \; \underset{\underset{H}{|}}{\overset{\overset{H}{|}}{N}}-\underset{\underset{R_2}{|}}{\overset{\overset{H}{|}}{C}}-COOH$$

$$\downarrow \;\; -H_2O$$

$$H_2N-\underset{\underset{R_1}{|}}{\overset{\overset{H}{|}}{C}}-(CONH)-\underset{\underset{R_2}{|}}{\overset{\overset{H}{|}}{C}}-COOH$$

amide
link

Scheme 4.4

$$H_2N-\underset{\underset{R}{|}}{\overset{\overset{H}{|}}{C}}COOH + H_2N-\underset{\underset{R_1}{|}}{\overset{\overset{H}{|}}{C}}-CONH-\underset{\underset{R_2}{|}}{\overset{\overset{H}{|}}{C}}-COOH + H_2N-\underset{\underset{R_3}{|}}{\overset{\overset{H}{|}}{C}}-COOH$$

$$\downarrow \;\; -2H_2O$$

and so on at each end
of the growing chain

$$\downarrow$$

$$H_2N-\underset{\underset{R_x}{|}}{\overset{\overset{H}{|}}{C}}-\left[CO-NH-\underset{\underset{R}{|}}{\overset{\overset{H}{|}}{C}}\right]_n CONH-\underset{\underset{R_y}{|}}{\overset{\overset{H}{|}}{C}}-COOH$$

acid group of the next. In the reaction one molecule of water is lost and an amide linkage is formed (Scheme 4.3). This process is repeated at each end of the new molecule, and thus the molecule steadily grows in length (Scheme 4.4). In effect the monomer unit is only one carbon atom long, and because the bonds of a carbon atom are arranged in space as a tetrahedron (Figure 3.4), keratin molecules in the normal state exist with their backbone coiled into a helix. This is alpha (α) keratin, and it will be indicated later how the alpha keratin helix influences the elasticity of wool fibres.

One particular amino acid has a significant influence on wool during wet processing. This is *cystine*, which has two atoms of sulphur in its molecule. The two sulphur atoms bridge the two halves of the molecule, each of which contains one acid group and one amino group. Because of its structure cystine can become incorporated into more than one wool molecule, forming a *disulphide bridge* between them. The formula of cystine and a diagrammatic representation of the

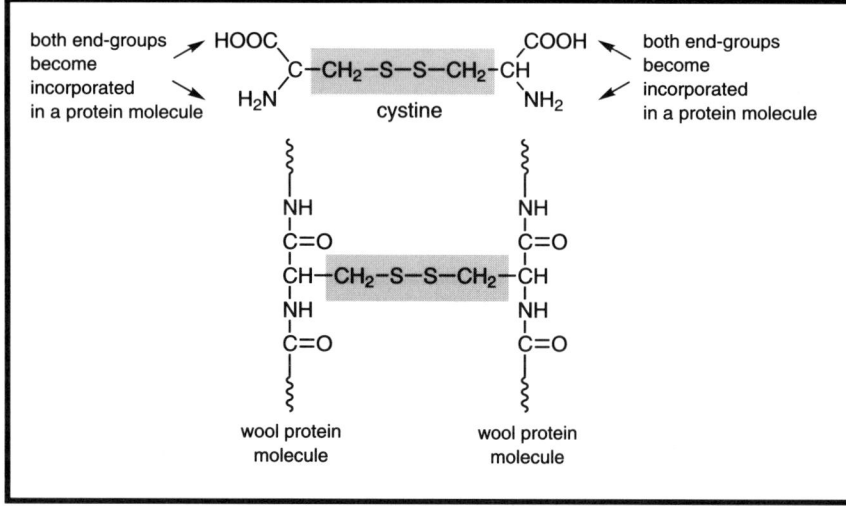

Figure 4.5 *The origin of disulphide crosslinks in wool molecules*

way in which it bridges (*crosslinks*) two wool molecules are shown in Figure 4.5. The disulphide bridge is susceptible to hot wet conditions and alkaline solutions, both of which split the crosslink; other reagents can have the same effect. If the reactions are

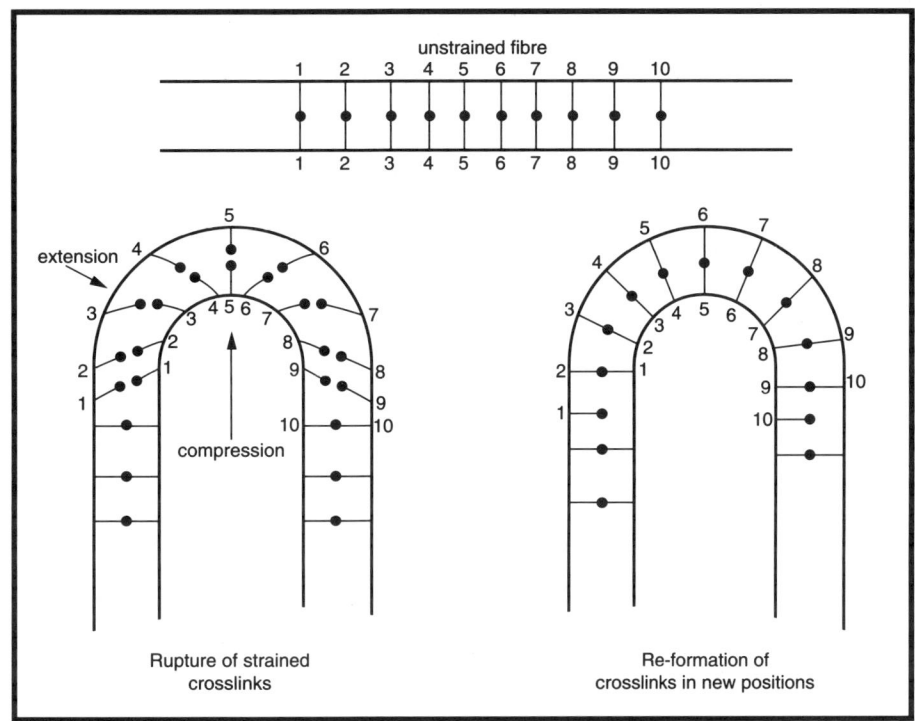

Figure 4.6 *The rupture and re-formation of crosslinks*

not controlled the properties of the fibre are harmed. With care, however, it is possible to manipulate conditions to advantage by allowing the crosslinks to be broken and to match up with different halves, thus forming a new crosslink in a different position (Figure 4.6). In this way creases and pleats may be fixed into the fabric by damp ironing, or fabric may be given a smooth flat appearance. This is also the principle of the permanent waving of human hair, but in this case a chemical reagent is used to split the crosslinks.

Amphoteric character of wool

All the side-groups of the constituent amino acids are found along the length of the wool protein molecule. Since these include both acidic and basic groups, wool is able to absorb and combine with acids through the basic groups and alkalis through the acid groups. Molecules with this ability are termed *amphoteric*. The acid and basic groups of adjacent chains also react with each other to form salt linkages, and their role in the dyeing of wool with acid dyes is discussed in Chapters 3 and 5.

At high pH values (alkaline solutions) the acidic groups ionise to form negative ions, leaving the wool with a net negative charge (Scheme 4.5). At low pH values (acidic solutions) the situation is wool—COOH + NaOH ⟶ wool—COO⁻ + Na⁺ + H₂O

Scheme 4.5

wool—NH₂ + HCl ⟶ wool—NH₃⁺ + Cl⁻

Scheme 4.6

reversed, the basic groups reacting with hydrogen ions in the solution to form positive ions and the wool is left with a net positive charge (Scheme 4.6). It follows that there must be a pH at which the numbers of negative and positive charges are equal. This pH is called the *isoelectric point* of the protein.

Fibre structure and elasticity

As well as the chemical differences between wool and cotton, there are also differences in the ways in which the constituent polymer chains are arranged in the fibre. These have a profound effect on their physical properties. Wool garments will easily stretch and recover during use, but their cotton counterparts have very little 'give'. The difference is largely due to the degree of alignment of the polymer chains along the fibre axis. In cotton fibres the cellulose molecules exist as fully extended chains aligned sufficiently close in register to enable crystallisation to occur within the fibre. The crystalline material is difficult to deform and this, together with the already extended configuration of the molecules, makes cotton fibres hard to stretch. All the molecules in the cross-section of the fibre take a share of the imposed stress, and consequently cotton fibres will withstand a high tensile force before breaking. But crystalline material is also brittle and cotton fibres are easily fractured on bending, a property that is associated with a reduced resistance to abrasion.

The protein chains in wool fibres are very different. Reference was made earlier to the coiled configuration of the protein chains and the way in which they are crosslinked through cystine disulphide links. Disulphide linkages also form bridges between coils within the same molecule, and so the fibre becomes an extensive molecular grid structure.

When the fibres are stretched the coils straighten out, but on release of the tensile force the crosslinks cause the chains to spring back to their original helical arrangement. Wool fibres can therefore undergo considerable reversible extension. With this molecular configuration there is very little crystallisation and any strain is distributed unevenly between molecules, which leads to a lower breaking strength. Wool is therefore weak but highly extensible; the balance between the tensile strength and elasticity of wool makes it a very desirable textile fibre.

Left from top:
indigo
indigo
cochineal/alum
cochineal/copper
indigo and weld
weld
quercitron bark
alder bark/iron/indigo
madder/alum
madder/alum
cochineal/tin
cochineal/tin

Right from top:
woad
Ochrolechia tartarea/alkali
Ochrolechia tartarea/acid
Ochrolechia tartarea
Xanthoria parietina (photo-oxidised)
elder leaves/iron
hedge mustard/alum
crab apple leaves/alum
Parmelia saxatalis
alder bark/iron
lady's bedstraw/tin
lady's bedstraw/alum

Plate 1 *Some natural dyes on wool*

Plate 2 *Standards for assessment of fading in light fastness testing*

Fastness Properties

	[1] Daylight ISO Std. Depth				[2] Washing ISO No.2		ISO No.3		[27] Dyeing Methods
	1/25 (a)	1/3 (b)	1/1 (c)	2/1 (d)	Effect (a)	Stain (b)	Effect (c)	Stain (d)	
Coomassie Milling Scarlet G 150 — C.I. Acid Red 97	2–3	3	3	3–4	4	5 (w) 5 (c)	3	4 (w) 4–5 (c)	4 5 8
					4–5	4–5 (w) 5 (c)	3	3–4 (w) 5 (c)	
Coomassie Fast Scarlet BS — C.I. Acid Red 111	3	3–4	4–5	5	4	5 (w) 5 (c)	4 WY	4–5 (w) 5 (c)	4 5 8
					4	4–5 (w) 5 (c)	4	4–5 (w) 5 (c)	
Coomassie Red PG 150 — C.I. Acid Red 85	3	3–4	4	4–5	4	5 (w) 4 (c)	3 WD	4–5 (w) 3–4 (c)	4 5 8
					4	4 (w) 3 (c)	3 WD	4 (w) 3 (c)	
Coomassie Red PR	3	3–4	4	4	4	5 (w) 4 (c)	3	4–5 (w) 3–4 (c)	4 5 8
					4	4–5 (w) 3 (c)	3	4 (w) 3 (c)	
Carbolan Crimson BS — C.I. Acid Red 138	2–3	3	3–4	4	4–5	5 (w) 5 (c)	3–4	4–5 (w) 5 (c)	5 7 8
					4–5	4–5 (w) 5 (c)	4	4–5 (w) 5 (c)	
Carbolan Rubine 2B 150 — C.I. Acid Red 129	3	3–4	4–5	5	4–5	5 (w) 5 (c)	3–4	4–5 (w) 4–5 (c)	5 7 8
					4–5	4–5 (w) 4–5 (c)	4	4 (w) 4–5 (c)	
Coomassie Bordeaux BS — C.I. Acid Red 134	3	4	4–5	5	5	5 (w) 5 (c)	4 Bl	4–5 (w) 4–5 (c)	4 5 8
					4–5	5 (w) 5 (c)	4 W Bl	4–5 (w) 4–5 (c)	

Left side labels: Test Depth 1/3 I.S.O.; Test Depth 1/1 I.S.O.; Acid Milling Dyes

Right side: Test Depth 1/3 I.S.O.; Test Depth 1/1 I.S.O.; I.S.O. Standard Depths — 1/25, 1/3, 1/1, 2/1

Swatch percentages by row:

Dye	1/25	1/3	1/1	2/1
Coomassie Milling Scarlet G 150	0·015%	0·13%	0·4%	0·75%
Coomassie Fast Scarlet BS	0·03%	0·3%	1·0%	2·2%
Coomassie Red PG 150	0·02%	0·18%	0·55%	1·1%
Coomassie Red PR	0·033%	0·3%	0·9%	1·8%
Carbolan Crimson BS	0·03%	0·25%	0·75%	1·5%
Carbolan Rubine 2B 150	0·025%	0·25%	0·75%	1·7%
Coomassie Bordeaux BS	0·03%	0·2%	0·65%	1·3%

98

Plate 3 *A typical shade card for acid dyes*

Plate 4 *Harris tweed fabric, frayed out to show the differently coloured component fibres of each yarn*

Plate 5 *'Photographic' printing permits subtle tone gradation*

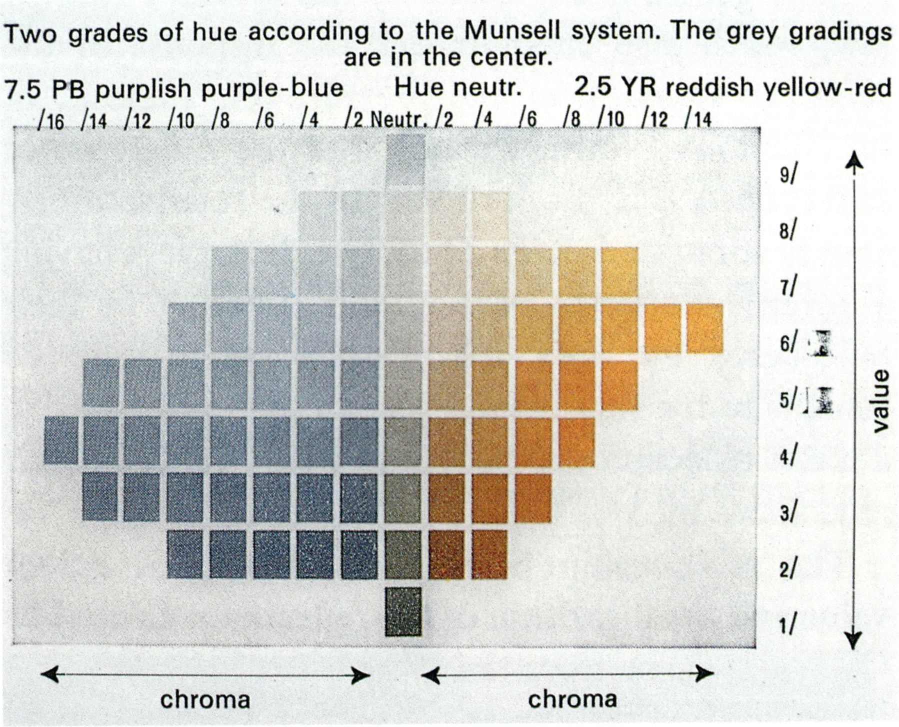

Two grades of hue according to the Munsell system. The grey gradings are in the center.

7.5 PB purplish purple-blue   Hue neutr.   2.5 YR reddish yellow-red

/16 /14 /12 /10 /8 /6 /4 /2 Neutr. /2 /4 /6 /8 /10 /12 /14

9/
8/
7/
6/
5/
4/   value
3/
2/
1/

chroma   chroma

Plate 6 *A page from a colour atlas,* The Munsell dictionary of colour

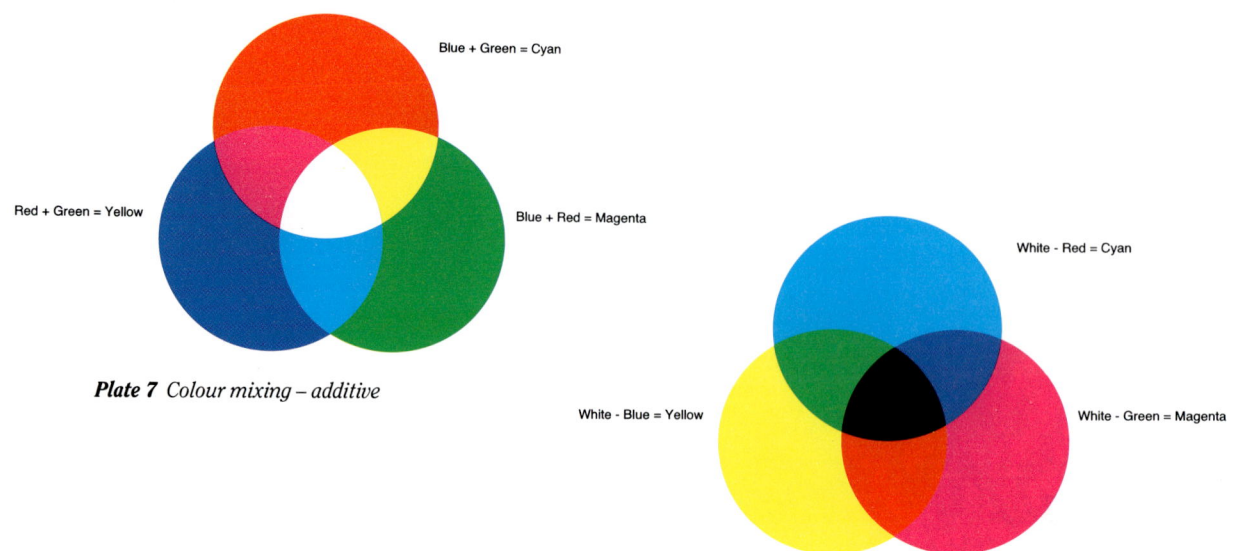

Blue + Green = Cyan

Red + Green = Yellow

Blue + Red = Magenta

Plate 7 *Colour mixing – additive*

White - Red = Cyan

White - Blue = Yellow

White - Green = Magenta

Plate 8 *Colour mixing – subtractive*

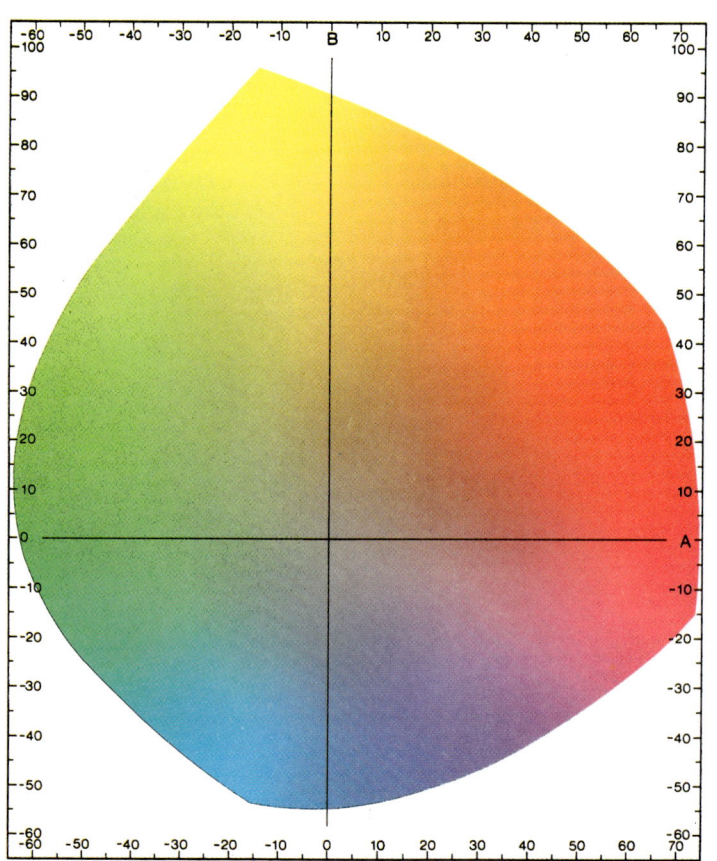

Plate 9 *CIE 1976 colour map (courtesy ICI plc)*

Amorphous and crystalline material

Crystalline material is very hard and resistant to the penetration of chemical reagents and dyes, but even with a highly crystalline material such as cotton there still remain some parts of the polymer chains that are less highly organised. This is regarded as amorphous material (a term that somewhat oversimplifies the situation), and it is within these regions that penetration and reaction take place. Any influence that changes the crystalline order also modifies the ease with which dyes and other agents are absorbed. The *mercerisation* process for cellulose is an example. Treatment of cotton with caustic soda causes a marked swelling, which is accompanied by a change to a round cross-sectional shape and a reduction in size, though not in total quantity, of the crystalline material. The fibre lustre is also increased, and there is a marked improvement in both the speed of dyeing and the quantity of dye taken up. On the other hand, the crystallinity and ordered orientation are less and the fibre molecules are more accessible.

Regenerated fibres

Clearly, taken together, cotton and wool possess a wide range of properties desirable for textile fibres. But for many years textile chemists dreamed of discovering how such properties could be obtained by design through synthetic routes.

The first step towards making fibres synthetically was the discovery of how to dissolve waste cellulose and regenerate it into the form of a fibre. The first successful venture of this kind was made by Chardonnet, who converted cellulose into a viscous mass of cellulose nitrate, which was forced through a spinneret to form a filament. This could be spun into a useful textile yarn once the solvent had evaporated, but unfortunately the product was dangerously flammable. The subsequent conversion of cellulose to cellulose acetate (ethanoate) avoided this problem, and cellulose acetate dope was first used by Wherry and Dreyfus for coating the canvas wing covers of aeroplanes in World War 1. Later they turned their attention to the conversion of acetate dope into a useful textile yarn, and such materials are still familiar today. Fabrics made from cellulose triacetate fibres met with particular interest at the time because, as the first hydrophobic fibres, they were the first to be endowed with quick-drying properties.

Fibres have also been regenerated from natural cellulose dissolved in one of two solvents. One was a solution of cuprammonium hydroxide, which gave the now obsolete fibre *cupro* (cuprammonium rayon). The other dates back to the discovery by Cross, Bevan and Beadle in 1892 that carbon disulphide can dissolve cellulose in the form of wood pulp to give cellulose xanthate. Some time later, in 1905, Courtaulds developed the process for the regeneration of the cellulose from the cellulose xanthate dope to produce the first *viscose* fibres, and their development continues to this day.

When wet the original viscose fibres suffered a drop in tensile strength, but this was later overcome with the development of *polynosic* fibres such as *Vincel 64*, a fibre which in water has properties similar to those of cotton. Polynosic fibres are used extensively in the form of knitted and woven goods for dress and a variety of other fabrics. They are also used in blends with cotton or polyester for sheets, shirtings and rainwear fabrics. A further version is *Sarille*, staples of which have a crimped configuration that imparts a warm handle to the fabric.

Eventually, however, fibres were developed from polymers synthesised directly from simple monomers, imitating the ways in which the natural molecules of cotton and wool are constructed, rather than by modifying natural polymers like cellulose.

Making synthetic fibres

Following the elucidation of the chemical structure of natural fibres, attention was turned to making fibre molecules using simple starting materials. The synthesis of cellulose molecules from carbon dioxide and water by photosynthesis (the chain of reactions that proceeds in all green plants in the light) and the production of fibrous protein from amino acids have so far eluded chemists.

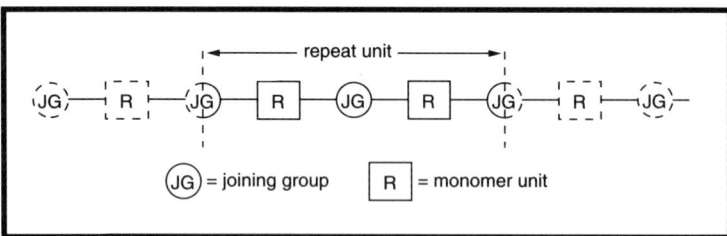

Figure 4.7 The molecular pattern of a step-growth polymer

Nevertheless, many useful textile fibres, such as the familiar and highly successful polyamide and polyester fibres, have been synthesised from simple compounds extracted from crude oil. The general pattern of their construction is shown in Figure 4.7, in which the repeat unit is first made by joining two simple compounds together and then repeating the process at both ends of the new molecule so formed. A simple analogy is a system of hooks and eyes (Figure 4.8).

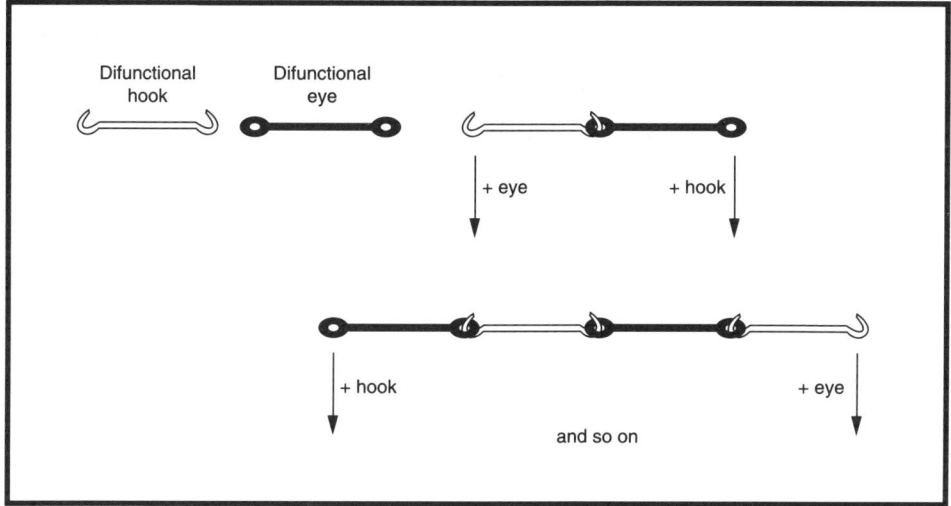

Figure 4.8 The stepwise construction of a 'hook and eye' chain

Step-growth polymers

Nylon fibres

Carothers' discovery nylon, already mentioned, is formed from a monomer made by the reaction of a carboxylic acid with an amine (a compound containing the amino group, $-NH_2$), with the loss of one molecule of water. Carothers deliberately started with difunctional reagents, that is, compounds containing identical functional groups at both ends of the molecule. For example, for the synthesis of nylon 6.6, the first nylon that was marketed, the difunctional acid is hexanedioic acid (adipic acid) and the difunctional base is 1,6-diaminohexane (hexamethylene-diamine). The joining process is repeated 100 times or more and the resulting polymer is designated by reference to the joining group. In the case of nylon it is the amide group ($-CONH-$). Consequently such polymers are called *polyamides* (Scheme 4.7). Nylon 6.6 is so called to indicate that both the diacid and the diamine contain six carbon atoms. This

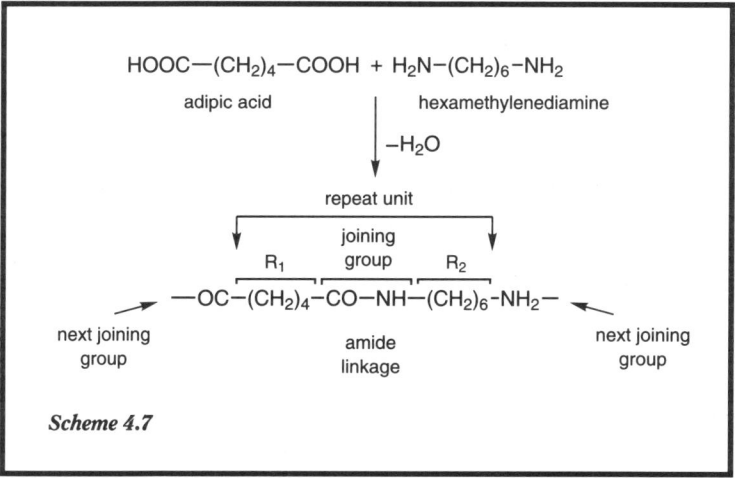

Scheme 4.7

distinguishes this particular polyamide from others made from different starting materials. For example, nylon 6 is made from a single kind of molecule, caprolactam ($H_2N(CH_2)_5COOH$).

Nylon fibres are widely used, particularly in clothing, overalls and menswear. Nylon also improves abrasion resistance when incorporated into a carpet pile.

Although the carbon atoms are represented here by a condensed formula, the actual structure of a row of six carbon atoms is a linear zig-zag arrangement in which the four bonds of each carbon atom point to the corners of a tetrahedron (cf. Figure 3.4). This allows the component carbon atoms to rotate about the carbon–carbon bonds, and it is this freedom of movement that gives the polymer molecules the flexibility usually required in a fibre. This flexibility is to a considerable extent lost in aromatic polyamide or *aramid* fibres, in which the amine component is a benzene ring carrying two amino groups (a benzenediamine). The *para* isomer, benzene-1,4-diamine (*p*-phenylenediamine), is used in the manufacture of *Kevlar* fibres. These have a much higher melting point than that of nylon, and good fire resistance; their textile properties are poor, however, in that their abrasion resistance and flex life are inferior and they cannot be dyed easily. They are nevertheless valuable because of their great mechanical strength and are used as reinforcing fibres for highly stressed articles (vehicle tyres, for instance) and for protective apparel such as bullet-proof vests. *Nomex* fibres are based on the use of benzene-1,3-diamines (*m*-phenylenediamines) as monomers. These fibres have better textile properties and can be used in protective clothing. Recent developments have produced a Nomex fibre which is more readily dyed. The two types of fibre can be combined to make a fabric for protective wear, which has exceptional fire and heat resistance; this provides a good example of a *synergistic* effect, that is, one in which the performance of the components in combination substantially exceeds that which is to be expected from an assessment of their individual properties.

Polyester fibres

Long polymer molecules have also been formed by combining a difunctional alcohol with a difunctional acid. The reaction of an organic acid with an alcohol gives an ester, and it is the ester group (— COO —) that acts as the joining group in the polymer (hence the name 'polyester').

The first commercially successful fibres of this kind were developed by J R Whinfield and J R Dickinson in the 1950s and, like polyamides, they rapidly became established as useful textile fibres. The starting materials in this case were ethanediol (ethylene glycol), a difunctional alcohol, and benzene-1,4-dicarboxylic acid (terephthalic acid), a difunctional acid (Scheme 4.8), which react together to form poly(ethylene terephthalate). Polyester fibres are noted for their easy-drying properties. They are used extensively in knitted and woven fabrics for apparel and household textiles and in the construction of functional articles such as car seat belts, ropes, nets and sails.

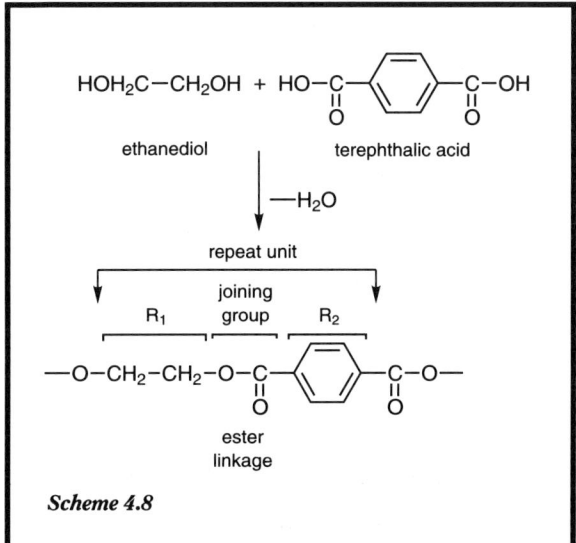

Scheme 4.8

Elastofibres

Elastofibres are based on polyurethane polymers, similar to those used in varnishes and paints. They are *copolymers*, in which long chains of a polyester or polyether (providing flexibility and stretch) are linked to urethane segments, which bond with each other and hold the structure together. This special molecular construction provides the fibres with a reversible stretch that rivals that of rubber. They are incorporated into activity wear, proving to be strong, hard-wearing and light in weight.

As indicated earlier, polyesters and polyamide polymers are formed in a series of steps, each step in the reaction adding a further unit on an end of the growing chain. For this reason they are called *step-growth polymers*. In theory the polymer chain will grow for as long as the reaction is allowed to continue. In practice, however, there are limits to the length of chain required for fibre formation. If the molecules are too short the fibres will be too weak. On the other hand, if the chain is too long the polymer becomes unmanageable because it can be neither melted at a temperature low enough to avoid decomposition nor dissolved in solvents to be formed into a fibre.

Chain-growth polymers

Other well-known synthetic fibres have been synthesised using a functional group that is very different in behaviour from those involved in step-growth polymerisation. *Acrylic* fibres and those based on *polypropylene* are synthesised through the reactions of *vinyl groups*, in which two aliphatic carbon atoms are joined by a double bond. *Vinyl polymerisation* is possible because of the

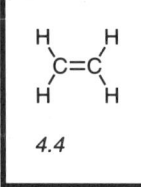

4.4

different character of the two bonds. The two shared electrons forming one of the covalent bonds are firmly bound, as usual in a covalent bond. As explained in Chapter 2, the electrons in the second bond are fairly readily displaced, thus making the bond less stable, i.e. more reactive.

The simplest vinyl monomer is the alkene ethene (ethylene, *4.4*). Molecules of ethene can be made to react together on the surface of a catalyst, where the two electrons of the less stable bond become unpaired and react rapidly with corresponding unpaired electrons in adjacent ethene molecules. This results in the formation of a stable single bond joining the two molecules together, in the same manner as shown for propene in Scheme 4.9.

One of the hydrogen atoms is added to the terminal carbon atom at one end of the new molecule, leaving the free electron on the carbon atom at the other end. But electrons cannot remain unpaired, and so a spontaneous reaction occurs with the next vinyl monomer. This continues until the process is halted by other reactions that terminate the growth of the chain. The end result is a long flexible chain some tens of thousands of carbon atoms in length. The polymer is called *polyethylene* or *polythene*, even though its repeat unit is the methylene group (— CH_2—).

polypropylene   repeat unit

Scheme 4.9

Olefin fibres

Some of the fibres based on alkene monomers (known collectively, from the traditional name for alkenes, as *olefin fibres*) are useful textile fibres. Polyethylene fibres have been produced, but since their melting point is below the temperature of the coolest iron they are not of much value for textile purposes. *Polypropylene*, prepared from propene (propylene, *4.5*) is a similar but more robust polymer that does have uses for textiles; the head-to-tail reaction of propene molecules forms the polymer (Scheme 4.9).

In this case the propene monomer is recognisable in the repeat unit. The production of polypropylene relies on the activity of special catalysts that ensure that the reaction takes place specifically in a head-to-tail manner. This catalytic intervention forces all the methyl side-groups to a position on the same side of the backbone of the polymer chain, thereby raising the melting point to 160 °C. These fibres are light in weight, and because they contain only carbon and hydrogen atoms they are very hydrophobic. They cannot be dyed and therefore colour is incorporated at the spinning stage. Polypropylene fibres are good for industrial uses such as ropes, filter fabrics and conveyor belts, but their textile applications are largely limited to carpet manufacture.

Thin films of both the above polymers can be converted into yarn. The films are converted into thread-like strips, either by slitting or by stretching them until they split (fibrillate), and the strips are then spun into yarn. As such they provide alternatives to string, twine and backings for tufted carpets. The resistance to weathering of olefin fibres also makes them useful for outdoor purposes such as deck chair covers.

Vinyl polymers derived from *propenonitrile* (acrylonitrile) are used more widely. Pure polyacrylonitrile (*4.6*) proved difficult to convert into fibres. Acrylic fibres cannot be produced from the melt (they decompose before melting) so they must be made from a polymer solution; a suitable solvent is thus essential. But polyacrylonitrile is insoluble in most of the common solvents that were available at the time it was first under investigation. It was many years after the first preparation before suitable solvents became available and acrylic fibres could be formed. Difficulties associated with the preparation and use of acrylic fibres are also eased by the incorporation of small amounts of a second monomer (a *co-monomer*), such as 1,1-dichloroethene (vinylidene chloride, *4.7*) into the polymerisation mix. In the resultant polymer (*4.8*) the side-groups on the backbone of the polymer include chlorine atoms as well as nitrile groups. *Teklan* is made in this way; the presence of chlorine atoms in the molecule results in a fibre with improved flame resistance.

Acrilan 16 and Courtelle

Acrilan 16 and Courtelle are two examples of copolymers containing up to 15% of a co-monomer. More recent developments have led to the production of copolymers containing between 35 and 65% of a monomer other than propenonitrile; these can be formed into filaments more easily than polyacrylonitrile itself, and can be dyed more readily. Acrylic fibres modified in this way are grouped together as *modacrylic* fibres, examples of which are given in Appendix 2. Acrylic fibres possess an inherent warmth and soft handle, and come closer to wool than any other fibre. They are used widely in carpet yarns and for knitted goods.

The reaction occurring in the formation of vinyl polymers differs from the step-growth process described for the formation of polyesters and polyamides. For example, when monomers react in step-growth polymerisation molecules of water are lost, whereas in the formation of vinyl polymers all the atoms of the monomer units are to be found in the polymer chain. The biggest difference, however, is in the manner in which the chains grow. In vinyl polymerisation the chain grows at one end only. Moreover, once the process begins it is so rapid that at any one time the reaction mixture consists of fully grown polymer chains and monomer: there are no intermediate stages of the kind found in the step-growth polymerisation of polyamides and polyesters. Consequently the reaction time allowed for vinyl polymerisation affects the amount of polymer formed but not the degree of polymerisation. Such reactions are referred to as *chain-growth polymerisations*.

Whatever the method of polymerisation, the final product is not a mass of macromolecules of identical length. There is always a distribution of molecular sizes, and figures quoted for the degree of polymerisation represent an average around which the values for the majority of molecules will fall.

Conversion of polymers to filaments

The synthetic polymer is presented to the manufacturer in the form of 'chips' or granules with the appropriate degree of polymerisation, and from this state it has to be converted to a filament in a manner akin to the spinning of a spider's web or a silkworm's cocoon. In this context spinning refers to the extrusion of a filament through a fine gland, not – as heretofore – to the twisting together of individual fibres or filaments to make a yarn. Thoughts about producing synthetic filaments in this manner were recorded centuries ago, but Ozanam was the first to describe a method in which a solution of real silk could be spun into fibres by extruding through small orifices. His invention,

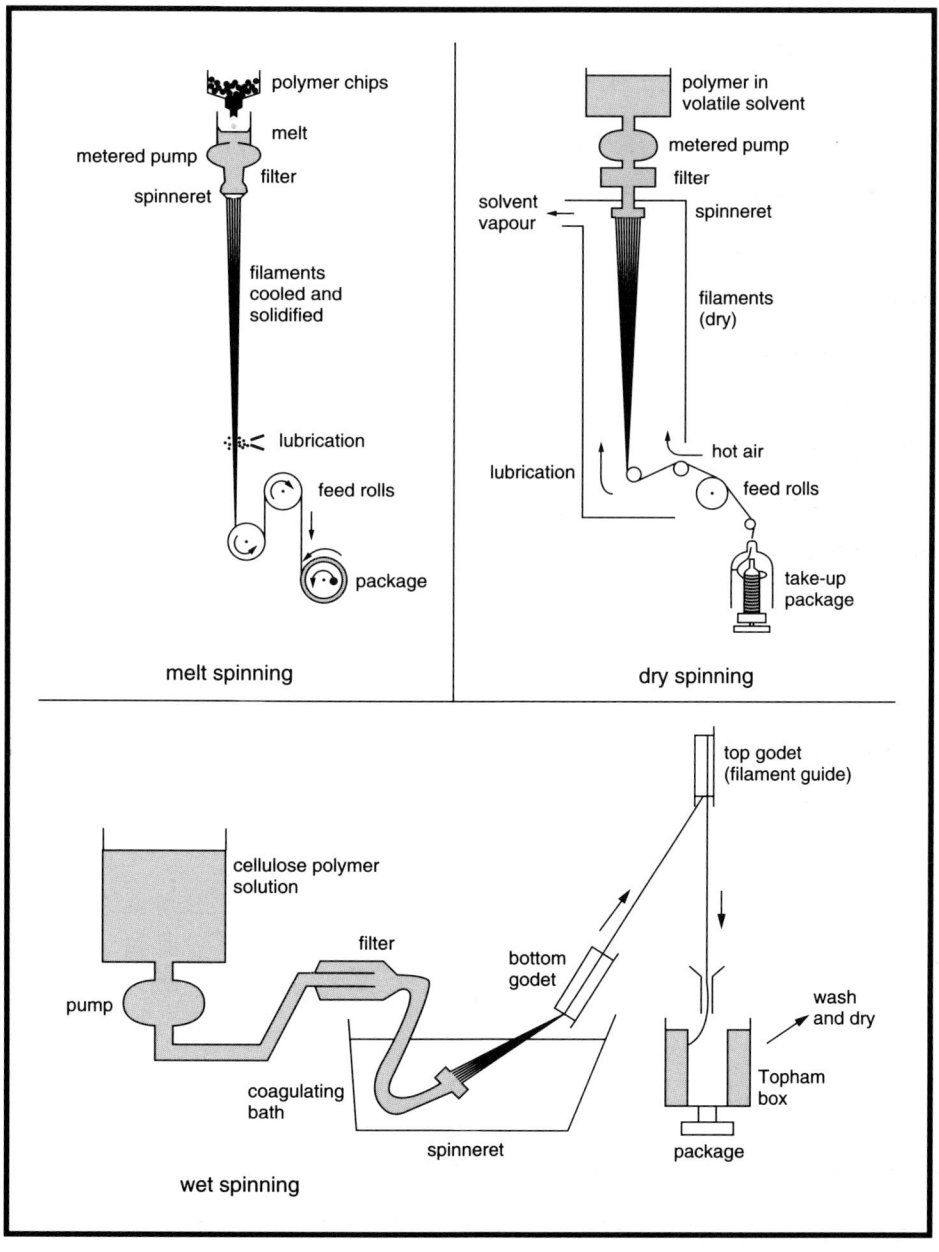

Figure 4.9 *Schematics of the three principal methods of spinning of synthetic filaments*

which was called the spinning jet or *spinneret*, made possible the present-day developments in spinning.

Three different methods of producing filaments are available at the present time: melt spinning, dry spinning and wet spinning, all of which are represented in Figure 4.9 (page 65).

Melt spinning is appropriate for polymers such as polyester or nylon, which do not decompose at their melting temperature. Molten polymer is pumped through a spinneret, which contains a number of small specially designed orifices. As the filaments enter the atmosphere they cool and solidify as they are wound up on to bobbins.

Dry spinning has been designed for polymers such as cellulose acetate, which are more difficult to melt. The polymer is dissolved in a volatile solvent to form a viscous solution, which is then extruded through a spinneret (Figure 4.10). Once the polymer 'dope' reaches the exterior the solvent evaporates in a current of warm air as the filament travels to the take-up bobbin.

Figure 4.10 *Filaments of cellulose acetate being extruded through a spinneret*

Wet spinning is reserved for those polymers that need to be regenerated by some form of chemical action after extrusion. Cellulose dissolved in carbon disulphide, for example, is regenerated in acid solution to form viscose fibre, after which it is dried.

Shape of fibre cross-sections

Extrusion of the filament is the stage at which the choice of cross-sectional shape is made, by choosing an appropriate shape for the orifice of the spinneret (Figure 4.11). The cross-sectional shape of a synthetic fibre is a function of both the method of production and the dimensions of the spinneret orifice; it is sometimes possible to identify which spinning method has been used simply from the cross-sectional shape of the filament. Orifices can be circular, crenellated, trilobal, convex, triangular and hollow, and each shape imparts particular characteristics. For example, ultrafine Trevira polyester filaments can be woven into breathable fabrics; since the cross-sectional area of the filaments is exceptionally low, the spaces between the filaments are so small that surface tension prevents water droplets from penetrating, whilst still able to allow water vapour to pass through. Other fabrics, such as reservoir linings, are designed to

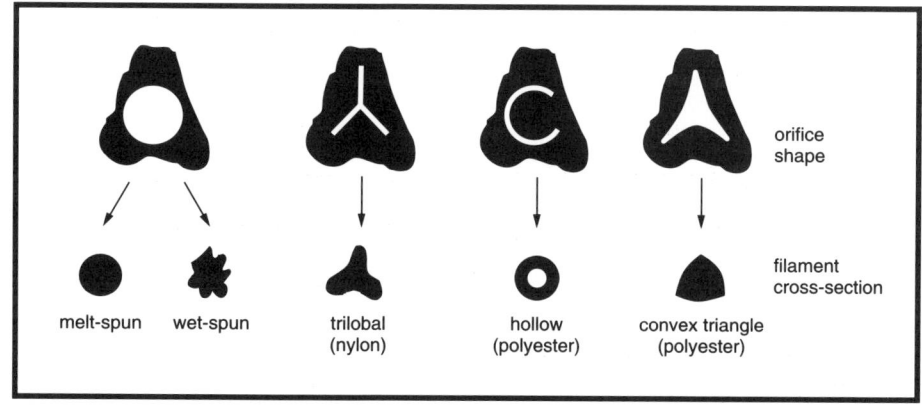

Figure 4.11 *Orifice shape and the cross-sections of the resultant filaments*

enable water to be retained, while still others prevent the evaporation of water and may, for example, be used for covers over crops in arid regions.

Multilobal nylon fibres are useful in carpet piles because they have a reduced lustre; moreover, some shapes increase their bulk and recovery from compression, in addition to being better able to hide soiling within the pile. The disadvantage is that dirt particles may become stuck in the crevices, thus making cleaning more difficult. The latter problem has been tackled by producing fibres with a smooth surface but four air-filled channels running down the length of the fibre. This reduces the visibility of the soiling through the multiple reflections inside the fibre, and at the same time produces a lighter fibre.

Fibres with a Y-shaped section are more resistant to bending and have better recovery than those with a circular or bean-shaped section, which makes them particularly suited to use as carpet pile. Other circular-sectioned polyester fibres have good insulation properties because of the air trapped within them, making the staple fibres (cut filaments) particularly suited for use as fillings in pillows, duvets and sleeping bags.

Cross-sections and surface appearances of some synthetic fibres are shown in Figures 4.12 (overleaf) and 4.13 (page 69).

Absorbent fibres

Modification of both the external and internal surface areas of fibres can also powerfully affect the absorption of water. The formation of regenerated cellulosic fibres with a hollow structure provides a method of meeting a demand for high-absorbency fibres for medical uses, such as swabs, and babies'

Figure 4.12 (a) Silk fibres seen under the scanning electron microscope (left) in cross-section, (right) longitudinal appearance; (b) viscose fibres in cross-section (magnified more than 700 times)

nappies. Various chemical expedients can be used to inflate the fibres at the regeneration stage and produce hollow fibres which collapse on drying. *Viloft* and *Courcel* are thin-walled fibres which can absorb an amazing 120 to 380% of their own mass of water [2].

Drawing of synthetic filaments

Fibre formation is incomplete after the spinning stage because the filaments are weak and dimensionally unstable. If they are pulled they stretch irreversibly. In this 'raw' state the polymer chains are disoriented and the structure lacks any coherent molecular arrangement. In the discussion of the structure of natural fibres on page 56 we saw that the degree of molecular alignment of the polymer chains along the length of the fibre axis is associated with the strength of the fibre. If a synthetic fibre is stretched after formation, the disordered polymer chains straighten and become extended along the fibre axis. The molecules slip past each other, but with the increasing order that the stretching imposes they eventually become close enough for intermolecular attractions to develop and to hinder further slippage without fracture. At this stage the filament has developed its maximum strength and the stretching is stopped. The individual polymer chains are now closely aligned and have become bonded to each other.

A process corresponding to this stretching is carried out by the fibre manufacturer, called the *drawing operation*. The filaments are passed around consecutive rollers, each of which rotates faster than the one before; the relative speeds of the rollers can be adjusted to impart the required degree of stretch to the filament (Figure 4.14, overleaf). In this way the length of a nylon filament may be increased five-fold, whilst its diameter is reduced and its breaking strength increased.

At this stage it is impossible to change one physical property without affecting others, so the degree of stretch needs to be

Figure 4.13 Cross-sections of polyester fibres (rod-shaped) and viscose fibres (hollow) in a fibre blend (× 442)

controlled. The close alignment of the polymer chains may allow some crystallinity to develop and this increases the brittleness of the fibre. Although crystallinity increases the strength of the fibre, if the fibre becomes too crystalline it will fracture when bent, and so will have poor abrasion resistance. The fibre will also be more difficult to dye or to be penetrated by chemical reagents or water (permeability to water is an important factor in the comfort of clothing).

Thus by adjusting the *draw ratio* (the ratio of the final length to the original length) these various properties can be controlled. In the final state, therefore, the fibres are composed of polymer chains aligned roughly parallel to the fibre axis with varying degrees of molecular order along the length of the fibre, ranging from crystalline through highly oriented noncrystalline to areas of low orientation (Figure 4.15, overleaf).

Conversion of filaments to staple

Once the filaments have been obtained they may be twisted together to form a yarn for use in knitting or weaving. Often, however, the properties required for the yarn are better obtained using staple fibre of a predetermined length. For the purposes of blending with natural fibres, the

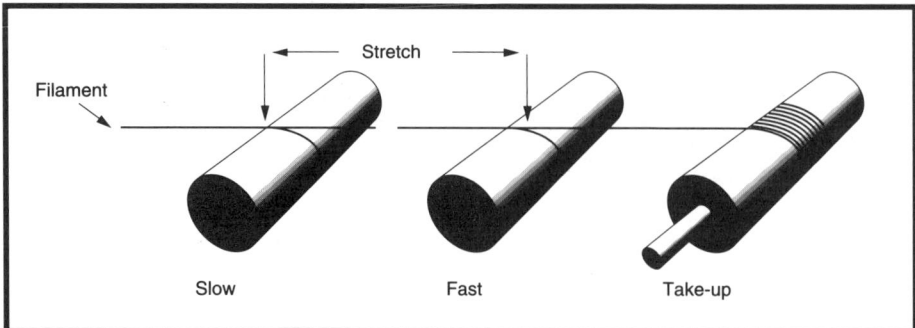

Figure 4.14 *Drawing filaments*

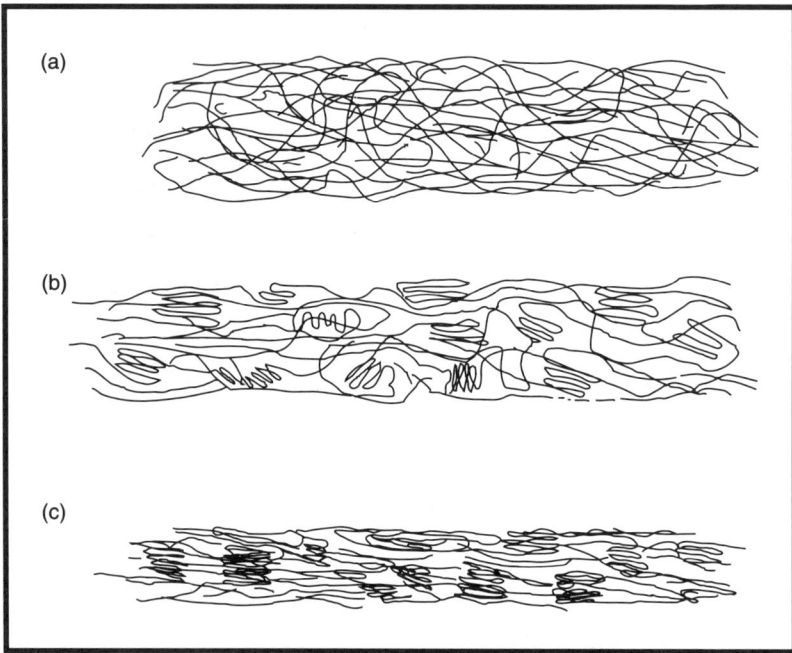

Figure 4.15 *Changes in molecular orientation in filaments during drawing: (a) as the filament emerges from the spinneret, orientation is mainly random (amorphous); (b) on cooling and stretching some crystalline order appears, with a degree of general orientation along the filament axis; (c) further stretching aligns amorphous and crystalline material along the axis*

synthetic fibres will be cut to correspond closely with the staple length of the natural fibre, but for other purposes such as the preparation of fibres for flocking the chosen length may be as short as a few millimetres. Special guillotine cutters are used for these very short fibres, but fibres intended for general textile uses are usually cut using helical-bladed cutters (similar in shape to those of a lawn mower) mounted on the periphery of a solid rubber roller (Figure 4.16). Hundreds of thousands of parallel filaments are formed into a web, which is passed between the bladed roller and a lower roller made of hardened steel. The length of the staple is governed by the spacing of the cutter blades. The cut is made at an angle to the direction of the movement of the web of filaments so that the cut ends are not coincident with each other. Having passed beneath the cutter, the web is loosened and rolled diagonally to form a continuous sliver for the subsequent conversion into yarn.

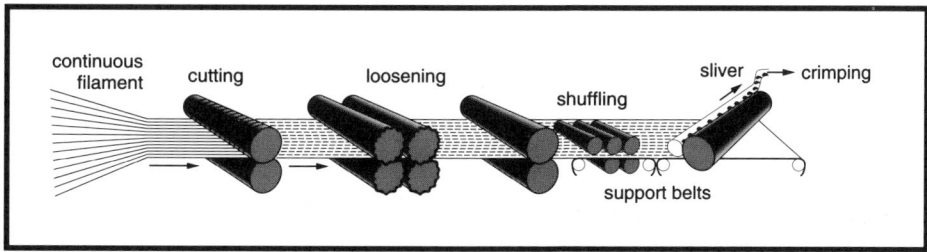

Figure 4.16 *A cutting sequence in making staple from filaments*

Imparting texture to synthetic fibres

Since the advent of the first synthetic fibres efforts have been continually made to meet consumer demands for synthetic fabrics with greater comfort in wear and pleasanter handle, more akin to those associated with fabrics made from natural fibres.

The effects of variation in the cross-sectional shape on handle have been mentioned already. A major influence on the texture of a fabric is the *crimp* of the fibre, and the 'loftiness' or 'bulkiness' of wool has been imitated with some success by introducing a crimp into the synthetic fibre through a variety of methods. This improves both the appearance and insulation properties of the fabrics subsequently produced, whilst the easy-drying properties are preserved. Furthermore, the greater air space in the fibre allows moisture to be transported more easily from the body to the surrounding air, thus helping to overcome the discomfort often associated with the hydrophobic nature of synthetic fibres worn close to the skin.

Many of the methods for texturising synthetic fibres depend on the fibres' *thermoplastic* nature. When synthetic fibres are heated they do not melt sharply at a certain temperature, as simpler substances do, since the extreme length of the polymer chains prevents them from separating easily. Instead the onset of melting is marked by a change in physical properties; in particular, the fibres become more readily deformed by mechanical stress. This is due to a general increase in the molecular movements of the polymer chains, which at lower temperatures were 'frozen' into position and unable to respond easily to external forces. At a certain temperature, which is a characteristic of the particular polymer, the polymer changes from a rigid substance into a material that is more easily deformed. This temperature is referred to as the *glass–rubber transition temperature* (designated as T_g) and is the temperature at which the polymer molecules become free to take up a new position in response to an external force. Consequently methods have been devised in which fibres held above the T_g are crimped mechanically and then allowed to cool. Such changes

71

in a thermoplastic material are reversible but will remain unaffected as long as the temperature of subsequent processing or aftercare treatments remains below the T_g.

Texturising processes

Various methods adopted for texturising are represented in Figure 4.17. In the stuffer box method (Figure 4.17 (a)), yarn is carried into a heating chamber at a rate faster than that at which it is removed, and the compressive action during heating leads to a bulky yarn. Another way of imparting texture is to drag the yarn over a heated knife edge (Figure 4.17 (b)), an action which imparts an unsymmetrical cross-section to the filaments or yarns. When they are subsequently relaxed in hot water curling results, providing the yarn with a stretch. In gear crimping (Figure 4.17 (c)) the heated yarn is passed between heated intermeshing cog wheels before cooling. Still another method

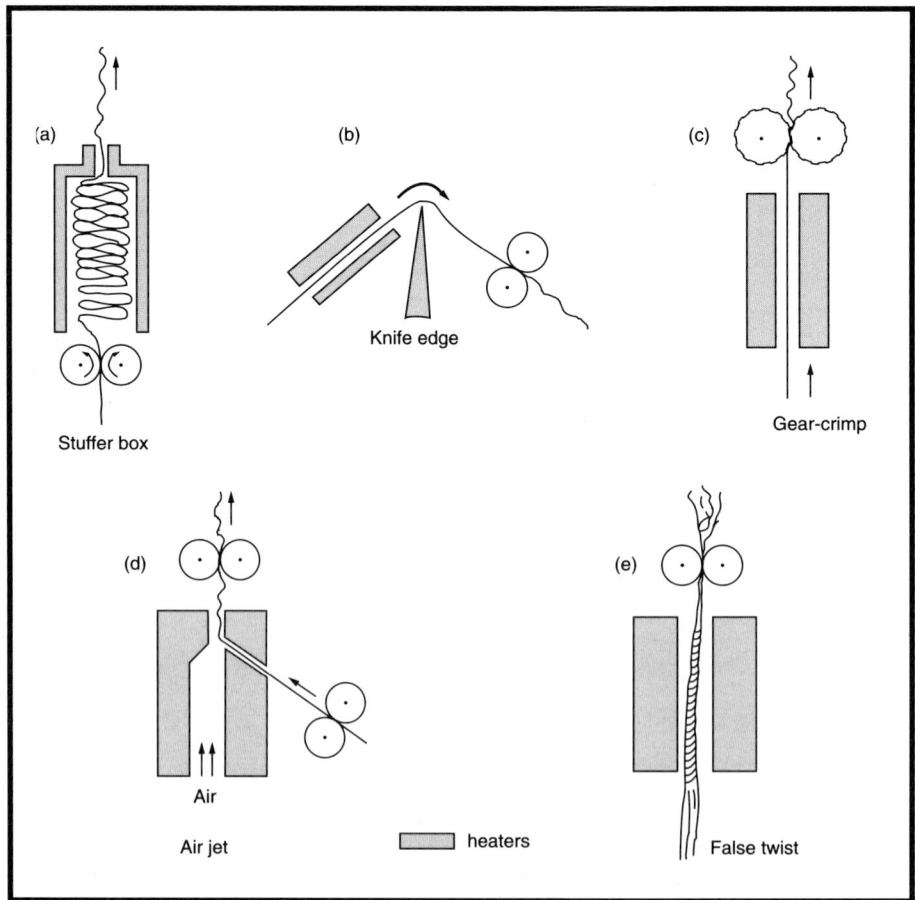

Figure 4.17 *Schematics of fibre crimping*

relies on the disorganisation produced in the yarn structure by a jet of air being forced through the yarn (Figure 4.17 (d)). In a widely used method, a twisted yarn is passed through heaters to set the crimp, and this is followed by an untwisting operation which separates the filaments as distorted coils (Figure 4.17 (e)).

Crimped fibres have also been produced by spinning dual-component fibres, made up of two different polymers lying alongside each other down the length of the fibre. Subsequent heat treatment shrinks both polymers, but to a different extent, and the differential effect leads to the development of a crimp. Such fibres are known as bi-component, conjugate, composite or hetero fibres.

Indicators of the quality of fibre and yarn

Once the yarn has been produced it is necessary to transmit descriptive details to the textile manufacturers, to show that it can meet the design requirements of their products. Yarn is sold by mass, but mass alone is insufficient to inform the weaver of the length of yarn being purchased. Without this information it is impossible to estimate how much yarn will be required for the production run. Consequently various ways of representing the fineness of a yarn (the *count* or *yarn number*) have evolved over the years. These traditional systems were many, varied and confusing; a detailed account has been published [5].

The ISO recommended *tex system*, now universally adopted, expresses the fineness of a yarn terms of the mass (in grams) of 1 kilometre of yarn. So, for example, 1 km of a 30 tex yarn will weigh 30 g.

To avoid the use of small fractions of a unit for very fine yarns a subsidiary unit, the *decitex* (dtex), based on the mass of 10 km of yarn, is used. Thus 10.0 km of yarn with a count of 20 decitex will weigh 20 g.

For single filaments the tex unit is impracticable because the counts involved are very small fractional values. For this purpose the *millitex* (mtex) unit is used, 1 mtex being equal to the mass in grams of 1000 km of filament.

Another important constructional detail for the weaver is the amount of *twist* inserted when spinning the yarn. The degree of twist influences several properties including strength, compactness, compressibility and lustre. The twist is expressed as turns per centimetre, and the

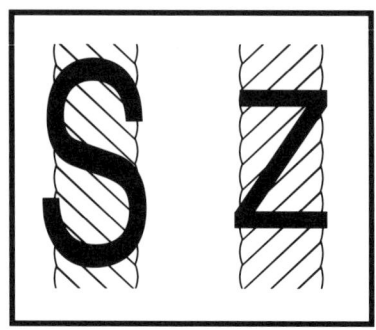

Figure 4.18 *S-twist and Z-twist*

direction of the twist is indicated by the term 'S-twist' when the fibres slope from left to right across the main axis of the fibre and 'Z-twist' when the slope is from right to left (Figure 4.18).

There are of course many other considerations inherent in the quality and design of yarns and fabrics. These include properties such as tensile strength, tenacity, elongation at break and elasticity, all of which are carefully monitored by the manufacturer. These fall outside the scope of this book, however; more specific works on fabric construction [3] and fibre physics [4] describe these properties and their measurement in more detail.

Presentation of information for the fibre manufacturer

The initial development work on fibres is carried out by chemists and physicists, who need to be aware of the chemical composition of the materials they are using. For this purpose precise chemical names, such as poly(ethylene terephthalate) for a particular type of polyester polymer, are required to confirm the likely chemical responses to any treatment or attempted chemical modification of the properties of the polymer with which they are dealing.

Generic names

Precise chemical names, however, are not essential for the designer or fabric manufacturer. They rely more on the agreed unambiguous generic names defined for international use by the ISO and BSI (ISO R/2076; BS 4815) in describing the chemical origin and type of fibre within any particular group.

Trade names

Very often the generic names of different polymers are also worded in terms of chemical nomenclature, and as such they convey very little information to the general public. A more reliable indicator of quality in this case is a familiar trade name. For instance, some well-known names for polyester fibres are Terylene, Trevira and Dacron, each of which is a polyester fibre from a different manufacturer. Such names are helpful to the consumer because they are often associated with certification schemes and other ethical merchandising procedures. Consequently through trade names the public can become acquainted with the reliability of a particular product in fulfilling its intended purpose.

Trade names often include the terms 'bright' or 'delustred'. The *bright fibres* are 100% polymer without additives. Fabrics made from these fibres transmit a certain amount of light, which is not always desirable in a garment. The difficulties are eliminated by making opaque or delustred fibres (usually called *dull fibres*) by incorporating a white pigment into the fibre at the spinning stage. Titanium oxide is used for this purpose and the particles of pigment are readily visible in such fibres under the optical microscope.

Some examples of generic, chemical and trade names for fibres are given in Appendix 2, and more extensive information is provided in other sources [1,6,7].

References

1.   *The identification of textile materials* (Manchester: Textile Institute, 1985).
2.   *Textiles*, **13** (3) (1984) 58.
3.   A T C Robinson and R Marks, *Woven fabric construction* (Manchester: Textile Institute, 1973).
4.   W E Morton and J W S Hearle, *Fibre physics* (Manchester: Textile Institute, 1985).
5.   J E Booth, *Principles of textile testing*, 4th Edn (London: Newnes Butterworths, 1979).
6.   J C Cook, *Handbook of textile fibres* (London: Merrow, 1964).
7.   R W Moncrieff, *Man-made fibres*, 6th Edn (London: Newnes Butterworths, 1975).

Further reading

N Hollen, J Sadler, A Langford and S J Kadolph, *Textiles* (New York: Macmillan, 1988).
J N Nicholson, *Chemistry of polymers* (London: Royal Society of Chemistry, 1991).
M A Taylor, *Technology of textile properties* (London: Forbes, 1979).

CHAPTER FIVE

The selection, classification and application of dyes

Nature of the textile coloration process

The value of most of the textile fibres destined for the domestic market is increased by coloration before they are sold. Unlike the impregnation of paper with coloured ink, the processes by which a molecule of dye becomes attached to a textile fibre involve far more than a simple impregnation process. Uniform impregnation of the fibre mass is only the preliminary requirement. It is the chemical interaction between a dye and a fibrous polymer, as well as the movement of dye into the fibre structure, which determines the suitability of the final product for the purpose in hand.

Most textile dyes are applied from water or a water-based printing paste. Many dyes for textiles are soluble in water and, like simpler electrolytes, their molecules split into positively and negatively charged ions. With most dyes (*acid dyes*) the coloured ion is negatively charged, i.e. it is an anion. Some dyes, however, form positively charged coloured ions, i.e. cations. Commercially these are limited in number but they meet specific needs, particularly with acrylic fibres. As a class they are referred to as *basic dyes*.

Interaction between dye and fibre

A dye is taken up by a fibre as a result of the chemical attraction between them, but as explained in Chapter 3 the dyebath conditions need to be adjusted before the attractive forces can operate efficiently. When fibres are immersed in water they develop a negative charge. Since the sign of this charge is the same as that on the dye anion, the fibre repels the dye, hindering or even preventing its close approach. With most water-soluble anionic dyes the addition of an electrolyte, such as common salt, enhances the attraction by masking the negative surface charges of the fibre, and the dye uptake is therefore increased.

Chemical combination through the formation of a covalent bond is the strongest possible dye–fibre attachment (Table 3.2, page 38). Next in strength are the salt links, which are less than one-quarter as strong as a covalent bond. Whilst covalent bonds can only be broken by a chemical reaction, other dye–fibre links can be split by the action of heat and water. It is therefore possible to control the rate of dye adsorption and ensure a uniform distribution of dye by raising the temperature of the dyebath. For this reason many dyeing processes are carried out at the boil.

Dyeing conditions are chosen to ensure that the final distribution of dye between the dyebath and the fibre always favours the fibre. But, like many other chemical reactions, the take-up of dye is reversible, and if the dyed fabric is placed in clean water the dye may bleed out in an attempt to re-establish equilibrium. Here therefore is a potential cause of poor wash fastness.

Affinity and substantivity

Information concerning the strength of the binding forces between dye and fibre is obviously valuable for dye selection, since it is relevant both to the colour yield obtained from the dyebath and to the fastness to wet treatments of the end result. The combined strength of the molecular interactions involved is referred to as the *affinity* of the dye for the substrate. This is a thermodynamic quantity that can be measured, so dye selection can be aided by ranking the members of any one class of dye in order of affinity.

Reliance on such measurements is restricting, however, because affinities are measured under precisely defined conditions of temperature, pH and salt concentration. The values obtained offer a comparison between dyes only under the conditions specified, and they do not apply to any other dyebath conditions. Conditions always change during a dyeing process, and the less specific term *substantivity* is more useful to the practical dyer because it can indicate the level of exhaustion (that is, the extent to which the dye has disappeared from the dye liquor into the goods). This in turn has a bearing on the wet fastness of the dye–fibre combination. Generally the affinity of a dye for a particular substrate does bear some relationship to the substantivity under practical application conditions, and the two terms are often, though strictly speaking incorrectly, used interchangeably.

Fundamental behaviour of dyes

In the dye–fibre reaction one reactant, the fibre, is a solid and the other, the dye, is dissolved in water. With any reaction, molecules (or ions) must collide before they can react together. In a solution, the molecules are in a state of constant random motion. But inside fibres the polymer structure offers marked resistance to the movement of the dye molecules, so that prolonged dyeing times are often needed before interaction is complete. Dyeing conditions therefore are always chosen so that they assist the movement of dye into the fibre, so enabling the forward reaction to go as efficiently as possible. The specific reactions concerned depend on the chemical character of the fibre, and therefore choice of dye is restricted to those capable of interacting in the appropriate manner.

Some colorants become retained within the fibre as a result of the mechanical entrapment of water-insoluble pigments, a mechanism which along with the formation of a covalent bond gives the highest level of fastness to wet treatments. Even so, the initial stages of application still depend on attractive forces between fibre and dye. In this case the colorant is initially applied in water-soluble form, and appropriate reactions in the fibre are then brought about. The colorant is chemically converted into the insoluble form at the end of the exhaustion step.

Once the appropriate dye class for the fibre in question has been chosen, attention has to be turned to the substantivity of the dyes required to provide the necessary level of fastness properties. This also involves choice of the method of application best suited to the dye combination. It is at this stage that the classification of dyes by appropriate dyeing procedures becomes especially relevant, and these matters will now be considered in more detail.

Selection of dyes for wool

In the coloration of wool the consumer generally benefits more from the requirements of the manufacturing processes than the demands made by the end use of the fabric. Both before and after dyeing, wool undergoes various wet treatments that concern the dyer even though they are not his responsibility. Efficient preparatory treatments of the material are the key to good dyeings, whilst the success of subsequent wet treatments is generally reliant on the proper selection and application of suitable dyes. Since the conditions of post-dyeing processes are usually more severe than those of any normal aftercare treatments, dyeings that have proved satisfactory during the processing will possess more than adequate fastness properties for consumer use.

Technical requirements also depend on whether the fibre needs to be dyed as loose fibre ('loose stock'), combed wool in the form of an untwisted strand of parallel fibres from the combing operation ('top'), yarn or fabric. With each type of substrate particular criteria have to be met in order to produce the required quality of colour, and this is usually achieved through variations in the dyeing conditions.

Loose fibre

When dealing with loose fibre, slight variations in depth of shade (*unlevelness*) from batch to batch may be dealt with by blending fibres from different batches. A uniformly coloured product is thus obtained before it is converted into yarn and woven into fabric.

There is less tolerance of batch-to-batch variations for some uses than others. For example, batch-to-batch variations need to be kept to a minimum with combed worsted fibres intended for high-twist yarns to be used in suitings and gabardines. On the other hand, in yarns for fabrics such as Harris tweeds different coloured fibres may be blended together to produce a multicolour effect (Plate 4). Clearly small variations in levelness from one fibre batch to another are not critical in this case, but since fabrics so produced are often destined for suitings, fastness to light and wet treatments become more important.

Yarn

The choice of dyes and dyeing conditions for the coloration of yarn is much more critical than for loose fibre because level dyeing and accurate shade control are of paramount importance. The fastness requirements will depend on the destination of the yarn. For example, hand-knitted or machine-knitted goods are never subjected to the severe processing encountered in woven fabrics, and some relaxation in wet fastness standards will therefore not detract from the expected quality of the knitted goods. Such yarns are usually dyed as hanks to preserve their characteristic softness and bulkiness, but yarns for weaving or for industrial knitting machines are dyed on wound packages (see page 114), which require more attention to dye distribution, liquor circulation and levelling.

Machine-washable wool demands careful attention to choice of dye class because the shrink-resist finishes often have the effect of reducing the wet fastness of deep shades; reactive dyes usually give satisfactory results, however (see page 86).

Woven fabric

Woven fabric requires both very level dyeing and excellent fastness properties, the latter being necessary to withstand the remainder of the finishing processes. These range from the removal of spinning oils by a scouring treatment of a few minutes duration in a weakly alkaline detergent solution to more severe treatments in steam (*decatising*), boiling water (*crabbing* and *potting*), chemical treatments (*setting*) and mechanical treatments of wet fabric (*milling*), all of which impart particular characteristics required for the end use of the wool fabric. It may be necessary also to treat the dyed fabric with 5% sulphuric acid solution, followed by drying and baking (*carbonising*), to facilitate the removal of burrs. None of these treatments will be encountered by the fabric after it leaves the factory and they are all more severe than conditions encountered in normal aftercare.

Acid dyes

The first synthetic dyes for wool were the acid dyes (see page 76), a class of dye that has since grown into a large, diverse, versatile and widely used group.

Acid dyes are sufficiently soluble to allow direct application from an aqueous solution. Some acid dyes may also be used for the coloration of other animal fibres, including silk, and also of nylon, which like protein fibres has both amide linkages and amino groups in its structure (page 59).

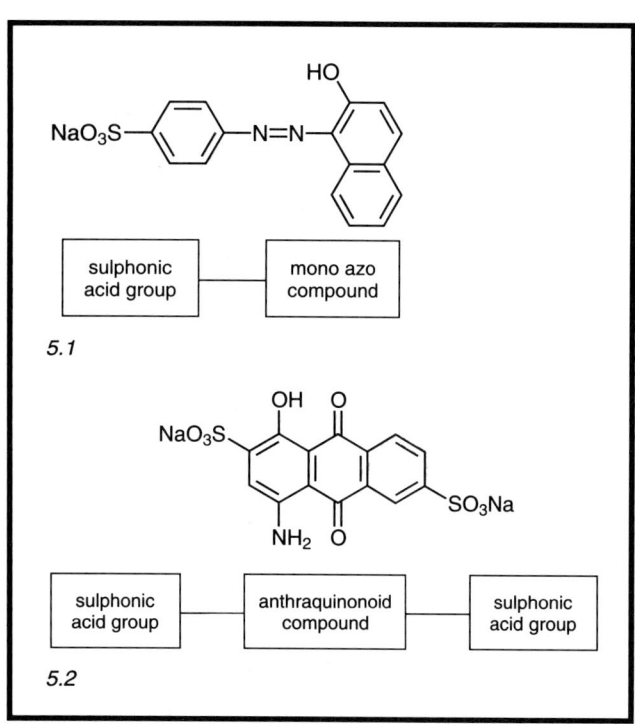

5.1

5.2

Nature of acid dye molecules

Acid dye molecules provide a wide range of colours covering several different chromophoric systems, based on anthraquinone, azo, triarylmethane and azine structures, and can also be applied under a wide variety of conditions.

All acid dye molecules have certain features in common. They all possess at least one group of atoms that imparts solubility in water to the large coloured component of the molecule. This is usually, but not always, the sodium salt of a sulphonic acid group, —SO_3Na (*5.1* and *5.2* are typical acid dyes, and further examples are given in Appendix 1).

80

The sulphonic acid group (or in some cases the carboxylic acid group) is also important in linking the dye to the fibre, since it can react with a basic group in the wool molecule and form a salt linkage, which thus becomes a point of strong attachment. For one group of acid dyes this is the most important reaction to be controlled during application. Sodium salts of sulphonic acids in general behave as simple electrolytes and dissociate into ions but, as explained above, the dye–fibre reaction is only achieved after the large coloured anion has diffused into the fibre.

Other factors in the attraction between fibre and dye include hydrogen bonds and van der Waals forces. The contribution of the latter is always present, and depends directly on the size of the dye molecule. Whichever type of bond predominates in the final stages of dyeing, the balance between one type of force and another can vary as the process goes on, and this fact is important in the formulation of dyeing methods.

Coloration of wool with acid dyes

Once the shade and the appropriate fastness properties have been selected, the dyer's attention turns to the production of level dyeings. Those dyes that attach to the fibre mainly through salt links are the easiest to dye level, but as the contribution from nonionic forces increases, so do the practical difficulties. In essence, dyeing methods adopted enable control of the rate at which dye–fibre interactions occur.

The easiest acid dyes to control are referred to as *levelling acid dyes*. Without the presence of a strong acid such as sulphuric acid in the dyebath, the important salt linkages between the wool fibre and the dye cannot form. The term 'acid dye' therefore refers to the necessary acidity of the dyebath rather than the chemical character of the dye. These dyes usually remain unaggregated.

Acid dyes are chosen whenever level dyeing is crucial to the quality of the goods. Yarn intended for weaving is one example, since unlevel yarn, when woven or knitted into a fabric, will give rise to localised areas differing in colour from the rest of the fabric. Both levelling and yarn penetration is especially important in carpet yarns, where the fibres of the pile are viewed end-on. Unfortunately their good migration, which makes levelling acid dyes suitable for the production of level dyeings, also means they may easily be removed from wet fabric. They cannot therefore be expected to show a particularly high degree of fastness to wet treatments. Since this factor is fully considered during the dye selection process, it does not usually offer a serious threat to the quality of the end product.

Once the group of dyes has been selected for level-dyeing properties, satisfactory fastness to light of the dyeing still has to be ensured. Articles like carpets will require dyes of high fastness to light, since they will be expected to keep their attractive appearance for many years. If they are intended for use on ships, then good fastness to salt water will be required as well. Garments also require a reasonable level of fastness to both light and perspiration, but since many are unlikely to need daily cleaning and dry cleaning may be used for aftercare, the fastness to washing need not always be of the highest order. With hosiery, on the other hand, fastness to light weighs less heavily than fastness to washing, and here rather more attention is paid to a group of acid dyes with dyeing properties different from those of the easy-levelling dyes, but which have better fastness to wet treatments.

Application of acid dyes

The connection between the levelling properties of the dyes and their subsequent fastness to wet treatments allows acid dyes to be classified into groups according to the application procedures that allow the best control of their levelling. The three groups are as follows.

(a)   *Equalising acid dyes*, which level well but have poor fastness to wet treatments. Sulphuric acid is incorporated into the dyebath.

(b)   *Milling acid dyes (acid-dyeing)*, which have poorer levelling properties than (a) but better fastness to wet treatments. They are applied using a weaker acid such as methanoic (formic) or ethanoic (acetic) acid, the acid chosen depending upon the substantivity of the dye.

(c)   *Milling acid dyes (neutral-dyeing)*; these are sometimes referred to as *supermilling* acid dyes. Their levelling properties are poor, but their fastness to wet treatments is excellent.

These groupings represent a transition in dyeing properties rather than clear-cut divisions. Nevertheless, the classification is useful to the dyer in dealing with a class of dye containing members ranging from easy-levelling dyes with poor wet fastness to dyes with very poor levelling properties but high wet fastness.

Equalising acid dyes

Their ease of fibre penetration, application and levelling, together with their bright shades, make equalising acid dyes (levelling acid dyes) the preferred choice for the coloration of wool, provided fastness requirements can be met.

For levelling acid dyes the dyebath is prepared with sufficient sulphuric acid or methanoic (formic) acid to give a pH of 2.5–3.5, which promotes exhaustion, and sodium sulphate (Glauber's salt), which aids levelling by providing sulphate ions to compete for the dye sites. The goods are entered into the bath and the temperature raised to the boil over a period of 15–30 minutes. During this time water and sulphuric acid penetrate the mass, and the dye begins to diffuse into the fibre. During the following 45 minutes at the boil, the dye continues to migrate from regions of high to regions of lower concentration until its distribution in the wool is uniform.

Milling acid dyes

More highly substantive dyes are required to produce a better degree of fastness. Adequate levelling through the controlled formation of ionic links using a strongly acidic dyebath is no longer possible, because the overall attractive forces are too strong. For these dyes the dominance of ionic forces then needs to be suppressed by reducing the acidity to a pH of 4.5–5.5 (by using ethanoic acid instead of sulphuric acid), and aggregation is controlled by raising the temperature.

Milling acid dyes give bright shades but their fastness properties are better than those of the equalising acid dyes. Their levelling properties are adequate for fabrics intended for uses such as dresswear, pale- to medium-depth knitting yarns and some types of upholstery. They offer some economy in production compared with the easy-levelling dyes because the similarity of the dyeing properties of the members of the class allows the dyer to reduce the number of dyes held in stock. If one red, one yellow and one blue dye (the primary colours) are chosen, a wide range of shades is possible by mixing the three dyes in appropriate proportions. This makes it easier to replace time-consuming laboratory shade-matching trials by instrumental colour measurements and computerised shade matching.

Another subdivision of milling acid dyes includes acid dyes at the higher end of the substantivity scale. Such dyes require more weakly acidic conditions still. Dyes in this subgroup tend to be more individual in character. Their poorer migration and higher wet fastness usually persuade the dyer to select a dye as near to the required shade as possible to minimise the necessity of shading to the correct colour with additional dyes.

The subgroup as a whole has good fastness to light and is often used to provide heavier shades for womenswear and loose-stock dyeing for carpet yarn and knitwear.

Milling acid dyes (neutral dyeing)

The highest standards of wet fastness are usually obtained using these milling acid dyes, a group that includes dyes able to withstand the very severe wet-milling processes associated with the preparation of wool fabric. Dyeing is carried out in loose wool and slubbing form because it is too difficult to obtain good levelling on fabric. Very careful control of the dyebath pH between 5.5 and 6.5 is required, and the temperature of the dyebath is raised very slowly in order to achieve level dyeing. These dyes remain aggregated throughout. 'Assistants' such as ammonium ethanoate or ammonium sulphate are used to help in control: these compounds decompose at the boil with the gradual release of acid, which reduces the pH of the dyebath and completes the exhaustion process.

The acid dye class therefore contains members that can meet a wide range of fastness and level-dyeing requirements, all of which are produced through very careful manipulation of dyebath conditions (Table 5.1).

Table 5.1 Conditions for dyeing with acid dyes

Acid dye type	Additive	Dyebath pH
Equalising	Sulphuric acid or methanoic acid	2.5–3.5
Milling	Methanoic acid or ethanoic acid	4.5–5.5
Neutral-dyeing	Ammonium sulphate or ammonium ethanoate	5.5–6.5

Other dyeing methods for wool

In general, menswear made from wool fabric will require good all-round fastness properties. For this purpose duller shades are usually more fashionable than those obtained by using levelling acid dyes but, as we have seen, the latter are unlikely to provide satisfactory wet fastness. The best fastness is obtainable with milling acid dyes, but they have poor levelling properties.

Craft dyers deal with this difficulty by using mordants for wool and silk, which enable the colourings extracted from natural products to display a reasonable substantivity. This is reminiscent of ancient and long-abandoned dyeing practices which, by comparison with the present-day synthetic colours, yield fabric with unacceptably poor fastness properties. Nevertheless, the principle can be used to advantage with synthetic mordant dyes in conjunction with more effective mordants.

The principle of mordanting is to form a bridging link between the fibre and dye; the mordants used today are metal ions. Since the most common metal used is chromium, those dyes applied in this way are called *chrome dyes*.

Chrome dyes for wool

There are several ways by which chromium may become implanted into the dyed fibre. But whichever method is adopted the dye molecule must contain suitably disposed chemical groups, otherwise the dye and chromium ions cannot combine. The reaction is called *chelation*, and some of the more substantive levelling acid dyes may be used in this way. It is therefore possible to have the advantages of level-dyeing acid dyes during exhaustion stage of the dyeing process, and then significantly to improve the fastness properties through aftertreatment of the dyeing with a solution of a chromium salt such as potassium dichromate. Conversion of the dye to a chromium complex substantially increases the molecular size, which prevents the outward diffusion of dye molecules even during severe wet treatments such as potting. The method is known as the *afterchrome* process.

In practice the advantages are accompanied by the pollution of dyehouse effluent by chromium residues, and also by difficulties in controlling and reproducing the final shade, which varies according to the chroming conditions. The afterchrome process is therefore generally used for loose wool or tops rather than for yarn or fabric, so that variations in shade can be eliminated by blending different batches before spinning. Moreover, because afterchroming is a two-stage process, extra time costs are incurred. Fibres also tend to be easily damaged, as the immersion of the wool in the acidic liquor is prolonged. Excess chromium adsorbed on the fibre may give rise to a harsh handle, which is detrimental to the spinning properties. Nevertheless, chrome dyeing is still preferred for some purposes because of the process can yield a product with excellent fastness properties more cheaply than most of the alternatives. It is favoured for the production of very deep shades on loose stock, and blacks and navies on yarn and fabric.

The alternatives to afterchrome dyeing are the so-called *Metachrome process*, in which dye and mordant are applied simultaneously, and *chrome mordanting*, in which the chromium is applied before dyeing. These offer no advantage over the afterchrome process, however, and their use is not widespread.

In the final analysis their economy of application, high fastness and level dyeing make chrome dyes among the most extensively used wool dyes.

Metal-complex dyes

Further developments aimed at avoiding the problems arising with chrome dyes have led to combination of the chromium with the dye molecules by the dye manufacturer. This eliminates variations in shade due to uneven afterchroming, and maintains the good fastness to both light and wet treatments of afterchrome dyeings. Such dyes are called *metal-complex dyes*, and their properties depend in part on the number of dye molecules attached to each chromium atom. The earliest complexes incorporated one chromium atom into each dye molecule (1:1 complexes) and could be applied as levelling acid dyes provided the dyebath was made strongly acidic. They combine the easy-levelling properties of the levelling acid dyes with improved light and wet fastness. Unfortunately the stronger acidic conditions inevitably lead to fibre damage and associated difficulties in spinning. Nevertheless, where the needs for good penetration, levelling and light fastness are paramount – as with gabardines and some high-twist carpet yarns – some fibre strength may be sacrificed. Moreover, dyeing acid-milled fabric or carbonised fabric in this way eliminates the need to neutralise the acidified wool before dyeing.

The necessity of a highly acidic dyebath was ultimately counteracted by further development of chrome–dye complexes in which each chromium atom is linked to two dye molecules (1:2 complexes). Such dyes may be applied from a weakly acid dyebath to produce higher wet fastness than the 1:1 complexes, and thus can provide good fastness without causing fibre damage. Unfortunately the improvements are also accompanied by a commensurate difficulty in producing level dyeings and consequently 1:2 complexes are not easily used for dyeing fabrics. They are often used along with dyebath additives to prevent the differential coloration of wool fibres from root to tip, a common phenomenon due to the slight changes in chemical composition caused by progressive weathering of the fibre tips during growth. It is referred to as 'tippy' dyeing, and 1:2 complexes often exaggerate the effect when applied without levelling agents in the dyebath.

Although the chrome dyes and chrome complex dyes are used extensively for wool dyeing, the development of machine-washable wool has brought even higher demands for wet fastness, and this is usually achieved using reactive dyes.

Reactive dyes for wool

Some of the most stringent demands of quality arise with the coloration of shrink-resist-treated wool that may be washed in a domestic washing machine. Much of the wool so designated is produced using aftertreatments that deposit polymeric compounds on the fibres. These have the effect of reducing the wet fastness of most conventional wool dyes, just where greater resistance to wet treatments is needed. This deficit can be effectively covered by the use of dyes chemically identical with, or similar to, the reactive dyes intended for cellulose (see page 91).

Reactive dyes are necessarily applied to cellulosic fibres under alkaline conditions, but alkaline conditions are usually inappropriate for wool because of the sensitivity of the disulphide crosslinks (page 54). Fortunately, the chemical nature of the functional groups in wool enables the reactive dyes to react with the fibres under mildly acidic conditions. Some are based on levelling acid dye molecules and others on 1:2 metal-complex dyes. Particular care is needed to achieve level dyeings because, once the dye has reacted with the fibre, migration is clearly impossible. Furthermore, any unfixed dye remaining on the fibre still remains sufficiently substantive to cause staining problems during use, and particular care is needed with washing-off after dyeing. Additives are included in the dyebath to avoid the danger of producing 'skittery' dyeings (an undesirable speckled effect arising from differences in colour between adjacent fibres or portions of the same fibre). The use of reactive dyes is generally limited by their cost, which is high compared with that of other wool dyes.

Selection of dyes for cellulosic fibres

The widespread use of natural cellulosic fibres such as cotton and linen, and also of regenerated cellulosic fibres, maintains a demand for a broad range of shades and different standards of fastness properties. For example, for many uses such as high-quality curtaining, military and naval uniforms and high-class gabardines good fastness to light is essential, but for others fastness to bleaching may be more important. Such a need may arise when bleaching is required to clean uncoloured parts of the design after weaving fabrics that incorporate both dyed and undyed yarns. Dyes may also require resistance to the bleaching ingredients included in commercial detergent preparations. For sewing yarns and furnishings intended for the cheaper end of the market, however, the demands on fastness properties are less stringent.

This diversity of requirements has led to the development of several different coloration principles for cellulosic fibres. There are water-soluble dyes applied by a one-bath process without the use of mordants (*direct dyes*), water-soluble dyes that form a chemical linkage with the fibre (*reactive dyes*) and water-insoluble pigments that are applied as water-soluble precursors which are converted to the insoluble pigment after diffusion into the fibre (*vat dyes, azoic dyes* and *sulphur dyes*). Here each dye class will be discussed in turn.

Direct dyes

The discovery by Böttiger of the dye Congo Red in 1884 was a landmark because this was the first dye to be used for colouring cellulose by a simple one-bath operation (i.e. directly) in the absence of a mordant; hence the term 'direct dye'.

Nature of direct dyes

The molecules of direct dyes are similar in structure to those of acid dyes but they are larger; structure 5.3, the dye Sky Blue FF (CI Direct Blue 1) is an example. They conform to the general formula R_1—N=N—X—N=N—R_2. It is their size that distinguishes them from acid dyes and makes them substantive to cellulose. Their attachment is through both hydrogen bonds and van der Waals forces and, as we have seen (page 81), the intensity of the latter increases with increasing molecular size. Their hydrogen bonding capability is

also aided by their long flat molecular structure which enables them to lie along a cellulose chain in register with hydroxyl groups.

The function of the sulphonate groups is limited to conferring water solubility on the molecule because, unlike wool, cellulose contains no cationic groups with which the coloured dye anions can form electrostatic linkages.

Compared with other classes of dye for cellulose the wet fastness properties of direct dyes are usually poor and where repeated washing of the dyed fabric is likely, as with lingerie, they are generally of use in pale shades only. A variety of aftertreatments is available to make the dye on the fibre less soluble in water to give improved fastness performance (page 106), but unfortunately such improvements are accompanied by a change of shade or reduced fastness to light.

The merits of direct dyes are their simplicity of application, the wide range of shades they can provide, and a cost that usually compares favourably with other alternatives. As a consequence, direct dyes are found in many different outlets, including cotton and viscose dress fabrics, sewing yarns, book cloths, pile fabrics and shoe canvas.

As with acid dyes, selection is aided by placing the dyes in groups with similar dyeing properties. Often a mixture of dyes is needed to produce the required colour, and sometimes the use of dyes from different groups cannot be avoided. In such cases the dyeing method is chosen to suit whichever component is most difficult to dye level.

Application of direct dyes

Direct dyes are usually applied by bringing the dyebath to the boil gradually and holding it at this temperature whilst the dye diffuses into the fibre. In the complete absence of electrolyte (i.e. with a

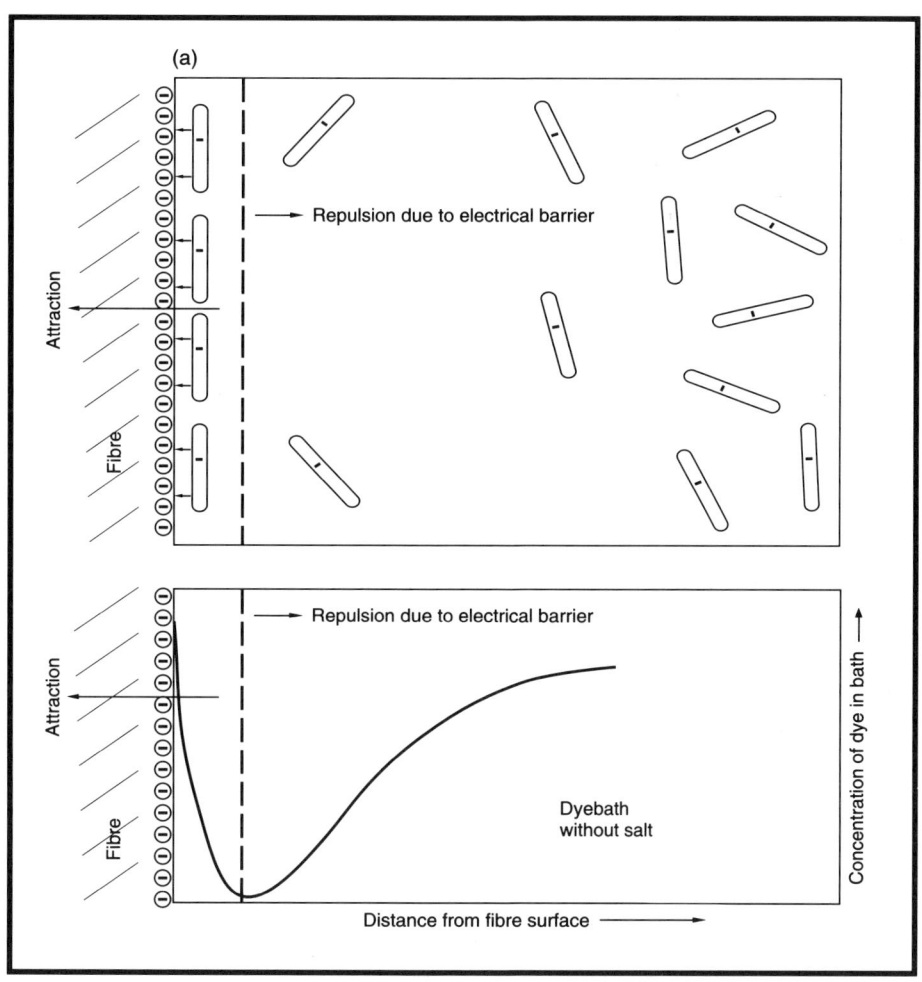

Figure 5.1 *The effect of salt on dye distribution at the fibre surface: (a) in the absence of salt, the initial adsorption of dye anions increases the negative charge on the fibre surface, and hence other dye anions are repelled; (b) (overleaf) in the presence of salt, cations redistribute around the electrical barrier to neutralise the charge and so allow other dye anions to reach the fibre surface, whence they can diffuse into the body of the fibre*

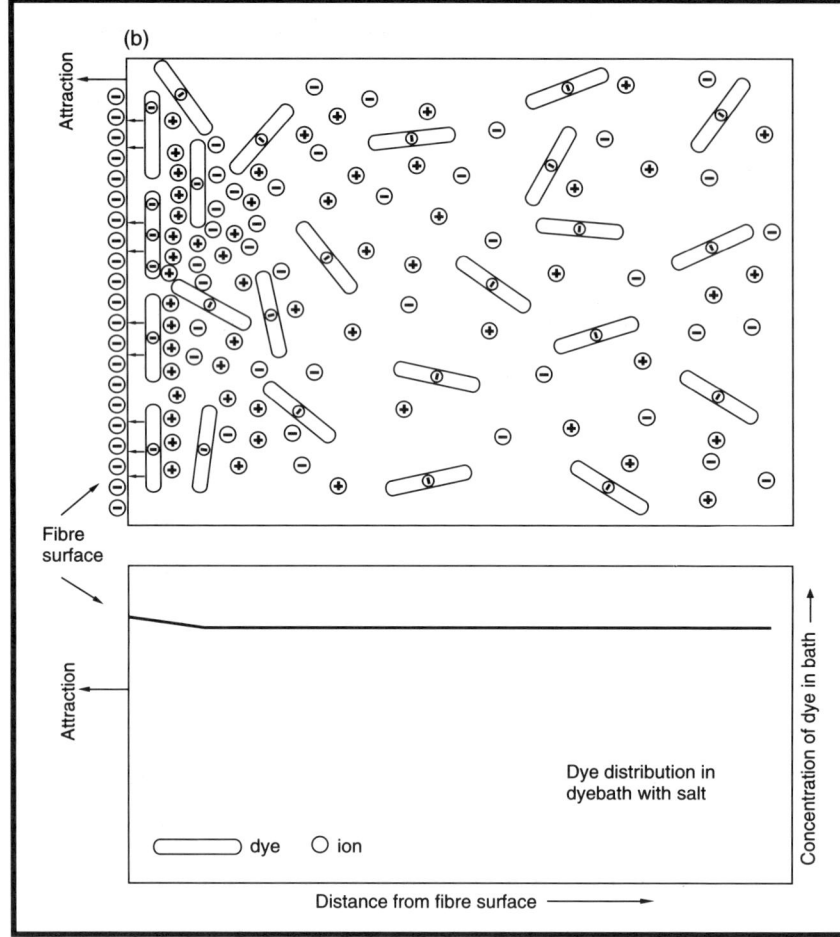

Figure 5.1(b)

chemically pure dye) some direct dyes will not dye cellulose at all, and all commercial direct dyes are absorbed much more readily if salt is added to the dyebath. This is because the dye anion is substantive but the sodium cation is not. The greater substantivities of the dye anions initially lead to their preferential adsorption, but once they start to be adsorbed their negative charge adds to that already acquired by the fibre when it is first im-

mersed in water. In the absence of other influences the consequence is repulsion of other dye anions near the surface (Figure 5.1 (a), page 89). Meanwhile, the positive sodium ions originating from the dye are attracted towards the negatively charged surface, but their concentration is insufficient wholly to neutralise the negative surface charge. Other dye anions can approach the fibre only when the charge is completely neutralised, and this occurs when further electrolyte is deliberately added to the dyebath. This is why the application of direct dyes always involves common salt (sodium chloride) or Glauber's salt (sodium sulphate) as a component of the dyebath (Figure 5.1 (b)).

In practice the rate of dyebath exhaustion is controlled by both the addition of electrolyte and the regulation of dyebath temperature. Individual dyes vary in their response to electrolyte: the more sulphonic acid groups there are in the dye molecule, the greater will be the effect of electrolyte and the greater the care needed to obtain level dyeings.

Direct dyes are classified into three subgroups, according to the effect of changes in electrolyte concentration and dyebath temperature on their dyeing properties. The three groups of the SDC classification are as follows.

(a)   Group A contains those dyes that can be applied easily, with electrolyte present from the start of dyeing. They are referred to as *self-levelling* dyes and are often used for the shading of faster dyes in hot dyebaths.

(b)   Group B contains those dyes for which the rate of addition of electrolyte throughout the dyeing process must be regulated in order to control dyeing. They are called *salt-controllable* dyes.

(c)   Group C contains those dyes for which regulation of both the rate of increase of dyebath temperature and the addition of electrolyte are essential for adequate control. Dyes in the latter group all possess very high substantivity, even in the presence of only small amounts of salt. Because of their marked additional dependence on the dyebath temperature, they are referred to as *temperature-controllable* dyes.

This scheme of classification is appropriate for the dyeing of both natural and regenerated cellulosic fibres, but since direct dyes are more substantive to regenerated cellulosic fibres than to cotton, there is a corresponding increase in the difficulty of producing level dyeings. A practical advantage may be taken of this difference by producing two-tone effects in the dyeing of cotton/viscose blends.

Reactive dyes for cellulose

Until 1956 the only known way of producing dyeings of very high wet fastness on cellulosic fibres was through the deposition of water-insoluble pigments within the fibre. But at this time I D Rattee and W E Stephen discovered that dye molecules containing certain chemical groups (*reactive groups*) could react chemically with cellulose under alkaline conditions. Thus for the first time it became possible to make a dye react with the fibre and become part of it, rather than remaining as an independent chemical entity within the fibre.

Rattee and Stephen's discovery was followed by the introduction of the Procion range of dyes by ICI, which illustrated the technical possibilities of producing bright shades of high fastness through a variety of application methods. Since then many similar dyes have become available. The

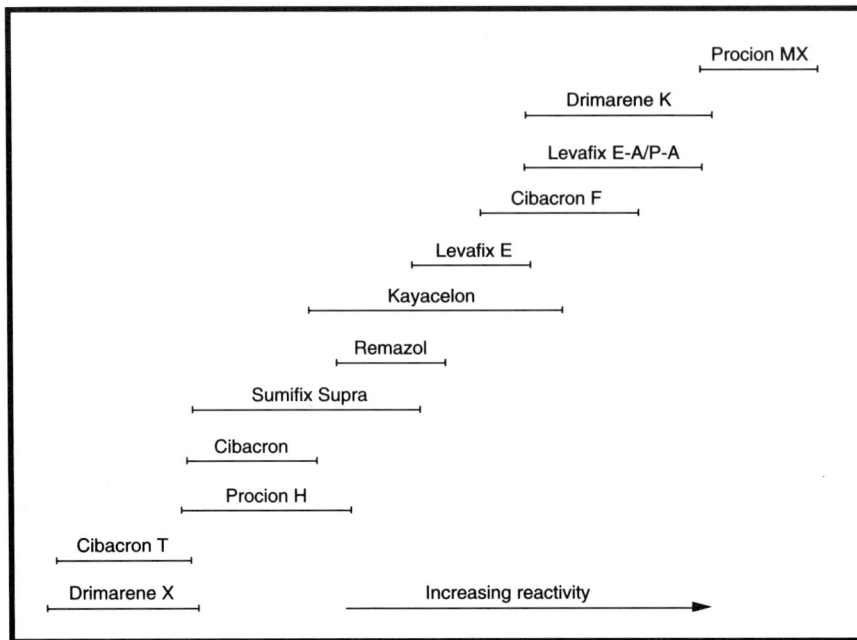

Figure 5.2 *Relative reactivities of reactive dyes for cellulose fibres*

Table 5.2 World consumption of dyes for cellulosic fibres by dye class

Dye class	Consumption (tonne $\times 10^3$/year)		
	1973	1979	1988
Direct	75	74	74
Vat	55	57	48
Sulphur	108	100	90
Azoic	29	29	26
Reactive	23	42	60
Total	290	301	300

Source: ICI Colours and Fine Chemicals, internal estimates

current ranges of reactive dyes include many that have a broad spread in their level of reactivity and substantivity. Some examples are shown in Figure 5.2, in which their respective levels of reactivity are compared. Since their introduction these dyes have played a dominant role in the dyeing of cellulosic fibres and, at the time of writing, their usage is still growing (Table 5.2).

Many reactive dyes possess a resistance to daylight previously only associated with vat dyes, and this is reflected in their use for top-quality curtains, furnishings and awnings. They also contribute to the colour quality of many domestic goods that require frequent washings, such as towellings, and are used extensively for shirtings, tapes, ribbons, dress goods and knitted sportswear; the last-named accounts for around 40% of the reactive dye market.

Nature of reactive dyes

The type of reactive group in a reactive dye molecule determines the level of its reactivity, whilst its substantivity is governed by the chromophore; both properties are equally important in controlling the quality of dyeings. The reaction of a reactive dye with cellulose is shown in Scheme 5.1. The cellulose reacts as the cellulose anion, which is formed under alkaline conditions only. That is, the dye–fibre reaction only takes place when alkali is added to the dyebath.

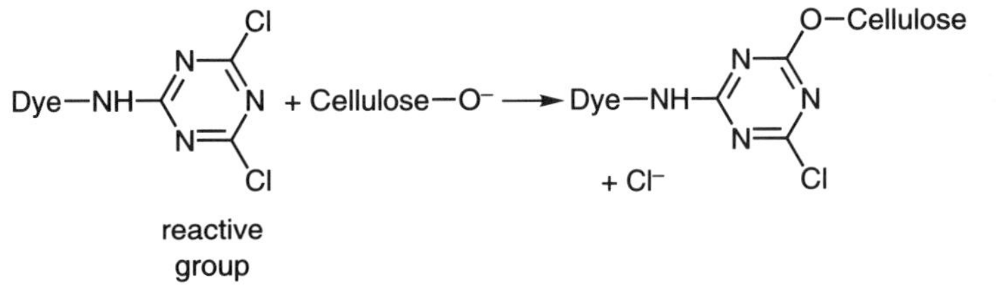

The molecules of reactive dyes are smaller than those of direct dyes, and their smaller size is accompanied by a correspondingly lower substantivity. The molecules of direct dyes are made deliberately large so as to

Scheme 5.1

build up the physical attraction between fibre and dye, thus making them more substantive. Much smaller molecules may be suitable for use as reactive dyes because one covalent bond is about thirty times as strong as one van der Waals bond.

As the size of a dye molecule becomes larger, the colour it imparts becomes duller. Reactive dye molecules therefore confer very bright colours to dyeings because their molecules need be no larger than those of simple acid dyes.

Selection of reactive dyes

Very many reactive dyes are now commercially available, with a variety of reactive groups. Their simplicity of application and broad spread of reactivity and substantivity makes them very versatile in application. But, as with other classes of dye, the quality of their dyeings depends upon careful dye selection. Appropriate levels of reactivity, substantivity and rate of diffusion are needed for the method of application best suited to the goods in hand. Indeed the dyeing of reactive dyes may be described quantitatively in these terms, but usually a simpler empirical representation is more appropriate on the shop floor.

The two essential stages in the application of reactive dyes are (a) diffusion of dye into the cellulose fibre, and (b) reaction between the dye and cellulose. The former is controlled by varying the dyeing time, the dyebath temperature and the salt concentration, and the latter is achieved by the selection of an appropriate alkalinity (pH).

Substantivity of reactive dyes

The low substantivity of the reactive dye molecules before fixation by alkali permits very easy levelling, but once they react with the fibre they cannot migrate further and they become resistant to normal domestic washing treatments. Inevitably, once alkali is added to the dyebath, reaction of the dye with cellulose begins. At the same time, however, the dye begins to react with water (*hydrolysis*), and the hydrolysed dye becomes a nuisance. It retains its substantivity but not its reactivity, and needs to be removed in the final washing-off. This situation is usually expressed in terms of the 'efficiency' of a dye or dyeing process, which is represented as a ratio of the amount of dye chemically combined ('fixed') to the amount of dye applied. This efficiency can never reach unity, because the presence of hydrolysed dye cannot be avoided even if the conditions could be adjusted to give 100% take-up (exhaustion) from the dyebath.

Dyeing temperature and reactivity

The decreased substantivity caused by raising the dyeing temperature aids both levelling before the addition of alkali and washing-off the unfixed dye at the end of the process. A great deal also depends upon the reactivity of the dye, however.

There are two groups of reactive dyes, differing in their level of reactivity. The first includes highly reactive dyes that can be applied efficiently at temperatures as low as room temperature; these are referred to as *cold-dyeing* reactive dyes. Dyes of the second group are approximately 1500 times less reactive and require temperatures of 80–100 °C for fixation; they are *hot-dyeing* reactive dyes.

The reactivity of a particular dye can be increased further by (a) increasing the alkalinity of the dyebath (i.e. increasing the pH value), and (b) raising the temperature. Although the initial discovery of reactive dyes held a promise of dyeings carried out at room temperature, difficulties with obtaining well-penetrated dyeings, free from skitteriness and streakiness, were encountered with tightly woven fabrics dyed to heavy mixture shades. Such fabrics include mercerised cotton fabrics containing highly twisted yarns, as used for rainwear, for instance. Packages of mercerised or densely wound yarns presented similar difficulties. In such cases a raised dyebath temperature is needed to aid penetration and hence level dyeing. Higher temperature increases the reactivity of the dye, which itself carries a danger of unlevel dyeing; this in turn requires further control of reactivity through a reduction in the pH of the dyebath. Thus substantivity and reactivity are manipulated together to control the quality of dyeings.

Effect of salt concentration

In a neutral solution reactive dyes are anionic in character (like direct or acid dyes), but their substantivity is low; it is of course this lower level of substantivity that confers the excellent levelling properties on reactive dyes. Compensation is made for this in batchwise dyeing by using much higher salt concentrations than are used with other dyes for cellulosic fibres. The lowered substantivity persists until the reaction between dye and fibre is initiated by the addition of alkali to the dyebath. Once fixation has taken place, however, mistakes cannot be rectified.

Reactive dyeing processes

The level of substantivity required for a particular coloration process depends on the amount of water required in relation to the mass of fabric, i.e. the *liquor-to-goods ratio*, often just called the 'liquor ratio'. With a liquor ratio of 50:1, 50 kilograms (i.e. 50 litres) of dyebath will be required for every kilogram of textile. In some methods a suitable quantity (batch) of goods is fully immersed in liquor throughout the whole process, and the liquor ratio can then be between 100:1 and 30:1. In other procedures the fabric is passed through the liquor repeatedly and the ratio is generally lower, around 20:1 to 5:1 depending on the particular machine used. Usually the higher the liquor ratio, the higher is the substantivity required to produce a good colour yield in a reasonable time.

Not all textile goods are prepared in small batches. Sometimes thousands of metres of identically coloured fabric may be needed, in which case it is impossible to immerse the entire bulk of the goods in one vessel. It is then more economical to resort to methods that allow a continuous movement of material through the entire process rather than split it up into more manageable batches. Such processes are designed to proceed from start to finish without interruption, and are appropriately referred to as continuous processes. For this purpose the fabric is passed through a trough containing the solution of dye and alkali (*padding*). It is then passed between the pressurised rollers of a padding mangle, a process in which the fabric becomes uniformly impregnated and the surplus liquid is removed. The continuous movement then carries the fabric into either a dry- or a steam-heated chamber to bring about fixation. As it emerges from the chamber it passes through the washing-off range and it is finally dried.

For continuous processes rapid washing-off is essential, and this is favoured by using dyes of a lower substantivity. This also avoids premature exhaustion of dye from the padding liquor during the time the fabric is passing through. If exhaustion were allowed to happen too rapidly, the fabric would develop a deeper shade at one end than at the other, a phenomenon known as 'tailing'. A low substantivity is also advantageous in textile printing (see page 126).

Control of batchwise dyeing

The rate of reaction between dye and cellulose is proportional to the concentration of dye in the fibre. Consequently the higher the substantivity, the greater the exhaustion and the quicker the reaction with cellulose when the bath is made alkaline. The need in batchwise dyeing methods is therefore to strike a balance between achieving the most efficient fixation, the most level dyeing and the most complete removal of hydrolysed dye.

As we have seen, there is room for control in deliberately reducing the substantivity by raising the temperature or by changing the reactivity of the dye through adjustments in pH. Conversely the substantivity can be increased by increasing the concentration of electrolyte before alkali is added to the dyebath. There are practical limits to the degree of control that can be exercised through each expedient, however, and as a general rule dyes of high substantivity can be induced to provide good yields by most methods involving the use of water. Dyes of low substantivity, on the other hand, give good yields only in padding operations. These are described below, and in further detail in Chapter 6.

The general principle of batchwise or exhaust dyeing with reactive dyes is to encourage as much dye as possible to move into the fibre over a period of 30–45 minutes by adding a high concentration of salt to the neutral dyebath. Consequently most of the dye is exhausted on to the fibre before the alkali is added, thus providing the best possible conditions for fixation before the dye–fibre reaction is initiated. Once the levelling process is complete, alkali is added and fixation continues for a further 30–60 minutes.

For highly reactive dyes, i.e. the cold-dyeing dyes, the temperature of dyeing can be set between 30 and 60 °C depending on the type of fabric and the strength of alkali. Typically, a pH of 10–10.5 and a dyeing temperature of 40 °C are used; fixation is achieved using sodium carbonate as alkali. The pH is modified to 9.9–10.0 by using sodium hydrogencarbonate (bicarbonate) when temperatures of 60 °C become necessary for certain fabric constructions. During fixation hydrolysed dye also becomes exhausted on to the fibres. To eliminate future staining which this loosely bound dye would otherwise cause, all reactive dyeings are subjected to a thorough washing-off process at the end of the dyeing cycle.

The method used with the hot-dyeing dyes is in principle identical, the difference being the use of a dyeing temperature between 65 and 90 °C and stronger alkali (i.e. a higher pH, generally 10.5–11.0); fixation is again with sodium carbonate.

A further variable is the liquor ratio, which in batchwise application can vary from 30:1 for yarn dyeing to 5:1 for jig dyeing (see page 117).

Clearly the mass of dye required for a given depth of shade is independent of the liquor ratio, and the concentration of dye used when dyeing at a low liquor ratio will be higher than for a high liquor ratio. A given mass of dye dissolved in a smaller volume of water will give a higher exhaustion. The choice of dyes for low-liquor-ratio dyeing may include those with a medium to low substantivity, whereas higher-substantivity dyes are generally employed at high liquor ratios. The high-fixation Procion HE dyes of ICI, for example, are particularly effective at high liquor ratios because they contain two reactive groups in each dye molecule. Hence they have double the chance of reacting with the cellulose before becoming hydrolysed.

Due allowance is also made for the kind of cellulosic fibre; the rate of dyeing decreases in the order: viscose fibre > polynosic fibre > mercerised cotton > linen.

The batchwise dyeing cycle is represented diagrammatically in Figure 5.3.

Control of the pad-batch process

The pad-batch process is essentially a semi-continuous one. A notable feature of the pad-batch process for reactive dyes is that a pad mangle is the only equipment required. Dye and alkali are padded from the same bath, the fabric is rolled on to a perforated or unperforated beam, covered with a plastic sheet to prevent drying out, and stored (batched) for long enough to allow dye diffusion and fixation to take place. The coloration process is then completed by washing the dyed fabric free of alkali and loose dye.

If the fabric was originally batched on a perforated hollow beam, it does not even need to be removed for washing since all the unfixed dye and chemicals can be washed away by pumping water

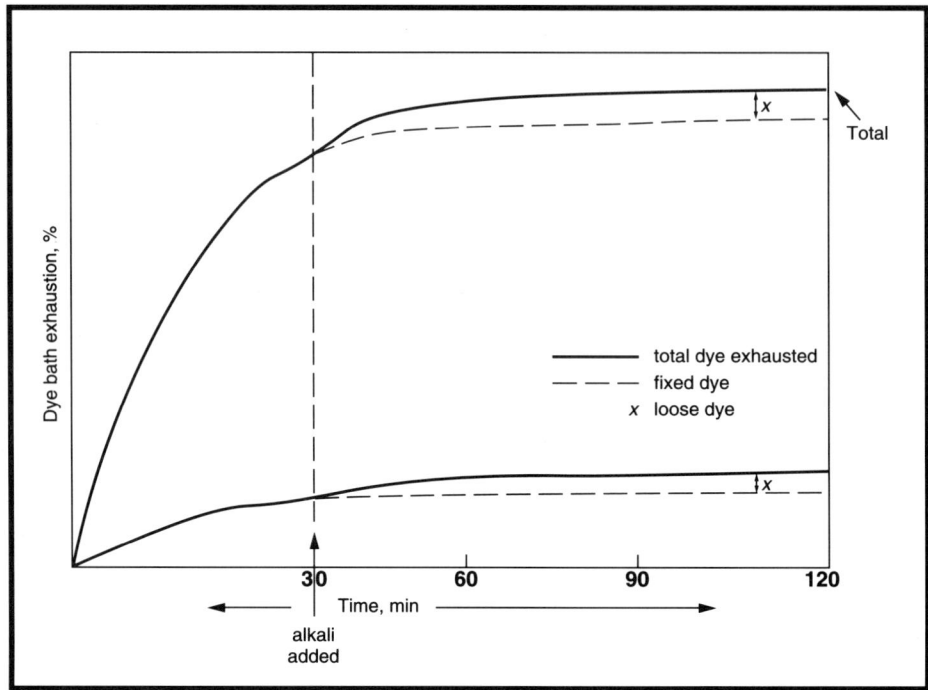

Figure 5.3 *Rate-of-dyeing curve for a reactive dye*

through the beam. Since the hollow beam is closed at one end, water is forced through the perforations into the bulk of the fabric. Within the fabric the slight positive pressure forces direct replacement of the existing dye liquor held between individual fibres with fresh water, thus flushing out the surplus dye and chemicals. This requires much less water than the conventional washing-off procedure, in which the fabric is passed through a large volume of water and which relies on the removal of loose dye and chemicals by water passing over the fabric surface.

Control of dye fixation

The pad-batch process is usually carried out at room temperature, and therefore the pH of the pad liquor is the most important variable in its control. Variations in pH of the padding liquor are used to accommodate variations in the batching time needed for penetration and fixation. Flexibility is essential for various technical reasons. For example, the greater resistance to the penetration of aqueous solutions offered by a tightly woven fabric at room temperature dictates that a longer batching time is required, but this is accompanied by a greater danger of premature hydrolysis; consequently where longer batching times are used the alkalinity is reduced. The conditions used for the cold-dyeing dyes are usually a 2 hour batching period for dye liquor at of pH 10.5–11.0 (using sodium carbonate) and 24 hours batching, or even longer, for a pH of 10 or below (using sodium hydrogencarbonate or sodium hydrogencarbonate/carbonate mixtures).

With the less reactive hot-dyeing reactive dyes a stronger alkali is called for and a pH as high as 12–13 may be required. Sodium hydroxide (caustic soda) is used as alkali, together with batching times of up to 48 hours. These conditions lead to a greater loss of dye by hydrolysis, and the colour yield is usually lower than that obtained with cold-dyeing types. Furthermore, the low colour yield cannot be counteracted by the use of the high-fixation Procion HE dyes because their high substantivity and enhanced fixation lead to 'tailing'.

Speeding up the process is possible by batching at between 50 and 70 °C with an additional piece of equipment called a pad–roll machine. This gives improved penetration, diffusion and more rapid fixation but has attendant technical problems. Variation in temperature across the width of the fabric, due to cooling of the edges of the roll, can bring uneven fixation across the width, a phenomenon called 'listing'. Dye may also migrate during the batching because of partial drying of the fabric from the edge. In general, therefore, the dyes chosen for application by the pad–batch process are those suited to cold batching.

Control of continuous dyeing

The simplest way of applying a uniform distribution of dye on a fabric is by a padding method, outlined above. The effort is minimal and the method is efficient in terms of dye consumption, levelling and water consumption, the liquor ratio being about 1:1.

Although padding is a mechanically simple operation, care has to be taken to avoid loss of quality of the dyed fabric due to 'tailing'. The effect can become serious with dyes of high substantivity. Consequently dyes of lower substantivity, which do not exhaust too readily, are preferred for padding operations. It is only in continuous methods that dyes of low substantivity give a high colour yield.

Padding operations are the first step for many of the continuous methods of application of reactive dyes in which the whole process is completed from start to finish without a break. After the initial padding stage the method of fixation varies but, whichever sequence of operations is chosen, the aim is still to allow dye to diffuse quickly prior to fixation. Conditions of fixation encompass the use of dry heat at up to 200 °C or heating by pressurised steam. Usually the levels of fixation achieved are higher than those obtained by batchwise methods.

The rapid outward movement of water in dry heat fixation tends to cause low-substantivity dyes to migrate to the surface of the fabric with the evaporating water. Consequently various proprietary pad liquor additives may be incorporated to increase the viscosity. The problem may be avoided by choosing dyes of higher substantivity.

The pad(alkali)-dry process

A padding process is the first step in the pad-dry sequence. The padding liquor contains sodium carbonate as alkali, sodium alginate as a migration inhibitor and a wetting agent to ensure rapid and efficient impregnation of the fabric by the pad liquor and dye. Since the volume of liquid is small, a high concentration of dye in the pad liquor is required to produce deep shades. The attendant problems of inadequate dye solubility can be counteracted by adding urea to the padding liquor. The reactivity of the cold-dyeing dyes allows fixation within a few minutes or less in hot air at 100–200 °C. Temperatures of 200 °C with urea and sodium bicarbonate are used for the corresponding pad(alkali)-bake process for hot-dyeing dyes. Persistent migration at these higher drying temperatures can often be avoided by introducing an intermediate drying stage at a lower temperature. Consequently a pad(soda ash)-dry-bake process is also available that complements the pad(bicarbonate)-dry process for cold-dyeing dyes.

Pad(alkali)-dry-steam process

Fixation by steam heating is also accompanied by a predrying process, which for cold-dyeing dyes becomes a pad(bicarbonate)-dry-steam sequence. For hot-dyeing dyes a pad(soda ash)-dry-high-temperature-steam sequence uses superheated steam at 220 °C to accelerate fixation.

The oldest sequence of all is a double padding system, i.e. a pad(dye)-pad(alkali)-steam process, in which a fixation time as brief as around 5–10 seconds is possible.

Principles similar to those that underlie pad dyeing methods are also appropriate for the fixation of reactive dyes in textile printing.

Dyes held as insoluble particles inside the fibre

The ultimate fastness to wet treatments on cellulosic fibres is obtained when water-insoluble coloured molecules become trapped mechanically inside the fibre, because diffusion out of the fibre during washing is then impossible. This principle underlies the action of several classes of dye, including vat dyes, sulphur dyes and azoic dyes. There are also the so-called ingrain dyes bearing the Alcian and Phthalogen trade marks. These are limited ranges noted particularly for their unique turquoise colour, provided by the remarkably stable copper phthalocyanine chromophore. Further discussion here is limited to the more extensive ranges of colours provided by the vat, sulphur and azoic classes.

Vat dyes

Vat dyes are used in the dyeing and printing of all types of cellulosic fibre, and also of blends of cotton with polyester. In their coloured form they are insoluble pigments, so their application depends on reversible reduction–oxidation (redox) reactions (page 42). In the dyebath the pigment is converted into a water-soluble form using a strongly alkaline solution of a powerful reducing agent. This forms the sodium 'leuco' compound of the dye, which is soluble in water but often different in colour from the original pigment. It is then allowed to dye the cellulose in this water-soluble form; once exhaustion is completed the leuco compound is oxidised to the coloured form.

Chemical nature of vat dyes

The large majority of vat dyes are based on the anthraquinonoid or the indigo (or thioindigo) chromophores; indigo, one of the oldest dyes still in use, remains popular through the wide use of indigo-dyed denim. Several of the anthraquinone dyes are complex polycyclic quinones (Appendix 1), and they all possess two carbonyl groups ($>$C=O) linked by alternate single and double bonds in a conjugated chain. This molecular arrangement is responsible for the easily reversible redox reactions on which the application of vat dyes depends.

In earlier centuries, when all textile colorants were obtained from natural sources, indigo plants were steeped in a large vat. It is from this ancient vatting process that the term 'fermentation vat dyes' is derived. Fermentation converts one of the plant constituents into the soluble leuco dye, which diffuses out of the plant. The replacement of natural by synthetic indigo at the end of the nineteenth century gave the impetus to research on other syntheses, and many synthetic vat dyes have since followed.

Synthetic vat dyes are costly because they are difficult to prepare, and so their use is usually directed to the higher-quality fabrics. Nevertheless, they are widely used and noted for their high fastness to light, in the dyeing of fabric for uses such as awnings, curtains, upholstery, military and naval uniforms, and high-quality gabardines.

High fastness to bleaching is another strong point of the anthraquinonoid group. This is exploited in the production of patterned fabrics from vat-dyed yarns in which the white areas of the pattern can be safely bleached out after weaving.

Anthraquinonoid vat dyes are widely used in the manufacture of, for example, good-quality shirtings, tablecloths, towels, sportswear, high-quality overalls, fabrics for women's and children's clothing and tropical suitings, and yarns and effect threads where repeated washing will be required. With careful dye selection, the use of vat dyes allows materials to be prepared with a guarantee against fading. A limitation, however, is that the range lacks scarlet, maroon and wine shades.

Application of vat dyes

Both the extent of reduction and the rate at which equilibrium between the reduced and oxidised form is achieved are of practical significance. Vat dyes vary in the speed with which they undergo reduction. The most common reducing agent used for the reduction of vat dyes is sodium dithionite ($Na_2S_2O_4$), which is capable of completely reducing even the most stable of vat dyes. As a result any difficulties in vatting can be overcome by raising the vatting temperature, increasing the concentration of reducing agent or prolonging the vatting time. The vatted dye must be kept in a strongly alkaline solution, because its leuco form is an insoluble acid. If, instead of being formed as its water-soluble sodium salt, it is formed as the free acid, it will not readily oxidise to the coloured form.

There are still some application methods in which reduction and adsorption on the fibre take place rapidly and almost simultaneously. Under these conditions the rate and extent of reduction can be decisive factors in the dyestuff choice – for example, in textile printing. Premature oxidation of the leuco compound in the print paste must also be avoided during both storage and steaming. This condition is usually met by using as the reducing agent sodium formaldehyde sulphoxylate (Formosul), a compound that is fairly stable in air at room temperature and develops the necessary action during steaming.

Variables such as pigment particle size and crystalline form can affect the rate of reduction, but these are controlled by the dye manufacturer. Consequently the colourist needs to concentrate only on the temperature and the concentration of reducing agent.

Leuco compounds can be applied by batchwise methods similar to those used for other dye classes, but there are difficulties in obtaining level dyeings. The necessary high concentrations of sodium hydroxide and reducing agent affect the exhaustion, just as the addition of salt does in direct or reactive dyeing. The difference is that the option of reducing the concentration of the additions is not available, because they are needed to form the leuco compound. Serious levelling problems can be lessened by raising the temperature of dyeing and then cooling to obtain satisfactory exhaustion, or by using a dyebath auxiliary that restrains the rate of exhaustion. A different approach is to use specially formulated stable dispersions of the pigment, in which form they are evenly distributed on the fabric by padding (*pigment padding*), followed by working the padded fabric through a solution of caustic soda and sodium dithionite on a jig. Pre-pigmentation can be carried out using package, jig, winch or beam dyeing machines (described in Chapter 6), provided specially formulated vat dyes are used. Once the pigmentation is completed, sodium hydroxide and sodium dithionite are added to the dyebath to reduce the pigment and allow the leuco dye salt to diffuse into the fibre.

Oxidation in air or in solution is then used to regenerate the pigment. A soaping treatment is given to the fabric at the end of the dyeing process; this is essential, both for cleaning the dyed fabric and for developing the final shade. In some cases a change in the crystalline form of the dye accompanies the change in shade.

Solubilised vat dyes

The need to reduce vat dyes before use makes their application a cumbersome process. Although it is possible to isolate the reduced form of the dye, it is too readily oxidised in air for the manufacturer to provide

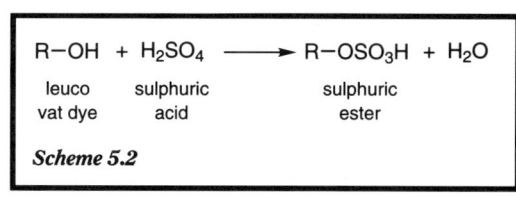

$$R{-}OH + H_2SO_4 \longrightarrow R{-}OSO_3H + H_2O$$

leuco   sulphuric   sulphuric
vat dye   acid   ester

Scheme 5.2

the dyer with the leuco compounds. It is possible, however, to convert the leuco acid into the leuco ester, a derivative that has greater resistance to oxidation and greater solubility in water. Such esters can be formed by the reaction of a hydroxyl group of a leuco acid with sulphuric acid, forming a sulphuric ester (Scheme 5.2). The sodium salts of such esters are stable and can be stored until required for use. Since the ester group is only weakly attached to the rest of the dye molecule, it is easily removed by the action of sodium nitrite in dilute sulphuric acid. The regenerated leuco compound may then be oxidised back to the pigment form.

Solubilised vat dyes are less rapidly taken up than are the more conventional vat dyes and are mainly used for the production of pale shades. As with ordinary vat dyes, application under alkaline conditions is essential, thus eliminating wool from the list of possible substrates because alkaline conditions modify the wool fibres. The low uptake and higher cost of solubilised vat dyes make them uneconomical for deep shades, however, and for these normal vat dye alternatives have to be used.

An interesting property of solubilised vat dyes is their sensitivity to light in the solubilised state. This is used to produce 'photographic' prints on fabric. Fabric dyed by padding (page 95) with one of these dyes may be placed on a suitable support with a photographic negative laid on its surface and exposed to ultra-violet light. Where the light penetrates the negative and reaches the surface of the dyed fabric the dye becomes converted to the insoluble pigment, and after washing the treated fabric free of dye a positive image remains (Plate 5).

Sulphur dyes

Deposition of insoluble pigments inside fibres may be achieved more cheaply using sulphur dyes, but with these the shade gamut is restricted to black, mauves, olives, bordeaux and reddish-browns. One of the earliest and best-known sulphur dyes is CI Sulphur Black 1, which is a popular black with good fastness properties still in use today.

Like vat dyes, sulphur dyes are reduced and applied as soluble leuco compounds that need to be kept under alkaline conditions, but sulphur dyes need only sodium sulphide to act as both alkali and reducing agent. A simplified version of the reaction is represented in Scheme 5.3. The structure of the chromophore of sulphur dyes is complex and unknown. Again like vat dyes, these

$$Ar-S-S-Ar' \xrightarrow[\text{with Na}_2\text{S}]{\text{reduction}} Ar-S^- + {}^-S-Ar'$$

Scheme 5.3

dyes cannot be applied to wool without damage to the fibres due to the action of sodium sulphide on the cystine crosslinks (page 54). After exhausting the dyebath for approximately 1 hour at 60–90 °C the fabric is thoroughly rinsed and exposed to the atmosphere, where oxidation generates the mechanically entrapped insoluble pigment.

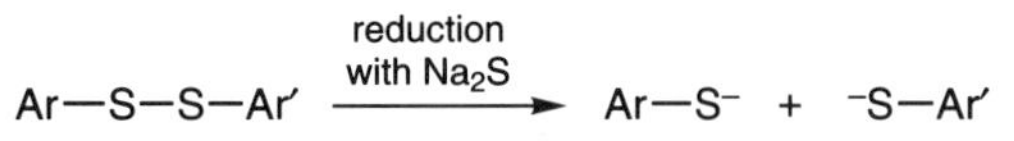

One disadvantage of certain sulphur dyes (although, strangely, this problem appears to arise with the black shades only) is that dyed material stored under conditions of high humidity and temperature can lose its natural strength. This is because inadequate washing-off after dyeing can lead to the slow generation of sulphuric acid in the fibre, arising from the presence of sulphur.

Sulphur dyes are used mainly in the dyeing of cellulose fabrics and in blends of cellulose with polyester, nylon and acrylic fibres. Typical applications are for heavy drill fabrics, corduroys, overalls, denims, awnings and canvas. Limited quantities are also consumed in the coloration of silk, paper and, more widely, leather.

Azoic colorants

In the early development of synthetic dyes a considerable impetus to progress came with the discovery by Peter Griess in 1858 that aromatic amines could be converted to *diazonium compounds* (page 35). These react readily with certain other compounds known as *colour couplers* or *coupling agents*, to produce insoluble dye particles within the fibre. Some years later, in 1876, Otto N Witt produced chrysoidine, the first commercially successful azo dye.

The commercial use of the colour coupling reaction had to wait until some years after the initial discovery when Read, Holliday and Co. described a process in which a 'coupler' was applied to cotton fabric, and the fabric was then dried and passed through an ice-cold solution of a *diazonium salt*. As a result, an azo dye was synthesised within the fibre.

Both coupler and diazonium salt are relatively small molecules and can easily penetrate the pores of cellulosic fibres, even in the cold. Once the dye is formed, it is trapped in the fibre. In subsequent soaping the dye particles aggregate into larger particles, giving dyeings with good wet fastness. Care must be taken, however, to ensure that too much insoluble dye does not form at the fibre surface, as otherwise the colour can be removed by abrasion.

A range of both colour couplers and diazonium salts is available, giving a variety of different colours. A full range of bright hues is possible with high fastness ratings to light, wet treatments and bleach, although relatively few members of the range lie in the blue-green sector of the colour gamut.

Earlier azoic dyeings were inconvenient to carry out because the dyer had to make and use all the diazonium salt solutions he needed in the winter, when ice was readily available (hence the name 'ice colours') – otherwise the very reactive diazonium salts decomposed. Later dye manufacturers were able to produce stabilised diazonium salts called Fast Salts, so avoiding the necessity of the ice-cold step. Instead the Fast Salts can be dissolved in water and applied to fabric that has previously been impregnated with a coupling agent. The range of substantivities of these agents covers products suitable for both printing and dyeing. Low-substantivity coupling agents are useful for printing applications, because after printing with the Fast Salt the unused coupling agent can readily be washed off to give a white background. Alternatively, level dyeing of a coupler of higher affinity will give a fabric that can be passed through the Fast Salt solution without bleeding-off.

For greater convenience a mixture is available that contains a coupler and a substance that generates a diazonium salt only under regulated conditions, thus providing the possibility of a one-bath process. Once the agents are exhausted on to the fibre, the addition of acid to the dyebath brings about the coupling reaction within the fibre. Even today, azoic dyes still make a significant contribution to the dyeing and printing of cellulosics.

Diazotisation and the aftertreatment of direct dyes

Although direct dyes are relatively easy to apply, their fastness properties often leave room for improvement. Various treatments have been used that are based either on enlarging the dye molecules or on making them insoluble once they are in the fibre. Discussion of these processes is relevant here because these treatments may involve either diazotising a primary aromatic amino group of the dye molecule, which can then react with a coupler, or allowing the direct dye to react with a diazonium salt, so that the dye itself becomes a coupling agent. The accompanying increase in molecular size improves the fastness to wet treatments, but is often accompanied by a change in colour and a deterioration in fastness to light.

The molecules of the diazotised and developed direct dyes are so large that any attempt to apply them directly in this form would involve difficulties of penetration and levelling. Enlarging the dye molecule in this way thus expands the possibilities for the production of deep black, brown and blue dyeings.

Diazonium compounds are also sensitive to photochemical degradation. This property can be exploited in the production of photographic textile prints, by a technique similar to that used with solubilised vat dyes described on page 104. This possibility was first demonstrated by Professor Green at Leeds University, who dyed a fabric with primuline, a yellow dye, and then converted an amino group in the molecule to a diazonium group. The fabric was then covered with a photographic negative and exposed to light. The diazonium compound in the dyed fabric was selectively destroyed in those areas where the intensity of the light reaching the fabric was highest. Aftertreatment with a coupler thus produced a printed image with tonal gradation.

Coloration of synthetic fibres

Disperse dyes

When cellulose secondary acetate and cellulose triacetate fibres were first produced in the late 1920s, they presented a serious problem to the dyer. Unlike all other known fibres of the time they were hydrophobic; since they could not be penetrated by water, they could not be dyed by water-soluble dyes. This threatened to limit the uses of the fibres, but the problem was eventually overcome by developing a new class of dye. The dyes concerned were nonionic and therefore, at the most, sparingly soluble in water. There was little point in treating the fibres with a mixture of the pure dye and water because the particles would not be distributed uniformly. Incorporating a surface-active agent with the dye powder ensures a uniform distribution of dye in the dyebath, allowing uniform dyeings to be obtained. The dye particles are thus held in dispersion by the surface-active agent and the dyes themselves are called *disperse dyes*. They are now the main class of dye for certain synthetic fibres.

Nature of disperse dyes

The main difference between the water-soluble dyes discussed previously and disperse dyes is that the latter do not contain the chemical groups (such as $—SO_3Na$ or $—COONa$) commonly incorporated to confer water solubility. Consequently disperse dyes are nonionic and as such are insoluble or only sparingly soluble in water, even at high temperatures. These hydrophobic dyes, however, are capable of 'dissolving' in the hydrophobic fibres; that is, the fibre acts like an organic solvent, extracting the dye from water. This is analogous to the simple solvent extraction of organic compounds from water by shaking up the aqueous phase with an appropriate water-immiscible solvent.

The inclusion of surface-active agents (page 31) in the dyebath is a crucial factor in the application of disperse dyes. The surface-active agents used with these dyes are usually anionic in nature. Once such a compound is added to water, its dual character results in the formation of micelles above a critical, but low, concentration. The hydrophobic 'tails' of the surface-active agent molecules are inside the micelle which, as a consequence, is able to solubilise the disperse dye molecules, so conferring a higher apparent solubility on the dye. The micelles, which thus carry negative charges on their surfaces, repel each other and consequently do not coalesce. The hydrophobic chains are also adsorbed on the surface of the solid dye particles, thus further stabilising the suspension. When used in this way the surface-active agents are referred to as *dispersing agents*.

The sublimation of disperse dyes at high temperatures gave problems with the early dyes (page 18), but such difficulties can now be avoided by careful dye selection. Indeed, the sublimation properties have been exploited in the development of novel methods that permit dyeing or printing through the vapour phase.

Application of disperse dyes

Disperse dyes can be applied to most synthetic fibres using simple immersion techniques. The dye transfers to the fibre from the micelles. As micelles empty their dye, they re-form and dissolve more dye from the solid particles (Figure 5.4).

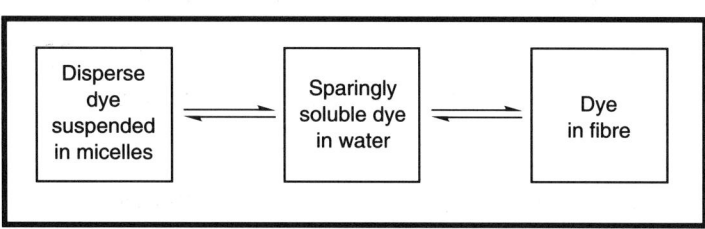

Figure 5.4 *Diagrammatic representation of the disperse dyeing mechanism*

Differences in dyeing properties between one fibre type and another are accommodated by changes in the dyeing temperature. Since neither ionic attachments nor covalent linkages are formed, the dyeing process is controlled through either accelerating dyeing by raising the temperature, or slowing it down by using a higher concentration of dispersing agent. The latter expedient assists levelling of the dye in the fibre and prevents the build-up of dye particles on the surface of the filament, a fault which that otherwise leads to poor rubbing and wet fastness.

Disperse dyes can be applied to cellulose secondary acetate readily over approximately 1 hour at 80 °C. Higher temperatures are avoided as otherwise acetate groups on the cellulosic fibre can be hydrolysed to hydroxyl groups, which can spoil the surface of the fibres and reduce their substantivity towards the disperse dyes. Cellulose acetate fabrics are best dyed in open widths (that is, with the weft threads fully extended) to prevent the formation of creases, which show up as darker markings.

Cellulose triacetate is more difficult to penetrate with disperse dyes because of its more compact molecular structure, but it can be dyed at the boil.

Nylon fibres can be dyed under conditions similar to those used for cellulose acetate fibres. Polyester fibres and acrylic fibres present more difficulty. The closely packed polymer chains of polyester and the presence of anionic groups such as $-SO_3H$ and $-COOH$ in acrylic fibres permit only pale shades to be obtained under normal conditions with disperse dyes.

One widely used way of overcoming the problem with polyester is to dye at temperatures above 100 °C, using pressurised vessels. Temperatures as high as 140 °C are attained in this way. At these temperatures the molecular structure of polyester becomes more flexible, allowing faster diffusion of dye into the fibre. (Unfortunately this approach is unsuitable for acrylic fibres because at these higher temperatures destructive changes take place in the molecular structure, imparting an unacceptably harsh handle to the fabric. Very often, therefore, acrylic fibres are dyed with basic dyes, as described on page 111.)

Instead of inducing polyester fibres to take up disperse dyes by the use of high temperatures, special dyebath additives called *carriers* may be used. Their effect on the polymer chains is similar to that of a raised temperature, allowing more rapid ingress of dye and the development of deep shades. Their smell is objectionable, however, and unless they are removed completely from the fibre they can damage the light fastness of the dyeing.

There is a correlation between the dyeing behaviour of disperse dyes and fastness to heat treatments that allows the dyes to be conveniently grouped into five main application groups: A, B, C, D and 'undesignated', based on their performance with polyester. The undesignated dyes are unsuitable for use with polyester, but can be used for dyeing cellulose secondary acetate, triacetate and nylon.

Class A dyes are suited to acetate, triacetate and nylon but are of limited value in dyeing polyester, giving poor fastness to heat. Class B dyes are excellent for use with polyester, particularly in covering variations in dyeing properties associated with textured yarns. Their fastness to heat is moderate, and some of them may be used for acetate, triacetate and nylon. Class C dyes have all-round suitability for polyester in all dyeing methods. Their fastness to heat is not the best possible,

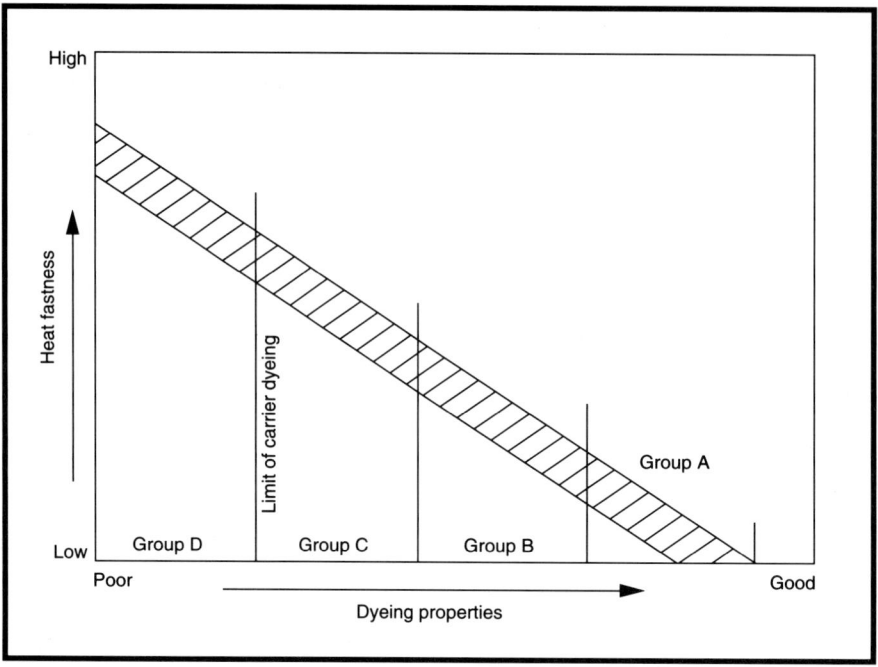

Figure 5.5 *The relationship between heat fastness and dyeing properties of disperse dyes; all disperse dyes have properties that place them within the shaded area on the diagram*

but all can be used with acetate and triacetate. Dyes of class D are used for polyester when maximum heat fastness is required. They are unsuitable for carrier dyeing and high-temperature methods or when a pad–dry–heat process is required. Thus, as a general rule, the dyeing properties of disperse dyes become more difficult to deal with as the fastness to heat treatments increases (Figure 5.5).

Sometimes attaining a particular fastness target can present major difficulties. For example, motor car upholstery may be exposed to extreme conditions of light and heat: in tropical countries it is not unusual for the seat covers in enclosed vehicles to reach temperatures of around 100 °C. These conditions can lead to weakening and severe fading of the fabric. The manufacturers therefore require a very high standard of fastness to light. Ratings of 6–7 on the blue light fastness scale are demanded, as compared with that of 4–5 usually associated with the demands of the domestic market. Dye selection must therefore take into account both light fastness and the likely effects of the dye on the stability of the fabric. Polyesters are widely used for these covers, so the high standards have to be achieved using disperse dyes. Intensive effort has been directed towards solving this problem so that suitable dyes can be selected with confidence.

Water-soluble dyes for synthetic fibres

Acrylics and nylon, being synthetic fibres, may be dyed with disperse dyes, but they also have sufficient hydrophilic character to permit entry of some water-soluble dyes. Consequently it is possible to find acrylic fibres dyed with basic dyes and nylon fibres dyed with acid dyes.

Basic dyes for acrylic fibres

Basic dyes are only occasionally employed for dyeing silk and wool, because they have poor light fastness on these substrates. As a class, however, their light fastness on acrylic fibres is very good.

Some basic dyes have been specially prepared for acrylic fibres, and whereas most water-soluble dyes are anionic in nature (negatively charged), basic dyes are cationic (positively charged) and are held on to the fibre by the formation of salt links with anionic groups deliberately built into the fibre to provide dye sites.

Rapid heating at around 60–70 °C is to be avoided because at this temperature the dye diffuses rapidly; since the dyes are highly substantive this can lead to unlevel dyeing if the control is inadequate. In fact the initial rapid adsorption of dye is controlled by adjustment of the dyebath pH and the use of colourless cationic *retarders* which compete for dye sites.

Acid dyes for nylon

Like wool, nylon contains amino groups which under acidic conditions become acid dye sites. Consequently certain levelling acid dyes have proved suitable for use with nylon. Nylon contains many fewer amino groups than does wool, however, and there is thus a limit to the amount of dye that can become attached to the nylon fibre. When this limit is reached, or as the dye molecules become larger, hydrogen bonding to amide groups (—CONH—) becomes significant.

Diffusion of acid dyes into nylon is slower than it is into wool, and the limited number of sites can cause problems in deep mixture shades where individual dyes compete for available sites. Under these conditions the faster-diffusing dyes may block entry of a second component.

Further reading

L P G Gohl and L G Vilensky, *Textile Science* (Harlow: Longman, 1990).
D Lewis, *Wool dyeing* (Bradford: SDC, 1991).
A Johnson (Ed), *Theory of coloration of textiles* (Bradford: SDC, 1989).
The dyeing of synthetic-polymer and acetate fibres, Ed. D M Nunn (Bradford: Dyers' Company Publications Trust, 1979).

Industrial coloration methods

Introduction

Coloration may be carried out at any stage in the manufacture of textile goods, including the spinning stage of synthetic fibres. Significant quantities of filament are coloured by mass pigmentation methods in which heat-stable pigment particles are dispersed in the molten polymer prior to extrusion. This is a particularly suitable method for olefin fibres that are too hydrophobic to be coloured from an aqueous dyebath, but it may also be used for polyester, nylon and viscose fibres. Other colorants are dissolved in the fibre-forming polymer and remain *in situ* after conversion of the polymer to filament.

A further variation used for acrylic fibres is to bring the freshly extruded filament into contact with a solution of basic dye before the filament is allowed to dry out. This process is referred to as *producer dyeing*, and has been used by Courtaulds and Monsanto in the production of acrylic filaments in tow form (untwisted aligned fibres or filaments collected together in the form of a loose strand).

More commonly, however, colour is applied from solution with the substrate in the form of loose fibre, tow, slubbing, sliver, yarn or fabric. Fabric may be dyed in all its forms, such as woven, nonwoven or knitted fabrics, or as hosiery or garments. Large quantities of fabric are also decorated with a pattern by printing (see page 126).

Batchwise dyeing

Machines intended for immersion dyeing are limited in the amount of goods that they can accommodate at any one time, and if the quantity to be dyed exceeds the capacity of the machine, the load has to be split into more manageable batches. Equipment for batchwise dyeing is constructed to ensure that the goods are in constant contact with the dye liquor. The liquor ratio (see page 95) of the various batchwise dyeing machines ranges from 5:1 up to 30:1 or even higher, and the dyebath composition is always formulated with a specific liquor ratio in mind.

It is important that a thorough movement of dye liquor through the goods continues throughout the dyeing process, particularly with highly substantive dyes. If the liquor circulation is inadequate and the rate of dyeing becomes reduced, the final dye distribution will be uneven. The situation is similar to the flow of water in a river. In the middle of the river the water flow is fast and turbulent, whilst nearer the banks it is usually gentler and smoother. When flood conditions arrive, however, the rapid flow and turbulence then extend from one bank to the other.

When there is insufficient force the liquid at the surface of the fibres is slowed down by viscous drag. This creates a *hydrodynamic boundary layer*, which rapidly becomes depleted in dye. Since no further dye can then reach the fibre surface except by diffusion from the main

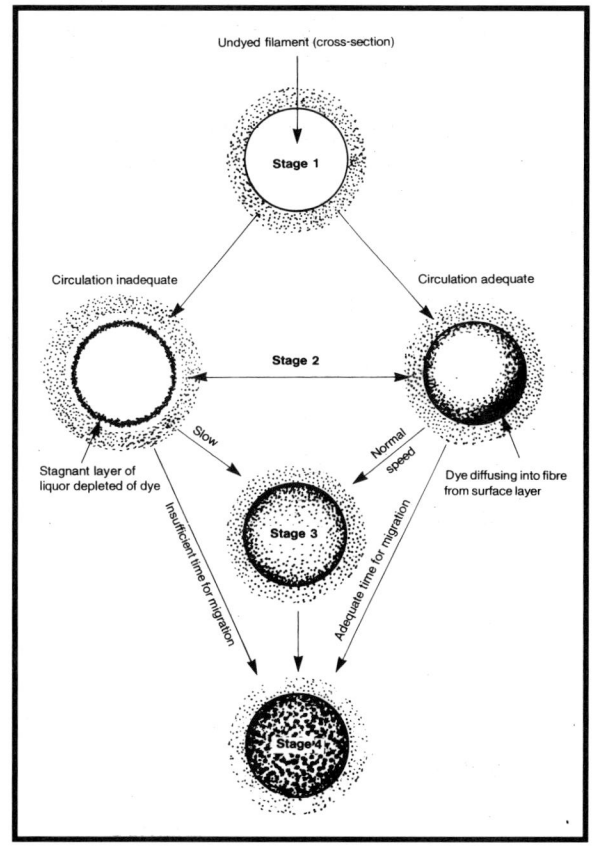

Figure 6.1 *The influence of rate of flow of dyeing liquor during the dyeing process:*
Stage 1 – dyeing begins
Stage 2 – initial dye adsorption at the fibre surface
Stage 3 – diffusion of dye into the fibre (the rate of diffusion depends on the concentration at the surface)
Stage 4 – the ideal end-point of completely uniform dye distribution

bulk of the liquid across this boundary layer (Figure 6.1), dye is not replenished at the surface quickly enough and the rate of dyeing is considerably reduced. The problem is eliminated by increasing the rate of flow to a point where it is sufficiently strong to overcome the effect of the hydrodynamic boundary layer.

There are two ways in which the flow of dye liquor relative to the goods is maintained: in some machines liquid is forced through and around the goods, while in others the goods are moved through a stationary liquor. In either case dyeing is allowed to continue until an equilibrium distribution of dye between fibre and dyebath is reached. Any aftertreatments required to fix the dye are then carried out in the same equipment before the washing-off process.

Dyeing loose fibre

The dyeing of staple fibre (*loose stock* or *raw stock*) or continuous tow is referred to as *pack dyeing*. The tow is usually formed into packages convenient for handling and dyed in machines similar to those used for dyeing packages of yarn. The hot liquor is circulated by the use of pumps through the fibrous mass packed into a large annular basket or cage. The cages are too bulky for manual handling and, as with other dyeing machines, some form of mechanical lifting device is mounted nearby for loading and unloading.

Equipment like this is not widely used, however, because the quality of the tow after dyeing is often disappointing. More often fibres are dyed in the form of yarn or fabric, and several different principles are employed for this purpose.

Yarn dyeing

Yarn is dyed either as hanks or, more usually, wound on to compact reels known as *packages*, mounted on hollow spindles. Packages can take a variety of forms, with names such as *cheeses*, *cones*, *cakes* or *muffs*. Muffs are very soft-wound packages prepared by first winding stretch yarns on to a frame, which is then removed to allow the yarn to contract. Up to a tonne of yarn can be dyed at one time in some machines.

Suitable pumps force liquor up the hollow spindles and through the packages. The flow is reversed from time to time. The whole system is contained in a cylindrical vessel with a dome-shaped lid. The vessel can be sealed to allow pressurised dyeings of hydrophobic fibres such as polyester, thus improving penetration and colour yield; temperatures up to 135 °C may be used. The liquor ratio is around 10:1, and an expansion tank at the side of the main vessel accommodates the increasing volume as the temperature rises. It is also a convenient point at which dyebath additives or further dye may be added.

The prime consideration in dye selection for yarn dyeing is always the economical production of a level dyeing with appropriate fastness properties. Free movement of the dye liquor is essential for the production of level dyeings and several factors can impede the flow if they are not taken into account when the package is being wound. In general permeability is low for regenerated cellulosic yarns, higher for staple yarns and packages, and highest for synthetic fibre packages. Provision must also be made for the effects of fibre swelling or yarn shrinkage, as these may cause a change in porosity as the dyeing proceeds. Other factors can be controlled more directly. For example, the package will be required to withstand frequent reversals of the forced flow of hot dye liquor without disruption of the orderly arrangement of the wound yarn. The porosity of the package must also remain uniform, because dye liquor will be able to flow more rapidly through less densely packed regions and this may lead to uneven dyeing. Obviously the use of a high tension during winding will produce a denser package. With nontextured yarns permeability increases with increasing tex, but the finer the filaments, the more readily the permeability is reduced due to flattening of the yarn. The same difficulty may occur with low-twist yarns. Packages of textured yarns and yarns with a rounded compact structure imparted by a high degree of twist are more permeable. Care is needed with nontextured fibres since their dimensional instability can also cause problems. Nontextured filament nylon, for example, is usually wound on to collapsible bobbins and relaxation induced by steaming. The increased tensions produced are then released before dyeing by rewinding on to fresh formers.

Nowadays most yarns are dyed in the form of packages mounted on a series of hollow, perforated, vertical spindles situated around the circular vessel containing the dyebath (Figure 6.2). When the dyeing is completed, the yarn is wound back on to bobbins ready for conversion into fabric by knitting or weaving. The packages are initially prepared in ways that help to overcome the difficulties sometimes experienced at this stage. For example, staple fibre yarns tend to cling on unwinding. Spun viscose yarns tend to swell considerably during dyeing.

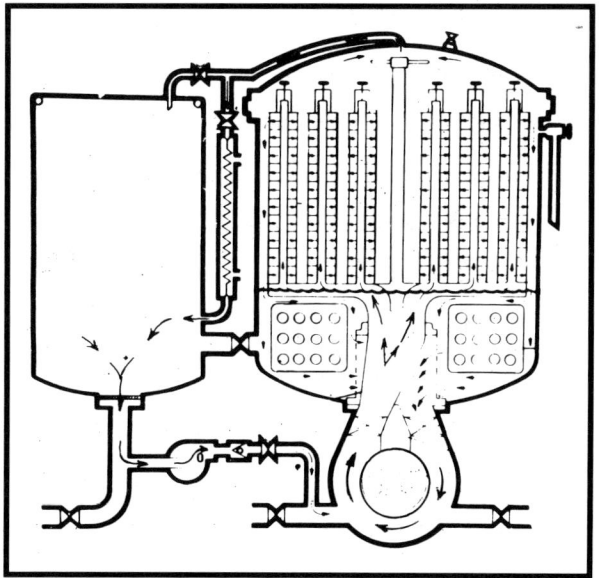

Figure 6.2 Vertical-spindle package-dyeing machine

This poses problems that can be eased by forming the yarn packages into the shape of a cone. Cones are unsuitable for taking up vertical compressions, however. Furthermore, flow of liquor through a cone is less uniform than through a cheese.

In some instances the central former of the cheese is removed completely to allow the wound yarn to reach a more relaxed state during dyeing. This is accompanied by an enhancement in the stretch properties of the yarn, and the associated improvement in permeability leads to more rapid dyeing. Such yarn packages are used as an alternative to the hank dyeing of high-bulk acrylic yarns and some wool carpet yarns. This procedure allows cost savings in processing because it requires only half the volume of water used in hank dyeing and there is a corresponding reduction in the consumption of energy to heat up the dyebath.

Hank dyeing

Nowadays dyeing of yarn in the form of hanks or skeins is mainly used for lofty yarns such as wool and high-bulk acrylic yarns for knitting and carpet manufacture. The hanks are usually mounted on horizontal bars and suspended in the dye liquor. Traditional machines have a rectangular bath in which dye liquor is gently circulated around the yarns using a suitably placed pump and overflow arrangement. Uniform dyeing is ensured by reversing the direction of flow from time to time.

Fabric dyeing

Beam dyeing

Fabric can be wound on to a perforated beam and dyed in an enclosed vessel. This enables the dye liquor to be forced through the substrate in a manner analogous to yarn package dyeing. The use of reversible pumps enables the flow to be in either the in-to-out or the out-to-in direction, but the former is favoured because compression of the fabric reduces the porosity of the goods. With some other methods of dyeing, delicate woven or knitted fabrics may suffer from creasing due to the way the fabric is manipulated in the liquor. In beam dyeing, however, the fabric remains in an open-width configuration (page 109) and is supported throughout the dyeing operation. Provided the porosity of the fabric mass remains satisfactory, good-quality dyeings are generally obtained. Any dimensional instability of the fabrics will lead to unlevel dyeing, however, because stretching allows localised increases in the porosity within the roll wherein liquor may flow more rapidly. If shrinkage occurs, then the increase in the internal mechanical pressure in the roll brings about flattening of the fibres. With thermoplastic fibres this results in deterioration of the appearance of the fabric surface. Synthetic fibres, particularly nylon, are given either a heat-setting treatment or a scouring treatment before dyeing to minimise such difficulties.

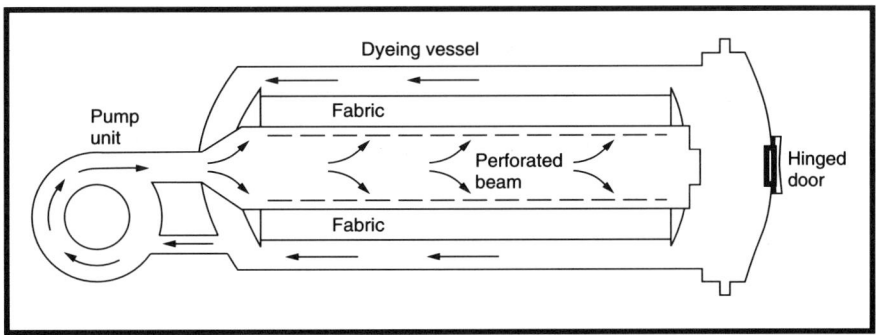

Figure 6.3 *Sectional diagram of a high-temperature beam dyeing machine*

A pressure beam dyeing machine is shown in Figure 6.3. A small expansion tank (not shown in Figure 6.3) is also fitted to enable additives to be introduced at the requisite point of the dyeing process.

Jig dyeing

The jig machine (Figure 6.4) is one of the oldest ways of dyeing fabric in open width. In this machine a batch of fabric is rolled backwards and forwards from one roller to another through the dye liquor. The direction of movement is automatically reversed as the machine reaches the end of the fabric roll. The duration of the dyeing process is monitored by the number of passages or 'ends' through the liquor. Machines open to the atmosphere can accommodate a roll of 500 to 1000 metres in length, but more modern enclosed machines can operate with a roll of 5000 metres. An enclosing lid helps to reduce heat losses and consequent temperature differences between the edge and the centre of the roll. Such differences lead to 'listing', a reduction in the dye uptake at the edges of the fabric. Pressurised jigs are available for the more difficult hydrophobic fibres. These operate at

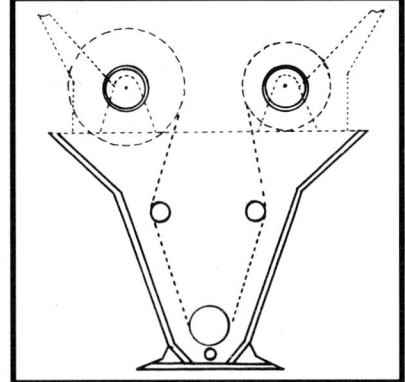

Figure 6.4 *Cross-section of a simple dye jig, showing the method of threading*

temperatures of up to 130 °C, but beam dyeing is usually preferred for high-temperature dyeing. A liquor ratio of around 5:1 is the lowest used in conventional jig machines. The method is well suited to the dyeing of fabrics that are readily creased, such as taffetas, poplins, suitings and satins, but less well for knitted goods because they distort so easily.

117

The mechanical action on the fabric is obviously limited in jig dyeing. Consequently the exchange of liquor inside the interstices of the fabric as it passes through the dyebath is less efficient than with machines in which liquor is circulated more forcibly through the goods. The jig is relatively inexpensive to install and convenient to use; moreover, since it operates at a low liquor ratio, it is economical on both water and energy consumption.

Winch dyeing

In winch dyeing machines, the oldest kind of equipment used for dyeing fabric, the fabric is dyed in rope form, gathered together across its width. The method is used widely for fabrics such as woollens, loosely woven cottons, synthetic fibre fabrics and most knitted fabrics. All these can withstand creasing during the dyeing process. The winch machine operates at longer liquor ratios than those employed in the jig, liquor ratios from 15:1 to 40:1 being commonly used, depending on the type of the fabric and the particular model of machine. The warp threads of the fabric remain under tension throughout dyeing, and as a result of this and of the mechanical action used to propel the fabric through the dye liquor the yarns in woven fabric often develop a crimp. With knitted goods there is an increase in loop length. Both effects lead to a fuller thicker fabric with a more resilient handle and improved crease recovery.

The principles of the operation of winches (also called becks, winces or vessels) are illustrated in Figure 6.5. The rope of fabric is looped over the winch reel, which lifts the fabric and allows it to drop into the dye liquor. The free-running jockey acts as a support for the fabric as it is pulled forward. As the fabric drops into the dye liquor it becomes folded over concertina-fashion ('plaited'), as shown. The folding and opening action, which persists for as long as the winch reel is turning, keeps the dye liquor in motion.

Variations in the design details of machinery have been introduced to suit the characteristics of different fabrics. Wool and heavy types are best suited to the deep-draught winch, where fabric piles up on the sloping back and pushes forward the fabric in front. For filament viscose, acetate or any fabrics which crease whilst wet, the shallow-draught winch is preferred because the lack of depth and flat base reduce the compressive pressure of the falling fabric. The design of the winch reel governs the movement of the fabric, which when wet grips the reel because of the gravitational pull and the friction between the wheel and the wet fabric. The reels are usually made of stainless steel.

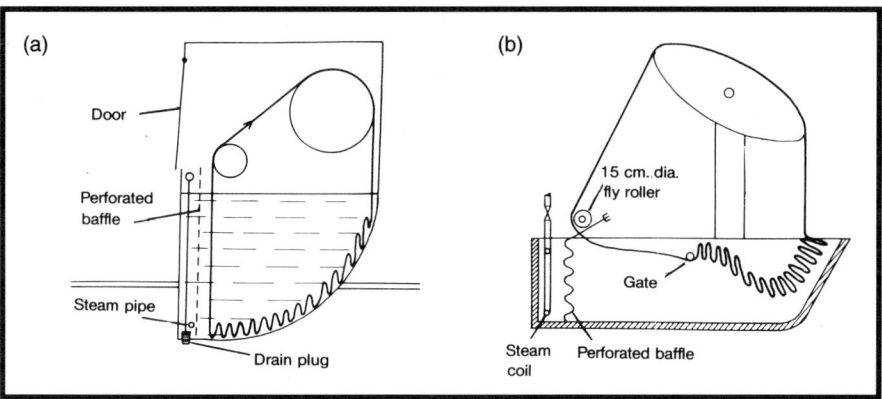

Figure 6.5 Winch dyeing machines: (a) deep-draught, (b) shallow-draught

With the deep-draught machine a circular or slightly elliptical reel is used to lift the fabric over the jockey roller, so that it falls straight into the dyebath from the reel with only a little plaiting action. Elliptical winch reels are better for other fabrics and provide greater plaiting. Mechanical action on more delicate fabrics is reduced by the use of a larger elliptical wheel. The presence of an adjustable horizontal bar (the 'gate') in the middle of the bath restrains the fabric at the back of the machine until it is pulled past by the revolving winch reel. This action minimises creasing by straightening the warp direction folds.

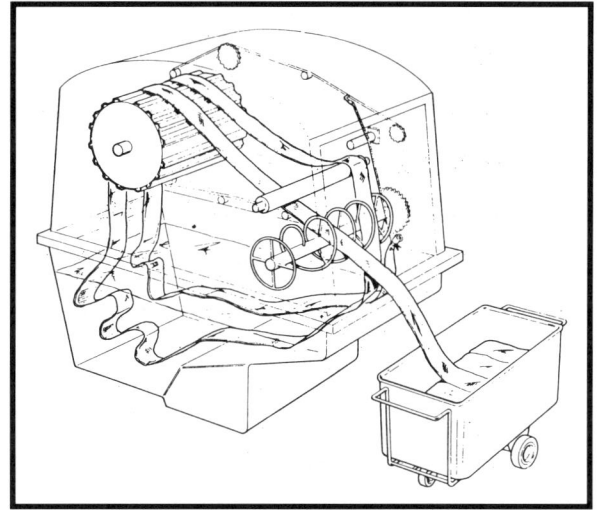

Figure 6.6 Winch dyeing machine with Autoloda

Figure 6.5 shows only one rope of fabric, but in most machines many such ropes are arranged side by side, in parallel. In others, a long continuous rope is used in a spiral configuration, and is presented to the machine with the aid of a helical Autoloda spanning the entry to the machine (Figure 6.6). This mechanism saves time in loading and allows a larger batch of fabric to be dyed, thus lowering the liquor ratio.

Jet dyeing

Recently designed machines have adapted the force from a strong jet of dye liquor to transport the

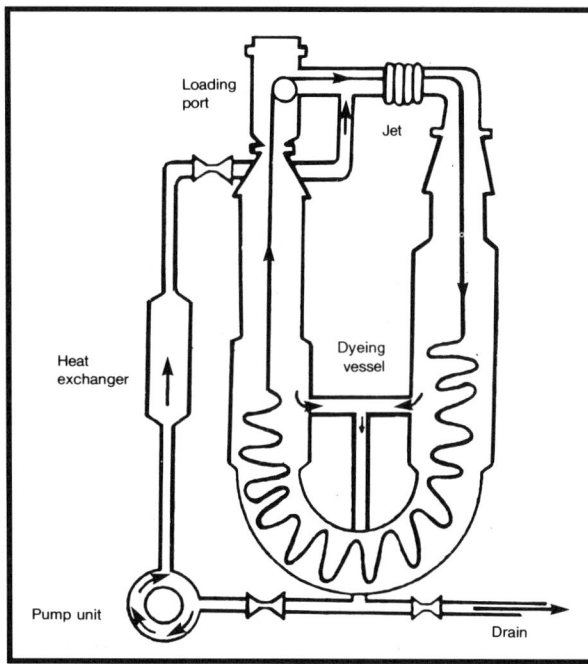

Figure 6.7 *Thies Jet Stream fully flooded dyeing machine*

fabric from the front to the back of the dyeing machine. Low liquor ratios can be used and the machines are designed to operate above atmospheric pressure with polyester fabrics, particularly when in the form of knitted goods.

The latest machines of this type keep the fabric fully immersed throughout the dyeing operation, eliminating the creasing and foaming that presented problems with the early models. Because the fabrics are constantly immersed and the machine fully flooded, delicate fabrics are supported throughout. The size of the jet may also be regulated to match the best requirements for a particular fabric.

An example of such a machine is shown in Figure 6.7. The goods in rope form are moved along by the force of the jet of liquid into the vertical chamber below, and the liquor is recirculated through the heat exchanger back into the jet. The rope moves slowly whilst in the main chamber, but very rapidly through the tube into which the jet is directed.

Soft-flow machines

A much gentler action is provided by so-called soft-flow machines, in which the force of the flow of dye liquor moving the fabric is reduced by circulating it into the main chamber from an overflow system (Figure 6.8). Soft-flow machines are notable for minimising the creasing of delicate fabrics and the lower overall strain imposed on the goods during dyeing. There are several versions of both jet dyeing and soft-flow machines, and further details may be found elsewhere [1].

Garment dyeing

Women's hosiery and socks are typical examples of textile goods that can be dyed in garment form, and the dyeing of knitted wool garments is equally long established. Nowadays it is common to dye more elaborate garments too, offering the retailer scope for a quick response to changes in current fashion and a reduction in the level of stock holding. The conventional approach of dyeing the fabric followed by making up is associated with a delay of at least two to three weeks between the preparation of fabric for coloration and its appearance as an artefact in the shop. The time between request and delivery may be reduced to four or five days, however, by holding a stock of undyed garments. Even after making allowance for the manufacture of the fabric and the making-up time, the garment dyeing approach is much faster. A full review of garment dyeing will be found elsewhere [2].

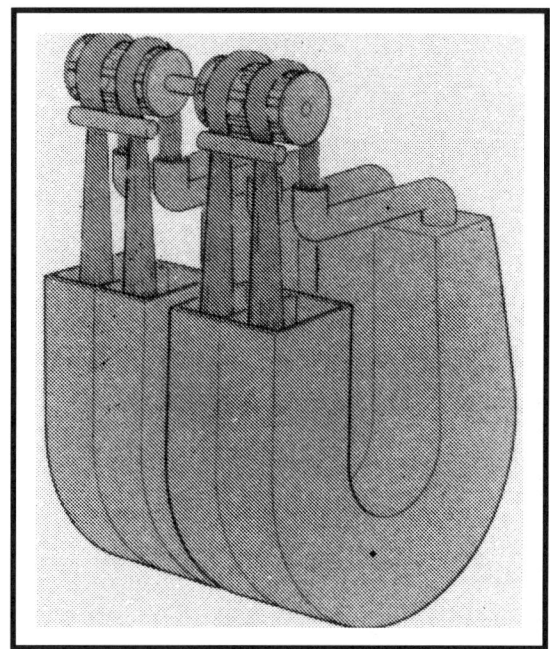

Figure 6.8 Longclose soft-flow jet dyeing machine

The current interest in garment dyeing has been encouraged by the growth in demand for casualwear and leisurewear. Although garments made from most fibre types can be dyed with commercial success, the main growth in this market has been with cotton goods.

The drawback of garment dyeing is its greater expense. Consequently success is dependent on reduction of the overall cost through retailing methods and attention to design features that are compatible with this method of production.

Adequate attention to fabric preparation is essential for satisfactory dyeing, and the fabric must be thoroughly scoured to remove contaminants such as spinning oils. With wool garments some form of shrink-resist treatment is usually applied before dyeing, and with all knitted goods pre-relaxation treatments are equally important for a good-quality end product. Careful selection of stitch type, stitch density, thread tension and thread type helps to reduce problems such as the development of seam pucker due to differential relaxation of the fabric and sewing thread during dyeing.

Other problems are entirely the responsibility of the dyer. For example, fabrics of different construction in the same garment must appear to be of the same intensity of colour, and the compacted fabric enclosed by the seam must be as well penetrated and dyed to the same depth as the rest of the garment. This calls for dyes with good migration properties and a dyeing method that will give good penetration of dye liquor. For this reason hot-dyeing reactive dyes are often used with cotton garments in preference to cold-dyeing types, since the higher dyeing temperature makes for more efficient penetration. For goods that will be subjected to hand washing, however, dyes will probably be selected using the Society of Dyers and Colourists' A and B classification of direct dyes in the dye selection process.

The sewing thread is also of concern. Usually it must remain inconspicuous, and this entails the use of dyes with a similar substantivity on both the sewing thread and the fabric. Occasionally, however, stitching is deliberately used to produce decorative effects, in which case differential dyeing of the thread and the fabric may become a desirable feature.

Knitted wool garments present similar problems of penetration, and in addition care is needed to avoid fibre damage, particularly when long dyeing times or low pH values are used. Again, dyes are chosen to match the requirements of the attached aftercare label. Thus levelling acid dyes are used for garments that will be hand-washed, whereas metal-complex and milling acid dyes provide better fastness and deeper shades for more robust articles. On the other hand, reactive dyes are generally the choice for wool fabrics finished to machine-wash standards (page 86).

Articles such as buttons or zip fasteners may present additional hazards to the dyer. The presence of metal ions in the dyebath from buttons or zips can influence the shade of the dye; conversely, dyebath ingredients such as acid, alkali or reducing agent (for vat dyes) may do irreversible damage to the appearance of such trimmings.

Machinery for garment dyeing

Garments are usually dyed in a simple system in which the dye liquor in a suitable vessel is agitated gently by means of a paddle arrangement. There are several types of machine, differing in the positioning of the paddles, but in all of them the action is gentle. The garments, being loose in the bulk of the liquid, move around freely with the flow induced by the paddle. Thus the liquid is not forced through the structure of the fabric in any way and there are predictable penetration problems with thick seams and with garments made from heavy fabrics. In the special machines designed for dyeing hosiery, the goods are placed in perforated drums with compartments. Some of the front-loading machines are useful for dyeing small garments. None, however, is ideal for present-day needs.

The Pegg Toroid machine has proved useful for dyeing fully fashioned Tricel and polyester knitted garments (Figure 6.9). Its gentle action is provided by pumping the dye liquor up the centre of the machine so that it is deflected at the top to cascade down the side of the dyeing vessel, giving a whirlpool-like movement of the liquor. A pressurised version allows dyeing temperatures of 130 °C to be attained but the actual relative rate of flow of liquor over and through the garments is still limited, since the goods are free to be carried along in the current of dye liquor.

Modern machines are more sophisticated and operate through electronic control systems; an example is shown in Figure 6.10. They have a rotary action during dyeing and a centrifugal action for eliminating dye liquor or water at the appropriate stages. This feature reduces the energy requirements for drying and the amount of rinsing required, thereby dramatically reducing the processing time. Various degrees and types of mechanical action are employed to suit the finishing operation required. Improvements in circulation have been effected through the introduction of pumps that force the dye liquor through external heat

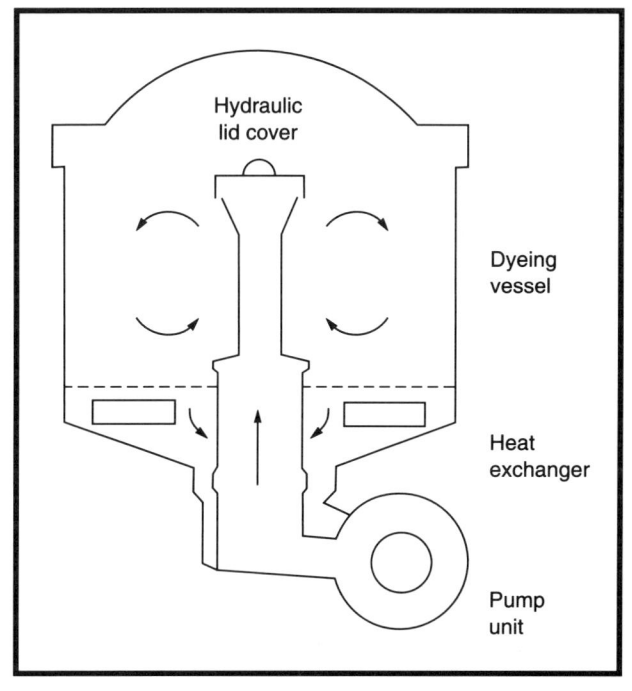

Figure 6.9 Pegg Toroid machine for garment dyeing

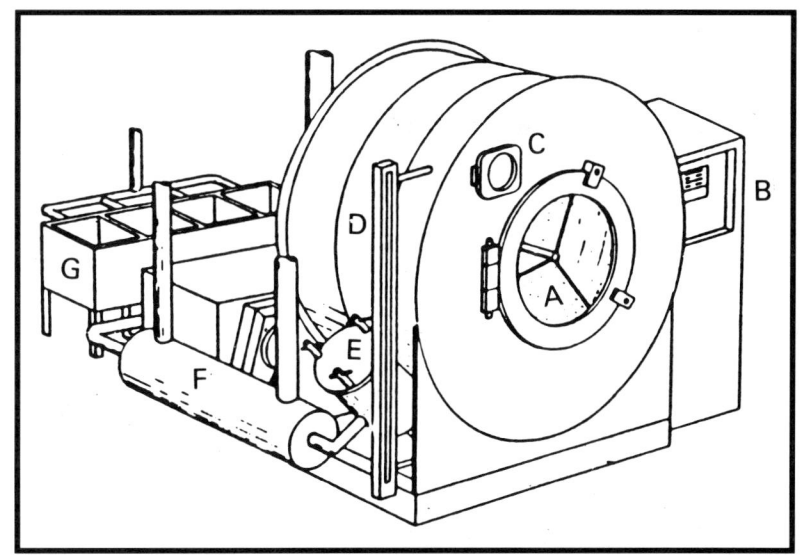

Figure 6.10 Typical rotary drum garment dyeing machine
A Perforated drum (with Y-pocket); B Machine controller; C Sampling port; D Liquor level indicator; E In-line lint filter; F Heat exchanger; G Addition tanks

exchangers. This reduces the mechanical action required, which is good for garments made from thermoplastic fibres (such as acrylics) that react adversely to the extension and compression experienced under the hot, wet conditions of dyeing. Moreover, better seam penetration is obtained with these machines. They are also equipped with an external filter to remove lint fibres which would otherwise adhere to and disfigure the garments.

Continuous dyeing

When there is a large volume of goods, it is usually better to process them continuously without the inconvenience of separating the job into batches and repeating the process several times. In this situation processing is arranged as a continuous uninterrupted sequence of events from start to finish. The goods move at a constant rate throughout, and on completion of the dyeing they are taken up mechanically at the far end of the equipment. The process is run until the whole length of textile has passed through.

Although most continuous coloration is carried out on fabric, equipment is also available for dyeing fibre in the form of loose stock, tops and tow, all of which have been reviewed [1,3]. At the start of each process fibre is sprayed with dye, fed on to an endless rubber belt and carried to the rollers of a padding mangle, where uniform impregnation is obtained as the surplus liquid is squeezed out. In the example shown in Figure 6.11 the loose fibre is carried through a tubular steamer, washed to remove surplus dyebath ingredients and, after the application of any special finishes, dried. This general scheme of impregnation followed by fixation, washing and drying is the same for each of the continuous processes.

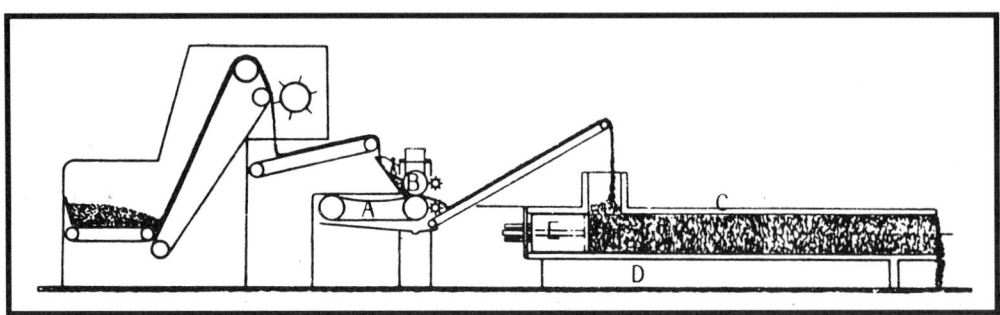

Figure 6.11 *Continuous fibre dyeing*
A Rubber conveyor belt; B Nip rollers; C Tubular steamer; D Front of steamer; E Piston

Various sequential operations are used for the continuous dyeing of fabric. These have already been outlined in Chapter 5, with reference to dyeing with reactive dyes on cellulose. An initial padding stage is common to all sequences. It involves immersion of the fabric in the dye liquor contained in a trough of minimal volume, which is kept constantly replenished from a stock tank. A liquor ratio as low as 1:1 may be used; in general, low-substantivity dyes are used in continuous dyeing processes (see page 96). Next, the fabric passes in open width through a 'nip'. The nip is the padding mangle, in which heavy rollers (called bowls), pressed closely together along their length, are rotated in opposite directions to carry the fabric through the system at a constant speed, squeezing out the superfluous dye liquor (Figure 6.12 (a)). Heavier fabrics are passed through two consecutive troughs and a second nip, using a three-bowl mangle.

The fabric, now uniformly impregnated with dye and the appropriate dyebath auxiliaries, usually passes directly to a steamer or dry heater for fixation (Figure 6.12 (b)). In some cases, however, where evaporation of the water in the fixation chamber causes unwanted directional migration of dye, the fixation step follows a preliminary drying operation. After fixing, the fabric passes from the fixing chamber to the washing range and is dried either on heated cylinders or by some other means such as radio frequency heating. Finally it is wound on to a beam ready for transportation. The sequence is similar for all processes, but of course the dyes, additives and operating temperatures vary from one situation to another.

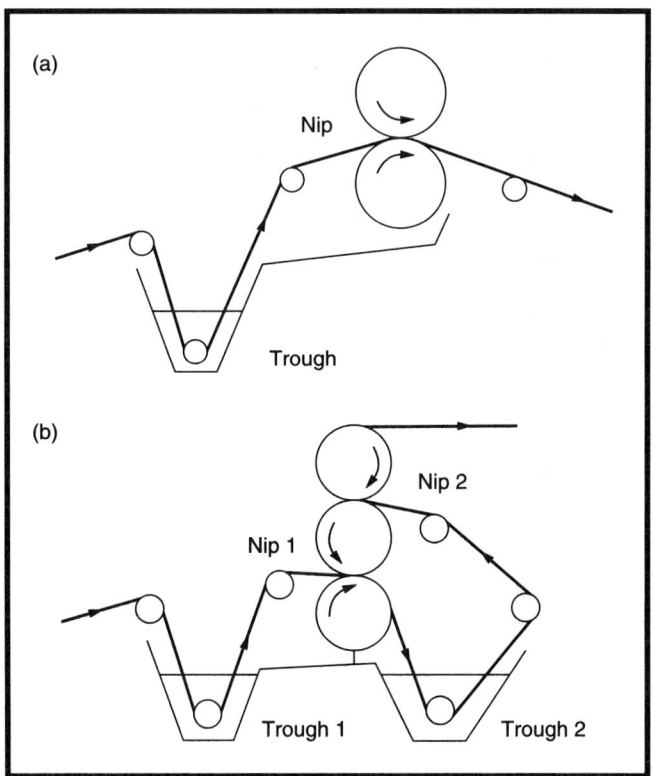

Figure 6.12 Principle of pad mangle operation:
(a) two-bowl mangle, (b) three-bowl mangle

Carpet dyeing

A serious difficulty in the coloration of carpets by conventional continuous dyeing methods is the very high pick-up of liquor required. This may range from 400 to 1000% of the mass of the carpet, and clearly can give rise to a very high consumption of water, processing energy and chemicals. Attempts have been made to alleviate these difficulties by replacing much of the bulk of the liquid with air by using surface-active agents that suspend the dye and chemicals as a stable foam. Various forms of foam applicator have been devised to produce plain-coloured carpets. Unfortunately the foam is required to be highly stable if the colour is to be uniformly distributed, but this very stability hinders the penetration of dye into the carpet pile.

Dispensing the dye liquor through a series of fine sprays is an alternative and more rewarding approach to the problem. Various spray applicator mechanisms have been designed, and these allow operation at much lower add-on values of about 150–250%.

Textile printing

Modern procedures for printing textile goods may be traced back to the block printing of silks in ancient China. In this method a wooden block with a raised pattern on the surface was dipped into the printing colorant and then pressed face down on to the fabric. The desired pattern was obtained by repeating the process using different colours. Printing by brushing colorant through thin metal stencils and the transfer of illustrations to the printed page from engraved rollers in a printing press were also widespread by the fifteenth century.

Block printing remained a practical proposition until the roller printing machine was invented by James Bell in 1783. This enabled six colours to be printed at a rate equivalent to that of 40 hand-block printers. The success of the machine depended on the hard rollers, each of which bore an engraving (i.e. an intaglio engraving, in which the depth of the recess on the roller determines the intensity of the print produced) corresponding to a particular colour component of the design. The machines were capable of continuously printing six different colours in sequence, with the rollers pressed against the fabric.

Traditional screen printing

The use of screens can be traced back to the ancient Japanese, who used fine threads of silk or human hair to 'tie' the freely suspended solid areas of the stencil in place. The threads were too fine to leave a perceptible mark in the final print.

The modern forms of screen printing began with the introduction of screens of fine woven fabric that allow colorant to be passed through any areas where a solid paper or painted pattern did not block the mesh. The dimensional stability and hydrophobic nature of modern synthetic fibres has made it possible to construct screens that provide a high precision in the placing of differently coloured components of the design. The high tensile strength of the filaments enables them to be stretched over a metal frame and remain taut during repeated use. This is a marked improvement over the older hydrophilic silk screen stretched over a wooden frame, and one that has led to the mechanical simulation of the older craft process. The screen can now be raised mechanically whilst the fabric moves into the next position, and then be replaced in exact register. A fully continuous operation was made possible by the development of electrodeposited screens in the form of hollow seamless cylinders, through which the print paste may be pressed from the centre as the screen rotates and beneath which the fabric is carried on a moving blanket.

Printing paste

In textile printing the printing paste on the fabric may be regarded as a miniature localised dyebath containing the dye and all the additives necessary for the coloration process. Thus print pastes for reactive dyes will contain alkali, those for vat dyes will contain reducing agent, and so on. Dye diffuses into the fibre from the paste, aided either by a rise in temperature and absorption of water within a steamer, or by the fibre becoming a more favourable environment as the paste becomes affected by the heat of a dry fixation process. To a certain extent the nature of the fixation process to be used influences the type of additive mixed with the print paste.

Textile printing pastes are usually water-based, but for paper printing a solvent base may be chosen since for this purpose rapid drying through evaporation is more important than substrate penetration. Compared with a dyeing process on a similar fabric, dyes of lower substantivity and high water solubility are often chosen, so as to ease the final washing-off process.

The viscosity of the print paste needs careful attention to ensure that it flows smoothly from the source of application on to the fabric. Too high a viscosity impedes transfer and penetration, and if the paste does not spread evenly on the fabric the surface appearance will be unsatisfactory. Most thickening agents are polymeric in nature, and the overall chemical composition of the paste must be compatible with the dye fixation mechanism. For example, there is little point in using a polysaccharide thickening agent (such as starch) for reactive dyes, because of its chemical similarity to cellulose: the dye would react with the thickener before it reached the fibre. Similarly thickeners with cationic groups will react with anionic dyes, and vice versa. A variety of thickening agents is available, ranging from polysaccharides (polymers of sugar monomers) such as starches and natural gums like locust bean gum, guar gum or gum arabic, the last-named being obtained from acacia trees, to alginates (from seaweed) and synthetic materials such as poly(vinyl alcohol) and acrylic polymers.

Roller printing

The principle of roller printing is illustrated in Figure 6.13. The fabric travels round a large cylinder (A) referred to as the pressure bowl. This is covered with a thick layer of textile material, the lapping, around the circumference of which the fabric to be printed is carried on an endless blanket, usually of polyester/cotton material. Thus a resilient backing is provided for the material during the impression stage. Any excess colour is absorbed by a layer of unbleached cotton (the 'back grey') placed between the printing blanket and the printed fabric. As the bowl revolves it carries the fabric forward from a roll situated behind the machine for as long as the engraved printing rollers are under mechanical pressure rolling over the surface of the fabric. In this way the resilience of the backing forces the fabric into the engraving from which the print paste is removed. Colorant is transferred from the

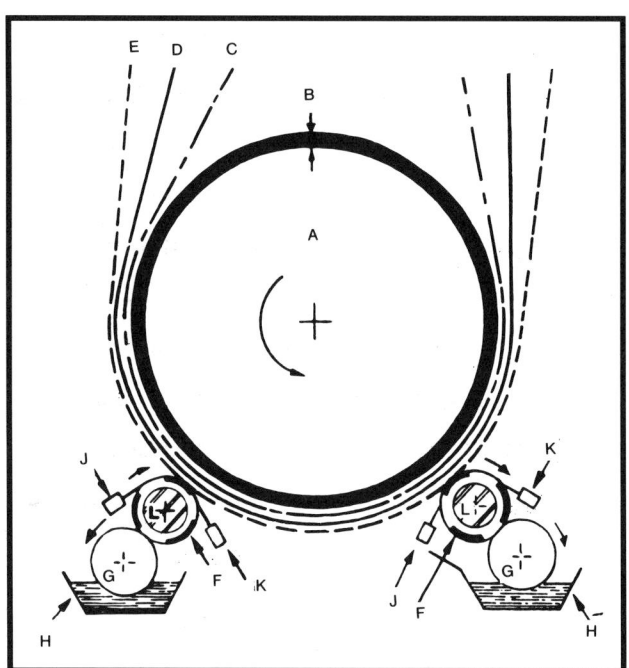

Figure 6.13 *Diagram of a two-colour machine*
A Pressure bowl (impression cylinder), B Lapping,
C Endless printing blanket, D Back grey, E Fabric to be printed,
F Engraved printing cylinder, G Furnishing rollers, H Colour box,
J Colour doctor, K Lint doctor, L Mandrel

trough containing the printing paste (the colour box) to the engraved roller through the intervention of a furnishing roller dipping into the printing paste.

Surplus print paste is removed from the printing roller by a sharp stainless steel 'doctor blade' before the roller makes contact with the fabric. Any loose threads or hairs that adhere to the roller after transfer of the print pastes are removed by a second doctor blade, the lint doctor, before the engravings are refurnished with print paste. Only two printing rollers are shown in Figure 6.13, but several rollers may be positioned around the bowl, each contributing its own coloured motif in the exact register required for the printed pattern.

From the bowl the fabric passes to a dryer, a steamer or any other treatment appropriate for fixation, from where the fabric travels to a washing range in which spent print paste, surplus chemicals and dye are removed.

In one machine the fabric passes over two bowls, so arranged that the inside of the fabric being printed on the first bowl becomes the outside when it reaches the second bowl. In this way the fabric may be printed on both sides to give a duplex printed fabric.

As we have seen, the composition and consistency of the printing paste are critical factors in the attainment of high-quality prints. In particular, a low viscosity can lead to frictional damage to both the doctor blade and the engraved roller. Any resulting imperfections in these metal components as a result are likely to lead to the unwanted appearance of fine lines of colour on the print. The absence of small particulate foreign matter in the paste and scrupulous cleanliness of the rollers are further requirements for perfecting the products.

Engraved roller printing is notable for high resolution and excellent reproduction of intricate patterns. Unfortunately the high cost of engraving the rollers and the need to adapt to shorter runs has gradually eroded the old supremacy of roller printing, to the advantage of rotary-screen printing.

Rotary-screen printing

The value of continuous rotary-screen printing first became apparent in the 1960s. The hollow screens, each applying the appropriate motif, are arranged sequentially as in roller printing, but they are aligned over a moving horizontal blanket that carries the

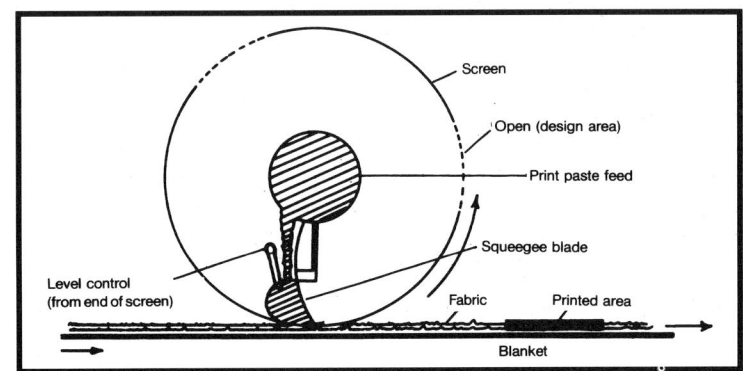

Figure 6.14 *Rotary screen printing section*

fabric between the two. As the fabric moves forward the screens rotate and apply the colour.

One arrangement for the delivery of print paste is shown in cross-section in Figure 6.14. The squeegee blade is flexible to accommodate any variations in pressure required to force the paste evenly through the mesh of the screen across the width of the fabric. In some models the squeegee is replaced by a metal rod held in position by a magnetic field. This is more suited to heavier fabrics, since the mechanism imposes a higher limit on the minimum amount of paste that can be delivered. In general the rotary-screen printing machine requires a lower pressure between roller and fabric than is used with engraved rollers.

As with all screen printing, some control of delivery can be obtained through variation in the mesh size, a larger mesh being appropriate for fabrics made from coarser fibres or areas of solid colour, whilst a finer mesh is better for producing fine detail or for fabrics made from fine fibres.

The advantages of rotary-screen printing machines over engraved-roller machines include faster production rates, greater ease of setting up and a lower dependence on experience for successful operation. Computer-aided design techniques for printing screens are now increasingly widely used (Figure 6.15).

Figure 6.15 A modern CAD system for digital processing of textile designs

Transfer printing

The ability of disperse dyes to sublime on heating (page 18) has led to a very different approach to textile printing. In this the design is first printed on paper using disperse dyes. The paper can then be inspected for faults; if any exist, that area of paper can be discarded to avoid wastage of fabric. The fabric is placed face down on the printed surface of the transfer paper, and the two are squeezed together in a heated press at a temperature high enough to vaporise the dye, which transfers in the vapour phase to the fabric. Transfer printing has the advantage that no printing paste is applied to the fabric and so no washing-off is necessary.

The production of transfer printing paper for textile purposes began to grow rapidly in the early 1970s but so far its use is restricted to the application of disperse dyes, and hence to the printing of synthetic fibres. The paper can be prepared by gravure printing, in a manner similar to the engraved roller printing of textiles (Figure 6.16). An alternative is flexographic printing, in which the image is formed in relief on a composite rubber moulding (Figure 6.17) using sophisticated methods for cutting the pattern; this method has the advantage that wide paper may be printed satisfactorily. Another method is lithographic printing, which involves the preparation of a discontinuous design on a plate by photographic techniques.

The fabric and paper are brought into close contact using a continuous calender type of processor (Figure 6.18). The fabric and paper are placed face to face and held close to a heated cylinder under

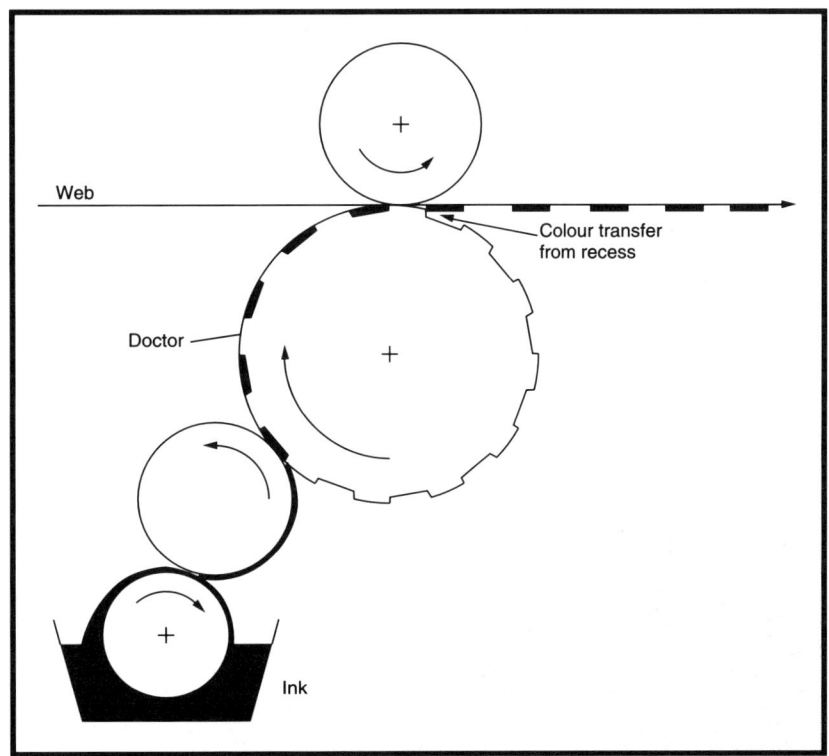

Figure 6.16 *Gravure printing: single colour*

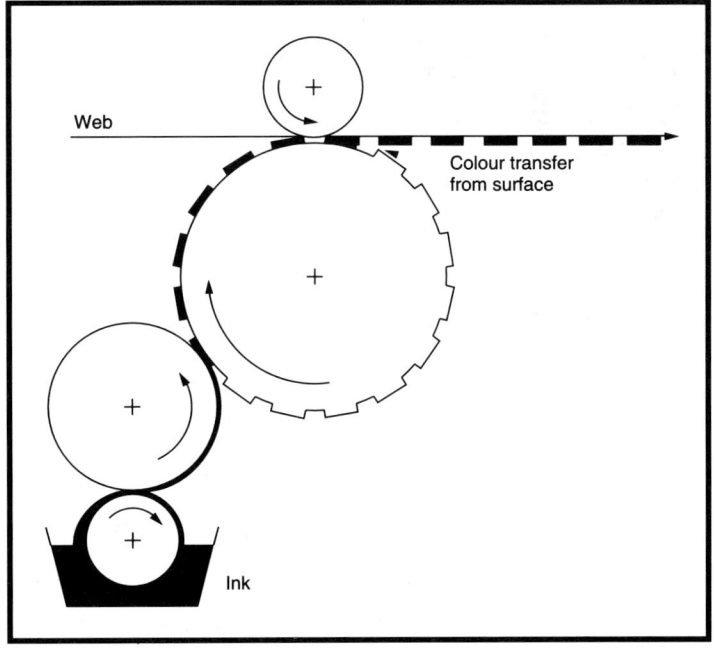

Figure 6.17 *Flexographic printing*

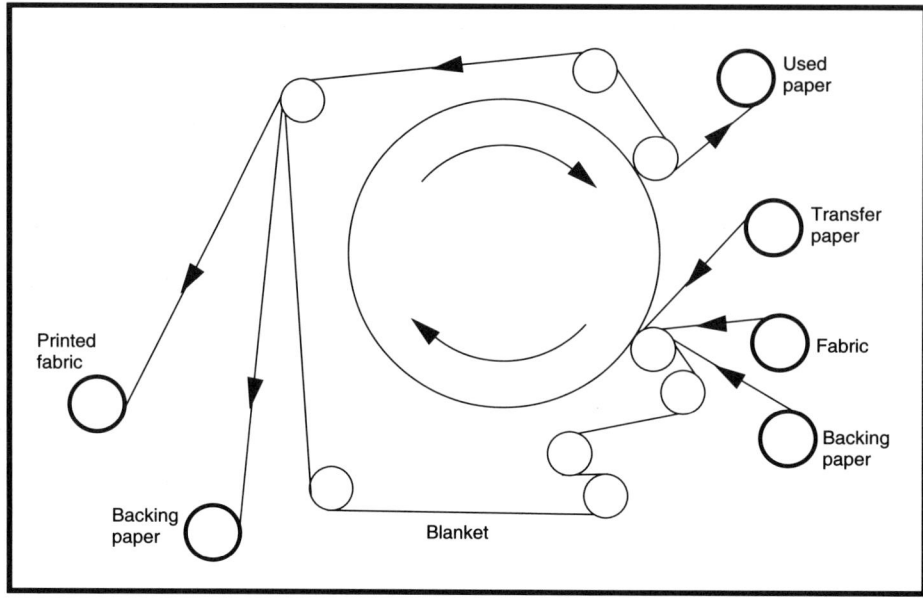

Figure 6.18 *Continuous transfer printing*

light pressure from an endless blanket, often made of the heat-resistant material Nomex (see page 60). Fast rates of production are possible with this system.

Discharge printing

In addition to the straightforward application of dye, textile printing offers the designer certain styles that can be used to obtain specific aesthetic effects. Discharge printing, for example, can provide intricate printed patterns on a coloured background (the ground colour). The new pattern may be white, or it may be a different colour from the original fabric, in which case it is referred to as an 'illuminated' style. Effective discharge methods have been developed for both natural and synthetic fibres.

Discharge printing is carried out where small areas of pattern are required on a large area of ground colour, too large to be produced efficiently by printing methods. It enables finely detailed patterns of good definition to be introduced on to the fabric, which adds significant value to the end product. The technique depends on the fact that some dyes may be chemically removed from the dyed fabric using a *discharge agent,* to leave a corresponding white area. The necessary discharge agent is mixed with a colour-free printing paste and the pattern printed on to the previously dyed fabric as usual. Drying or steaming and then washing follow. For illuminated styles a discharge-resistant dye is incorporated into the paste so that discharge and coloration with the illuminating colour occur simultaneously.

The efficiency of the discharge reactions is critically dependent upon the selection of suitable dyes. Easily discharged dyes are required for the ground shade, while discharge-resistant dyes are needed for the *illuminating discharge*. The method can be used on fabric dyed with indigo vat dye either by destroying the colour with an oxidising agent, or more commonly by converting it to a leuco compound using a reducing agent, which then combines with the leuco compound and prevents its reoxidation.

Selection of the thickening agent for the print paste is also more critical than for direct printing because it must remain chemically resistant to the reducing action and retain its viscosity throughout. If the latter proves unsatisfactory, migration of the print paste beyond the required area carries the reducing agent with it, blurring the definition and fine detail of the pattern. This effect is called 'flushing'. In illuminated discharges it appears as a white surround to the printed pattern, in which case it is referred to as 'haloing'. It can be controlled, however, with proper attention to preparation of the print paste.

Resist printing

Resist printing offers a way of producing an effect similar to that of discharge printing. It also uses dyes that can withstand the discharge process, so that high fastness standards are possible.

The principle of resist printing depends on preventing dye from reaching, or becoming fixed on, defined areas of fabric. Both mechanical and chemical techniques are adopted to provide the resist. Inert compounds such as waxes, resins, fats, china clay, zinc and titanium oxides, and salts of lead and barium all act as mechanical resists for the dye.

Chemical resists, on the other hand, act to prevent the fixation mechanism from operating. Consequently their use requires an awareness of the chemical reactions involved in dyeing the ground shade. A nonvolatile acid, for example, will prevent the alkaline fixation of reactive dyes on cellulosic fibres, an oxidising agent will prevent the reduction of vat dyes, and so on. A more detailed review of discharge and resist printing has been provided elsewhere [6].

'Burnt-out' printing techniques have also been developed in which part of the fibres themselves is chemically removed to produce a clear-cut, shaped space in the fabric. Effective results are obtained in this way with polyester/cotton blends, with areas in which the cotton fibres have been 'burned away' leaving the coloured polyester threads behind. The effects produced depend on the original colours of the two types of fibre and they are achieved without undue loss of fabric strength.

There are many other possible printing styles available, notably those producing African prints, some of which have evolved from tie dyeing or the mechanical wax-resist 'batik' style. A full discussion of these and other styles is given elsewhere [4].

Carpet printing

The introduction of carpet printing was stimulated by the desire to expand the possibilities for producing patterned tufted carpets. Various machines have been designed, similar in principle to those used for printing fabric.

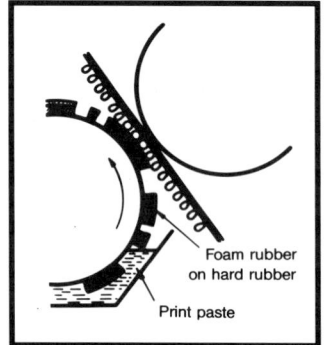

Figure 6.19 Carpet printing: one type of roller action

Figure 6.19 shows one type of roller, in which a sponge rubber or nylon flock fibre design caps the cut-out pattern in the rubber surface of the roller. The face of the carpet is pressed successively on to the upper surface of each of four rollers arranged one above the other in a line at 45° to the horizontal. The principle has proved popular but its application is restricted by the relatively poor resolution of detail that it can achieve.

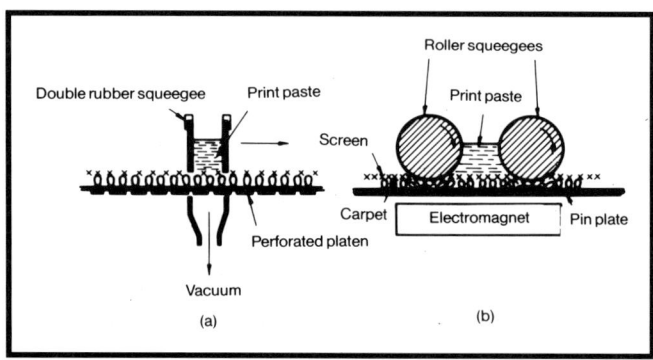

Figure 6.20 Principles of the (a) BDA and (b) Zimmer machines

Flat-screen printing

Penetration of the pile is important in carpet printing and there are two principles upon which flat-bed machines have been constructed. The BDA machine, which is no longer widely used, employed an ingenious arrangement in which the reservoir of dye was trapped between the blades of a double squeegee passing over the screen, penetration of the pile being assisted by the application of a vacuum from beneath (Figure 6.20 (a)). In the Zimmer machine the print paste is trapped between the electromagnetic rollers that form the double roller squeegee (Figure 6.20 (b)). Penetration in this case is encouraged by the pressure created by the second roller running over the wedge of paste, which it traps as it moves forward over the screen. Shorter pile lengths are preferred for this machine. There are also other versions of the rotary-screen printing machines with heavier gauge screens and rollers.

A more novel method for applying colour to carpet substrates is through the use of a bank of miniature jets of dye. This principle was first used in the Millitron machine of Milliken & Co., although other similar machines are now available. The jets are controlled by computer-operated electromagnetic valves, and the mechanism has eliminated the need for screens. Since there is no distortion of the pile, optimum surface appearance is maintained and the pattern can be changed simply by the use of different computer software.

A more detailed discussion of the printing of carpets has been published [4].

Coloration of fibre blends

The properties of synthetic fibres have been exploited in many different ways since their first appearance. They have given a much greater degree of freedom to the designer faced with the task of matching the properties of textile goods with the requirements of a particular end use. Very often this involves blending mixtures of natural and synthetic fibres in the same yarn, or including natural and synthetic yarns together in a fabric. A variety of benefits may be gained from blending fibres of different chemical origin, including economy – blending natural with cheaper synthetic fibres enables a yarn to be produced at a lower cost. Very often, however, the main attraction is the combination of the unique advantageous properties that each fibre has to offer.

Blends of polyester and cellulosic fibres are particularly popular. Polyester confers good tensile strength, abrasion resistance, dimensional stability and easy-care properties to the goods. Cotton is responsible for good moisture absorption properties (and hence comfort in wear), antistatic properties and a reduced propensity to pilling. Combinations of acrylic fibres with wool are noted for their good dimensional stability, wear resistance and pleat retention. Nylon fibres are often included in carpet yarns alongside wool to give improved durability and elastic recovery whilst retaining the warmth and bulk usually associated with pure wool.

These and many other widely used fibre blends add complexity to the dyer's task. Often the requirement is to colour hydrophobic and hydrophilic fibres in the same fabric – yet, of course, they need completely different approaches. Sometimes this may require a separate dyeing operation for each fibre component, but through ingenuity on the part of both dyer and dye manufacturer some single-bath operations have been developed. For example, it is possible to find conditions under which a combination of disperse dyes and vat dyes, or of disperse dyes and reactive dyes, may be applied together from the same bath. Dispersol T dyes (ICI), for instance, were designed to dye the polyester portion of cotton/polyester blends but to become soluble in the hot alkaline conditions required for applying a reactive dye to the cotton component after the dyeing of the polyester was complete: thus on washing the residual disperse dye could be removed from the cotton component. Subsequently ICI developed the Procion T dyes, which react with cellulose under acidic conditions. Thus the Dispersol T and Procion T dyes could be applied in one bath and fixed simultaneously.

Other combinations of fibres may require the use of anionic dyes for one component and cationic dyes for another, which without proper control could lead to chemical interaction between the different dye classes or dyebath auxiliaries, thus preventing or at least hindering the attainment of the desired effect.

The most frequent requirement is for a solid shade, where each fibre component is of exactly the same colour. But this does not preclude requests for reserve effects (in which one component remains undyed), contrast effects (where each component is dyed a different colour) or shadow effects (with each component dyed the same colour but to different depths). The situation may be compounded further by the use of three different fibres in one blend.

A systematic approach to the formulation of dyeing methods is therefore adopted through a classification of fibres into groups according to their dyeing properties. Thus the 'disperse dyeable' group includes the cellulose acetates and polyesters, the 'anionic dyeable' group contains wool, nylon and cellulosic fibres, whilst the 'basic dyeable' group contains acrylic fibres and some modifications of nylon and polyester. Reference to these groupings may then be made to indicate whether the components of a blend require dyes from the same or different dye classes. The dyeing of ternary blends may be formulated on similar principles.

The dyeing of fibre blends is a vast and complex subject, and those with a special interest in this area are directed to more advanced texts [5].

Control of coloration processes

In the finishing of textiles, as elsewhere in industry, moves towards greater efficiency have led to the automation of many aspects of production. Over recent years the various mechanical devices used to ease the physical work required have increasingly incorporated equipment that aids or even replaces human mental effort. Fully computer-controlled systems are well established in many large chemical plants, oil refineries, steel works and paper mills, so it is not surprising that microprocessor technology is also growing in textile processing organisations.

Computer control involves monitoring processes and initiating corrective action towards specified targets in an attempt to 'get things right the first time round'. This can lead to reduced costs in plant and raw materials, increased safety, improved working conditions, savings in manpower and improved plant management and supervision. Computer monitoring of temperature, flow, pressure, pH and concentration of dyebath chemicals is becoming commonplace.

One of the most dramatic transformations witnessed by dyers over recent decades is the replacement of lengthy preliminary laboratory dyeing trials, formerly routinely required to match a customer's shade, by instrumental measurements of the coloured pattern. These are coupled with information concerning the adsorption properties of the available dyes on the given substrate to provide a recipe for precise matching of the shade, together with information concerning fastness properties and cost, within only a little time. The basis of this aspect of quality control in textile coloration is the subject of Chapter 7.

References

1.   D H Wyles in *Engineering in textile coloration*, Ed. C Duckworth (Bradford: Dyers' Company Publications Trust, 1983).

2.   J A Bone, P S Collishaw and T D Kelly, *Rev. Prog. Coloration*, **18** (1988) 37.

3.   G Clarke, *A practical introduction to fibre and tow coloration* (Bradford: SDC, 1982).

4.   *Textile printing*, Ed L W C Miles (Bradford: Dyers' Company Publications Trust, 1981).

5.   J Shore in *The dyeing of synthetic-polymer and acetate fibres*, Ed D M Nunn (Bradford: Dyers' Company Publications Trust, 1979).

6.   J R Provost, *Rev. Prog. Coloration*, **18** (1988) 29.

CHAPTER SEVEN

The modern approach to coloration

Introduction

With most textiles intended for the domestic market the attention of the purchaser is first arrested by their aesthetic appeal, and at that instant colour is often a persuasive factor. If the manufactured goods are of satisfactory quality they will conform to predetermined specifications appropriate to the intended use. Overall satisfaction therefore demands a design process capable of integrating both aesthetic and technical judgements, and it is in this area that the manufacturer realises the real worth of modern technology. Recently the accent on quality assurance and quality control has been underpinned by various technological developments. These have enabled producers to transform their organisations and production methods in their attempt to optimise costs, prevent the occurrence of defects, obtain a high degree of precision in predicting the performance of their goods and develop the necessary flexibility for a rapid response to the volatile demands of fashion.

Developments in most areas of activity in the coloration industry bear witness to the effective application of modern technology, starting in the colour kitchen where dyes and chemicals are dispensed and ending with delivery of customer service. For example, high-precision electronic balances make for a more accurate recipe composition where weighing is done manually. There are also facilities for dispensing dyebath chemicals through computerised control valves that have the ability to adjust the flow of dye liquor automatically from a large flow rate at the beginning of the dyeing cycle down to dropwise additions towards the end of the operation, where precision is most needed. This may be accompanied by automatic recording of the consumption of dye and chemicals for convenience in the administration of storage and purchasing.

Computer-aided design systems are more elaborate examples noted for their ability to produce digitised patterns from original artwork. There are also systems for textile printing that will either scan an image for reproduction or allow the creation of a free design, and translate the information into commands that initiate practical activities. Such a system is adapted to receive colour measurement information from a spectrophotometer that can be processed to provide a formulation for the colours needed. The set-up enables the user to maintain full control of the design input, design correction and colour formulation; the commercial reward is a drastic reduction in response time. Most computer-aided design units can be linked to colour printers that enable the coloured designs to be inspected on paper before starting production. In some cases the initial concept for the garment design is simulated on a three-dimensional model, and when this is complete it can be converted directly into the two-dimensional pattern corresponding to the shapes of the fabric pieces needed to make the garment. Simulation of the expected drape, the appearance of yarns or the effects of other construction details on the final garment may thus be assessed along with visual effects of any possible variations in colour. A similar principle can be applied to a carpeting contract. A three-dimensional presentation of the room layout can be prepared on-screen for the client's acceptance, and from this the area of carpet required is calculated directly.

In some arrangements the design can be analysed and a program produced automatically for direct transfer to either a computerised knitting machine or a loom. The possibilities are expanded further by the inclusion of a vast directory of colour to facilitate colour coordination or colour matching. This provides the manufacturer has the ability to reduce to one hour the time needed for a design operation that formerly would have required several days' work.

Parallel developments are to be found at different stages of the manufacturing process within the carpet industry. The capabilities range from the initial design process to simulation of the final appearance, thus enabling the contract carpet producers to illustrate the design to their clients in a variety of different colour combinations before starting manufacture.

Direct transfer of a pattern to the carpet coloration process has been accomplished through computerised control of spray nozzles or jets, the provision of which enables quick colour or pattern changes to be made without undue loss of production time.

Coloration processes have been at the forefront of many very successful applications of new technology to the overall design process. They are developments made possible by the advanced levels of theoretical insight, experimental methods and technology developed in various areas of textile and colour chemistry well before the advent of microprocessors. An outline of the background of colour measurement is therefore provided here to familiarise the reader with the relevant principles that have become embedded in everyday coloration practice.

Objective assessment of colour

At the end of the dyeing process judgements have to be made about the success achieved in matching the customer's required shade. Before embarking on the full-scale operation it was once the standard practice for past generations of dyers to reach the final shade via a range of laboratory trials to accommodate successive corrections in the dyebath formulation. During the trials the assessment of the corresponding changes in the appearance of the colour were recorded for future reference using verbal descriptions of the colour.

It has long been realised, however, that the human perception of colour is a physiological sensation that defies absolute verbal definition. Sir Isaac Newton during his investigations into the nature of light came to the same conclusion, and he held the belief that light is uncoloured but that each wavelength has the power to stimulate unique sensations in the brain. Nevertheless, in the past a methodical approach to the verbal expression of subjective colour assessment was the only means available for transmitting opinions about the appearance of colour; this is reflected in the nomenclature of commercial dyes (Chapter 4).

Describing colour

Changes in colour are expressed qualitatively through the use of the three variables hue, strength and brightness. *Hue* is defined as 'that attribute of colour whereby it is recognised as being predominantly red, green, blue, yellow, violet, etc.' [1]. Changes in hue therefore may result in the pattern being described as bluer, yellower, redder, greener, and so on. The term *strength* relates to the amount of colour present while *brightness* refers to the greyness of a colour.

The magnitude of any colour change may also be qualified using further terms such as 'trace', 'slight', 'little' or 'much' – for example, 'much redder', 'a trace bluer', and so on. Further aid to the visualisation of a colour is given by the designatory letters that follow the names of commercial dyes and by the provision of coloured samples in the dye makers' pattern cards.

Colour solid

Precision in the description of a colour is enhanced considerably by the organisation of colours in a three-dimensional array using lightness L, chroma (or saturation) C and hue H, as the coordinates describing a colour solid. Lightness is defined as 'that property of a coloured object which is judged to reflect or transmit a greater or smaller proportion of the incident light than another object', whilst chroma is 'the nearness of a colour in purity to the associated spectral colour (i.e. the sensation caused by monochromatic visible light of known wavelength)' [1].

The concept of a colour solid was first used by Munsell, and is represented diagrammatically in Figure 7.1, with the various hues contained by the perimeter of a circle. The lightness increases to white at the

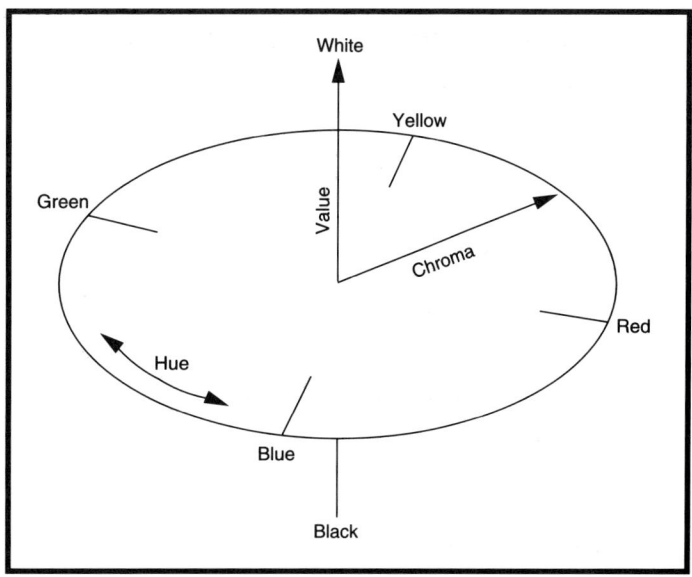

Figure 7.1 The Munsell Colour Solid

top end of a central vertical axis and decreases in ten steps to black at the bottom, the position of mid-grey coinciding with the centre of the solid. Colours falling on the same horizontal plane of the solid are of the same lightness.

In any one plane the purity, or chroma, of the colour increases with increasing distance from the centre. Other names used as an alternative to 'chroma' have been 'saturation', 'purity', 'intensity' and 'vividness', but 'chroma' is the preferred term adopted by the colorant-using industries. The value ascribed to the chroma for white, greys and black is zero but the chroma of the perceived colour increases with movement towards the perimeter, where the most vivid or saturated versions of the spectral colours are placed. In practice each hue is represented on a page of a colour book or colour atlas (Plate 6). The lightness and chroma axes are calibrated using scale numbers, so that the spacing between successive units of chroma represents incremented changes of equal magnitude in visual appearance. Small coloured chips varying in lightness and chroma are prepared and positioned at the appropriate coordinates of each hue page. A complete visual colour atlas is formed in this way [2]. A representation of the Munsell coordinates and the corresponding hue qualifiers is given to illustrate the relationship between visual appearance and the corresponding verbal description in Figure 7.2, overleaf.

Although the Munsell chips provide a more objective way of describing colour, the level of precision they provide is still inadequate for denoting the location of a dyed textile in a colour space.

Ultimate precision can only be attained with a system using continuously variable coordinates rather than stepwise scales.

There have been many efforts to develop a more suitable scale for the colour coordinates, and it is now possible to obtain a precise objective assessment of the extent to which trial dyeings differ from the required shade through instrumental measurements. This is a clear advantage and the replacement of verbal descriptions by unambiguous measurements has led to a significant improvement in the efficiency with which colours can be selected and matched to a customer's request.

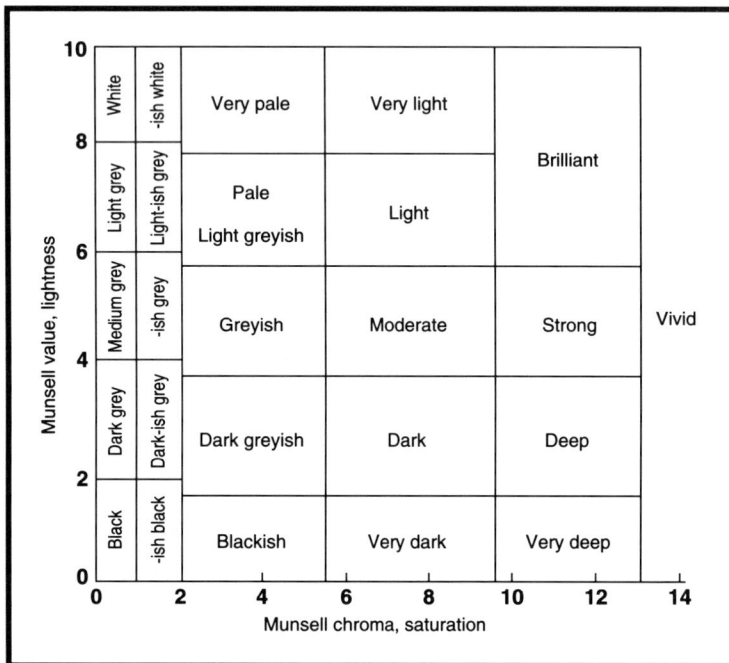

Figure 7.2 *Munsell coordinates and hue qualifiers*

ICI colour atlas

In 1970 ICI produced a colour atlas that enabled its customers to convert the colour of its patterns into colour coordinates. The values could then be transmitted to ICI and used by its Instrumental Match Prediction service to provide the customer with a suitable recipe. This form of colour atlas was constructed using the brightest hues, and a series of neutral-density filters were provided to place over the atlas to reproduce duller shades. This was equivalent to moving up and down the lightness/darkness axis of the colour space (Figure 7.1).

Development of such systems had become possible through an understanding of the nature of light and its interaction with dye molecules on the one hand, and application of the theoretical concepts concerning the human perception of colour to the design of colour-measuring instruments on the other. Accordingly the nature of light and the elementary principles of colour vision are described below to provide a background for later discussion on perception of colour and colour measurement.

Nature of light

A clear definition of the nature of white light has proved very elusive, but it is known that light is a form of electromagnetic radiation and that visible light is only a small section of a much broader band

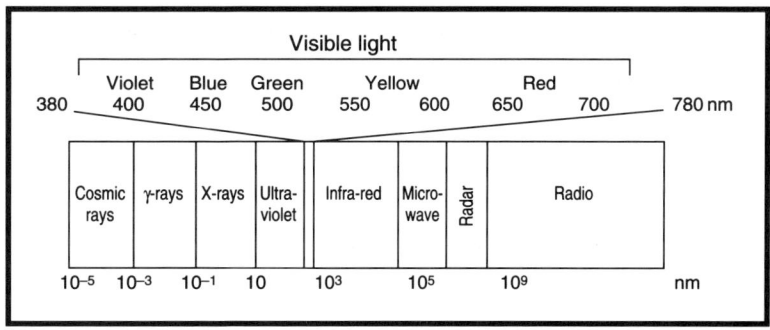

Figure 7.3 *The electromagnetic spectrum*

of electromagnetic radiation travelling as a wave motion. The electromagnetic spectrum covers wavelengths from 10^{-5} nm[1] (cosmic rays) to wavelengths greater than 10^9 nm (radio waves). Within this spectrum the only visible radiation is that within the wavelength range between 380 nm (ultra-violet) and 780 nm (red), each wavelength representing a different hue (Figure 7.3).

Colour perception

Various theories of colour vision have been proposed, none of which describes all the observed effects, but their development is a fascinating subject [3]. Here we will look only at modern theories of colour perception on which instrumental measurements are now based.

Trichromatic theory

The combined ideas of Thomas Young and Hermann von Helmholtz are expressed in the hypothesis that the human eye contains three different types of photoreceptor. This proposition received practical support some years later from James Clerk Maxwell. He demonstrated how to match various colours by mixing just three 'primary colours' presented as coloured sectors on a rapidly rotating disc. This long-standing theory is referred to as the Young–Helmholtz trichromatic theory of colour vision, but it is only in more recent times that physiological evidence has become available to support the theory. This evidence is an unambiguous distinction between red-, green- and blue-sensitive receptors (cone cells) in the retina, the sensitivity of which is indicated in Figure 7.4.

---

[1]The wavelength of an electromagnetic wave is measured in nanometres (nm); 1 nm = 10^{-9} m, i.e. 1/1 000 000 000th (one billionth part) of a metre.

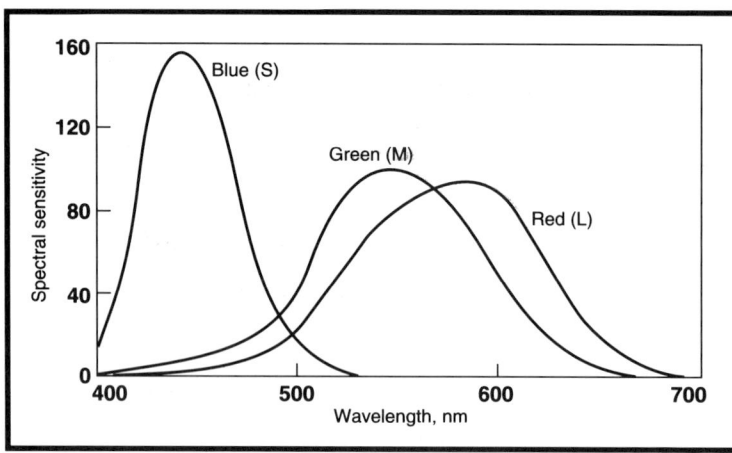

Figure 7.4 *Cone sensitivity curves. S, short wavelength; M, medium wavelength; L, long wavelength*

The other essential contribution was that of Sir Isaac Newton, who demonstrated that white light is dispersed into a spectrum of rainbow colours when passed through a glass prism, and is recombined unchanged when passed through a second prism. To this he added the philosophy mentioned previously that light itself is not coloured, but that light of each individual wavelength is responsible for creating a characteristic sensation of 'colour' within the human brain. Nevertheless, the established convention is that perceived colours are a property of the object with which they are associated, rather than a physiological sensation originating in the retina, and this convention will be adopted here to avoid confusion.

Table 7.1 Relationship between wavelength of absorbed light and hue

Absorbed wavelength (nm)	Hue of absorbed light	Perceived hue
400–440	Violet	Greenish-yellow
440–480	Blue	Yellow
480–510	Blue-green	Orange
510–540	Green	Red
540–570	Yellow-green	Purple
570–580	Yellow	Blue
580–610	Orange	Greenish-blue
610–700	Red	Blue-green

The perception of different hues is a consequence of the absorption of electromagnetic radiation of wavelength between 380 and 770 nm by an object. If the coloured object is transparent (or a solution) the incident light after the selective absorption is transmitted through it. If it is opaque then the residual light is reflected back from the surface.

The perceived colour of the object is determined by the wavelength(s) of the absorbed light. The extent of absorption at a given wavelength is known as the *absorbance*. Light of the remaining wavelengths is transmitted, perceived by the eye and interpreted by the brain as colour. The principle is illustrated in Table 7.1, which summarises the hues produced by the selective absorption of particular wavelengths.

144

Table 7.1 accounts for a wavelength range of about 400 nm in the visible spectrum but, as mentioned earlier, the final appearance of the colour is also dependent upon the brightness and the degree of saturation. The three important stimuli may be quantified as the dominant wavelength, spectral purity and luminance.

The *dominant wavelength* of a shade is the wavelength of the spectral colour that needs to be diluted with different amounts of white light to produce variations of shade from the spectral colour through pale shades and finally to white. The *luminance* is defined as 'the luminous flux emitted per unit solid angle or per unit projected area of a real or imaginary surface' [1]. For a coloured object luminance is a measure of the apparent overall reflectance. For a light source it is a measure of the apparent brightness of the light.

The term *spectral purity* refers to the percentage ratio of the luminance of the mono-chromatic light to the total luminance. Thus the purity would be 100% if the light consisted of only one spectral wavelength – that is, the colour would be saturated.

All three quantities are related, and a change in the value of any one has an effect on the other two. Thus a change in luminance will also affect the hue and saturation. It has been calculated that because of this fact the number of unique hues associated with the visible spectrum is around 7 million for a person with normal colour vision! Obviously, even if it were possible, precise definition of each unique colour by name is impractical. This emphasises the merit of the colour solid as a means of specifying colour, and various efforts have been made to devise a quantitative description of a colour through its location in the colour solid.

Measurement of colour in terms of continuously variable scales is now carried out using colour-measuring instruments. These work on the principle that the sensation of all colours may be stimulated by adjusting the intensities of light of three primary wavelengths, the essential property of any three primary colours being that they cannot be matched by mixing the remaining two. There are several such triads within the visible spectrum, but for experimental convenience the wavelengths chosen are widely spaced in the spectrum and consist of a long, a medium and a short wavelength.

The sensitivity of the human eye at these three chosen wavelengths is very high and the corresponding sensitivities of the red-, green- and blue-sensitive receptors (cones) in the retina are illustrated in Figure 7.4 [3]. The practical consequence is that any colour perceived by the human eye may be imitated with a mixture of red, green and blue lights of appropriate intensities. This concept was used as the basis for the specification of colour in terms of primary colours by the Commission International de l'Éclairage (CIE) in 1931.

The convention used when applying a quantitative description to a particular hue is that the three stimuli in question are signified by the use of a bracketed letter preceded by the same letter without brackets, the latter representing the amount of that stimulus required to match the pattern. Thus C units of colour C are represented by $C(C)$, X units of the primary X as $X(X)$ and so on.

Quantitative representation of the colour is achieved using three *tristimulus values*, designated as X, Y and Z, to represent the amounts of the chosen primaries required to match one energy unit for each wavelength. X, Y and Z are the *imaginary primaries* used in instrumental measurements. Their derivation from the real primaries R, G and B for an equal-energy spectrum is necessary in order to avoid the need to use negative tristimulus values (Figure 7.5). For example, consider a situation in a tristimulus colorimeter where light of a particular wavelength is shining on to half of a white surface and the other half is made to match by adjustment of the amounts of the real primaries. There may be a point at which it is impossible to match the wavelength in question by the three primaries alone, in which case the only way to bring about a match is to add an appropriate amount of one of the primaries to the colour being matched. This is equivalent to saying that in some cases negative tristimulus values are required, and this presents instrumental difficulties. For this reason and because of the variations in perceived colour between individuals, originating from physiological differences, the proposed CIE tristimulus values are manipulated mathematically so that they are always positive in value. The result is the X, Y and Z set of imaginary primaries representing red, green and blue, which are used in defining the colour-matching properties of the hypothetical standard observer. The result is similar to the sensitivities of the cones represented in Figure 7.4.

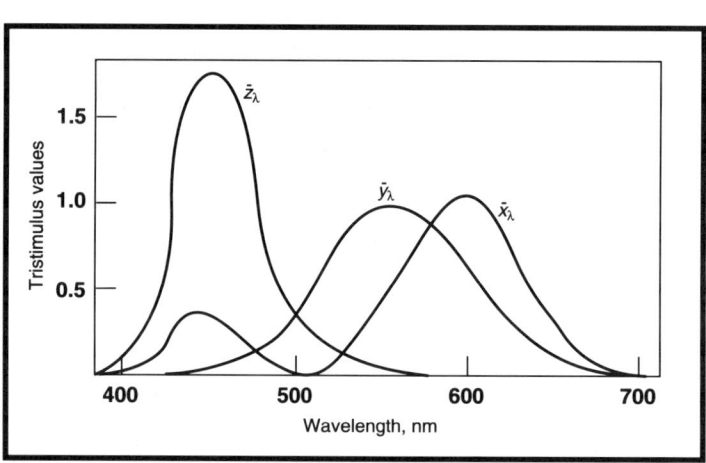

Figure 7.5 *Tristimulus values for each wavelength in a constant-energy spectrum; the results represent those of an average observer with normal colour vision using as primaries [R] 700 nm, [G] 546.1 nm, [B] 435.8 nm*

Additive colour mixing

In additive colour mixing all colours can be matched by using appropriate amounts of primary colours corresponding to X, Y and Z. Thus for *C* units of colour C, we can write Equation 7.1:

$$C(C) = X(X) + Y(Y) + Z(Z) \qquad (7.1)$$

where the symbols have the significance previously defined.

The scales for X (the red stimulus), Y (the green stimulus) and Z (the blue stimulus) are adjusted so that the quantities of each component required for white light are equal. Thus 1 part X + 1 part Y + 1 part Z = white.

If we therefore direct equal amounts of red, green and blue light on to a white surface it remains white, but if the intensity of any of the three is varied the sensation of colour is produced. Thus if only red and green lights are used a yellow sensation is produced; green and blue produce cyan; red and blue produce magenta (Plate 7). This is the principle of *additive mixing*.

Subtractive colour mixing

Obviously, the appearance of dyed fabric in daylight is not contrived by illuminating the fabric using primary coloured lights of appropriate intensity. The sensation of colour in this case occurs because the dyes absorb some of the wavelengths of the incident white light. That is, the light reflected back to the observer is no longer white, and the fabric is perceived as being coloured. In this case the origin of the colour arises from a subtractive process. The principle of *subtractive colour mixing* is illustrated in Plate 8.

In subtractive mixing the primary colours used are magenta, yellow and cyan. Comparison of Plate 8 with Plate 7 shows that cyan may be obtained additively by mixing the green and blue primaries, yellow by mixing the red and green primaries, and magenta by mixing the red and blue primaries. Thus each additive primary is representing one of the three components of white light. The subtractive primaries are different because they represent a mixture of two of the additive primaries, i.e. one of the three components of white light is absorbed whilst the two remaining are reflected (or transmitted through a solution). For this reason the subtractive primaries are often designated as negative primaries:

magenta   =   – green (1 part red + 1 part blue transmitted/reflected)

yellow   =   – blue (1 part red + 1 part green transmitted/reflected)

cyan   =   – red (1 part blue + 1 part green transmitted/reflected).

This nomenclature has the advantage of indicating which of the three additive primaries has been absorbed.

In subtractive mixing, therefore, the colour perceived is determined by what has been removed from the incident white light. Thus if the cyan (– red, i.e. blue + green remaining) and magenta (– green, i.e. red + blue remaining) are superimposed, only the blue component remains unabsorbed and the perceived colour is blue. Similar reasoning shows that superimposition of magenta and yellow results in the transmission only of the red component of white light, and the superimposition of cyan and yellow only of the green (Plate 8).

The functioning of the human eye and of colour-measuring instruments, however, are both based on the use of additive primaries irrespective of the process by which the colour is produced. The spectrophotometers used for colour measurement are designed to enable a coloured pattern and a standard white surface to be illuminated under conditions that conform with carefully considered geometrical requirements, using a standardised source of illumination. Reflectance measurements for both the pattern and the white standard are made over appropriate intervals of the visible spectrum. The information from the sensors is transmitted to a microprocessor where the results are converted into X, Y and Z values for display on a monitor.

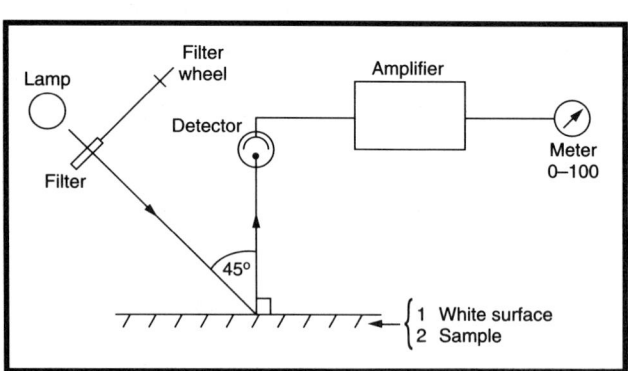

Figure 7.6 *Basic trichromatic colorimeter*

Alternatively a tristimulus colorimeter may be used. This also enables reflectance measurements to be made of the coloured pattern alongside a white standard, but in this case appropriate red, green and blue filters are inserted successively between the collimated beam of the standard source of illumination and the surface in question (Figure 7.6). The instrument is readjusted as each filter is placed into the beam. The reflectance of the white surface represents 100% reflectance. The lower reflectance of the coloured sample is then measured and compared with the result for the white surface. The reflectance values are transmitted to a microprocessor and displayed as the tristimulus values.

For opaque coloured objects the relationship between the spectral power of the standard illuminant at wavelength λ (E_λ) and the spectral reflectance characteristic of the coloured object (R_λ) are related to the tristimulus values as shown (Equation 7.2):

$$X = \Sigma E_\lambda \bar{x}_\lambda R_\lambda$$

$$Y = \Sigma E_\lambda \bar{y}_\lambda R_\lambda$$

$$Z = \Sigma E_\lambda \bar{z}_\lambda R_\lambda \qquad (7.2)$$

where $\bar{x}_\lambda$, $\bar{y}_\lambda$ and $\bar{z}_\lambda$, the spectral response characteristics of the standard observer, represent the number of units of X, Y and Z required to match one unit of energy of wavelength λ. The sigma (Σ) sign indicates that the appropriate values for each increment of wavelength, between 380 and 760 nm, are added together to obtain the final value. The X, Y and Z tristimulus values therefore indicate the relative quantities of light of the red, green and blue regions of the spectrum reflected from the surface, as perceived by the eye.

On this basis a perfectly white surface viewed under an equal-energy light source would be represented by the expression $X = Y = Z = 100$, and a black surface by $X = Y = Z = 0$. The situation with a real light source differs from this ideal situation, however, and in reality X and Z do not equal 100.

In all accurate colour matching, consistency in both the quality of the incident light and the conditions of viewing is of particular importance. The energy distributions in the spectra of different sources are, in practice, different. Consequently the energy distribution of light reflected back from the pattern from each source will have its own distinct profile, and both the visual appearance and tristimulus values will be affected. The quality of various illuminants has therefore been extensively studied; those with defined spectral energy distribution are now specified by the CIE. The source designated as illuminant A represents the light from a tungsten filament lamp. Those designated as illuminant B and illuminant C correspond to direct sunlight and average daylight respectively. An improved series of sources, the D illuminants, are based on a mixture of both sun and skylight and their use is now becoming more widespread.

Chromaticity diagrams

The concept of a colour space has proved to be invaluable in colour measurement. Although a three-dimensional representation is inconvenient, the practical solution has been to convert the tristimulus values into fractional quantities referred to as *chromaticity coordinates*, as shown in Equation 7.3:

$$x = X/(X+Y+Z)$$
$$y = Y/(X+Y+Z)$$
$$z = Z/(X+Y+Z) \qquad\qquad (7.3)$$

It therefore follows that $x + y + z = 1$ for all colours. Thus only two chromaticity coordinates, x and y, need to be defined; since $x + y + z = 1$, z can always be found by a simple calculation ($z = 1 - (x + y)$). Values of x and y can be plotted on a two-dimensional graph, and X and Z can also be calculated from x, y and Y, the latter three parameters being used to specify any colour on a two-dimensional plot. A colourist regards this as a statement of the *quality* of the colour. (The use of the term 'quality' in this context should not be confused with the broader statements concerning factors such as fastness and levelling properties, discussed in previous chapters.)

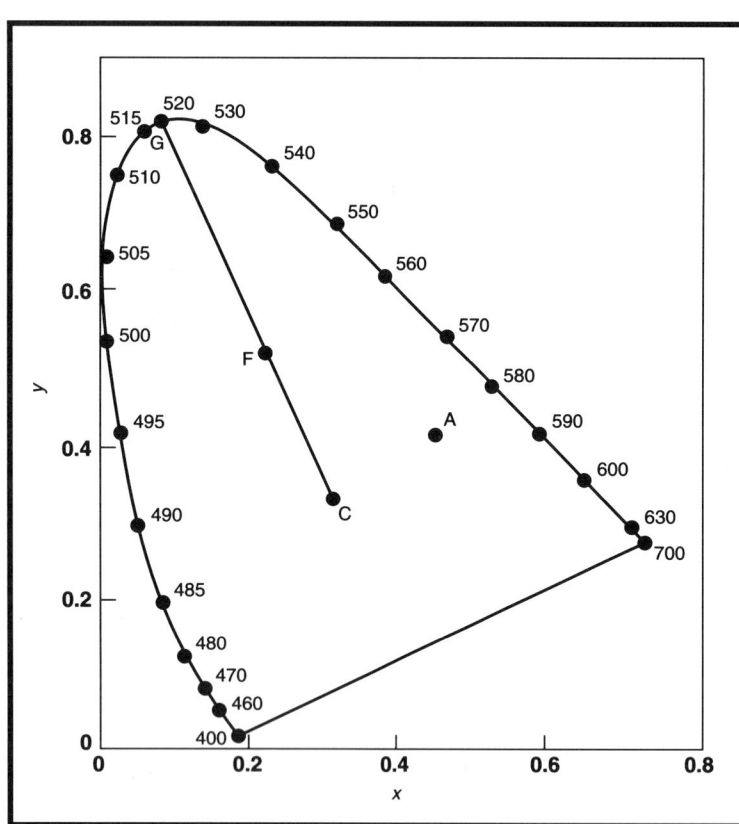

Figure 7.7 Chromaticity diagram

A plot of x against y is called a *chromaticity diagram*. The line joining the spectrum of colours plotted as values of x and y obtained from the tristimulus values of the standard observer is called the *spectrum locus*. The position of each wavelength on the spectrum locus is shown in Figure 7.7.

The effect of illuminant source on appearance is also emphasised in Figure 7.7, since point A and point C represent the appropriate values for the same neutral pattern under illuminant A and C respectively. A further property of the chromaticity diagram is that if white light from illuminant C is mixed with monochromatic light of wavelength, say, 520 nm (green), all the possible greens will fall on a line CG; they will appear as various shades of green, ranging from white through pale green to the saturated hue at the spectrum locus. The same principle holds good for any other wavelength on the diagram. A defect of this system is that equal changes in the numerical quantities do not produce equal differences in the perceived colour.

Various attempts have been made to improve the visual uniformity of the colour space, and in 1970 the Society of Dyers and Colourists, and later the ISO, recommended a colour space that provided the precision necessary for specifying colour-difference measurements for coloured textiles. At the present time tristimulus values X, Y and Z, for a particular combination of illuminant and observer, are transformed into alternative units in relation to the corresponding values for a sample reflecting 100% of the light at all wavelengths (denoted X_0, Y_0 and Z_0) in the CIE system. The new so-called *CIELAB coordinates* are represented by Equation 7.4:

$$L^* = 116(Y/Y_0)^{1/3} - 16$$
$$a^* = 500[(X/X_0)^{1/3} - (Y/Y_0)]^{1/3}$$
$$b^* = 200[(Y/Y_0)^{1/3} - (Z/Z_0)]^{1/3} \tag{7.4}$$

where the asterisk signifies that CIE-defined units have been used. This covers all colours except those with very low tristimulus values.

The relationship between the coordinates in the colour space is shown in Figure 7.8. In this more uniform system a^* and b^* are plotted instead of x and y, and a representation of the colour map that this produces is shown in Plate 9.

A further customer aid has been provided as part of the ICI colour atlas (page 142) in the form of a grid that can be placed over a CIE colour map. The grid consists of a card of the same dimensions of the colour map into which are cut viewing holes coinciding with the coordinates of the appropriate dyes on the colour atlas. Lines are drawn between adjacent dyes to indicate the various hues that may be obtained by mixing the dyes in different proportions. With three dyes the

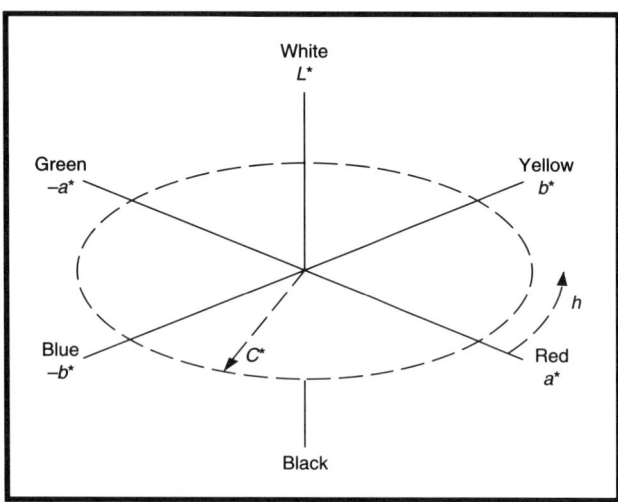

Figure 7.8 *CIELAB colour space*

triangular area contained by the three lines drawn on the **colour map** represents the range of colours **or** the 'colour gamut' that can be obtained by mixing these dyes in different proportions. An example of the position of **vat** dyes on the colour map is given in Figure 7.9.

Colour differences

The colour coordinates now developed are sufficiently accurate to be used to quantify the colour differences between two patterns. This entails using the sets of the L^*, a^* and b^* values and substitution in the colour-difference equation (Equation 7.5):

$$\Delta E = [(\Delta L^*)^2 + (\Delta a^*)^2 + (\Delta b^*)^2]^{1/2} \qquad (7.5)$$

where ΔL^*, Δa^* and Δb^* represent the differences between the corresponding units of each sample.

In this way the grey scales described on page 8 for assessing the visual effect of a treatment on a coloured pattern may be quantified; these are given in CIELAB units in Table 7.2.

In industry there is usually greater tolerance towards depth and/or brightness variation than towards hue variation. Consequently further equations have been developed that take into account differences in lightness and in chroma, one of which, the CMC equation, has been issued as a draft British Standard. The subject of colour difference is very complex, however, and readers requiring more detailed information are advised to consult a more advanced treatise [3,4].

Table 7.2 Grey scale ratings represented as colour differences in CIELAB units

Grey scale rating	Effect (ΔE)	Stain (ΔE)
5	0	0
4	1.7	4.3
3	3.4	8.5
2	6.8	6.9
1	13.6	34.1

Colour constancy and metamerism

At one time or another, nearly everyone has carefully chosen and purchased a coloured article from a store only to find that in another location the colour was not exactly what had been expected. The disappointment may have been due either to poor colour constancy or to metamerism. Both phenomena are related to a change in the spectral energy distribution of the light reflected back to the eye from the article in question in moving from one light source to another.

Colour constancy refers to the extent to which the appearance of an individual coloured article remains the same when viewed under different light sources, irrespective of the dyes used. *Metamerism*, on the other hand, refers to a change in the appearance of two

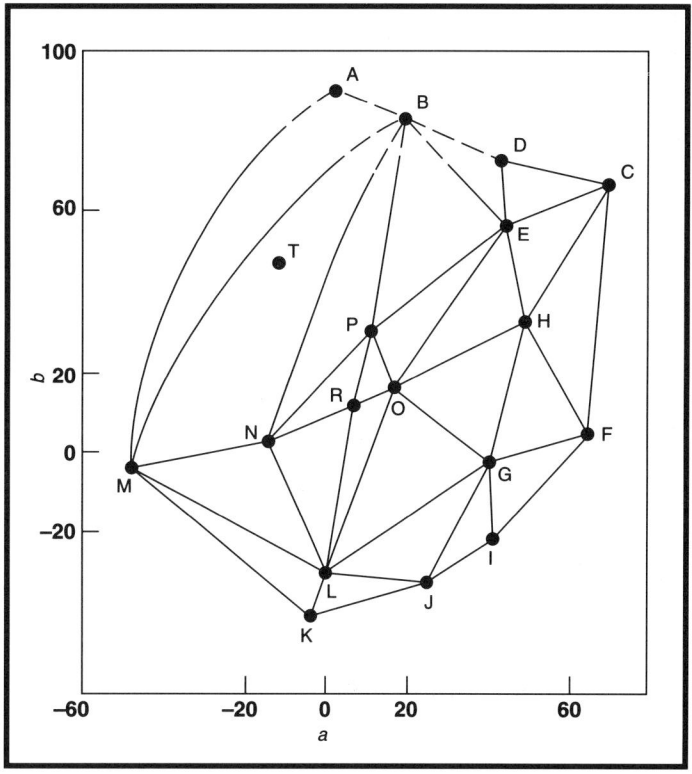

Figure 7.9 *Dye map for vat dyes on mercerised cotton (L planes 48–74)*

A	CI Vat Yellow 2	J	CI Vat Violet 21
B	CI Vat Yellow 12	K	CI Vat Blue 6
C	CI Vat Orange 7	L	CI Vat Blue 64
D	CI Vat Orange 15	M	CI Vat Green 1
E	CI Vat Orange 17	N	CI Vat Green 30
F	CI Vat Red 1	O	CI Vat Brown 1
G	CI Vat Red 13	P	CI Vat Brown 30
H	CI Vat Red 14	R	CI Vat Brown 49
I	CI Vat Violet 3		

patterns dyed with different dyes that have been matched under one light source, when they are viewed under a different source. It may be that the two patterns are no longer a match because, although they have identical visual appearances and tristimulus values under a specified illuminant, their reflectance curves are very different.

Both the perceived colour and the corresponding tristimulus values derived from the hypothetical standard observer are a function of a balance between the spectral qualities of the illuminant source and the wavelengths absorbed by the coloured object. Thus, if some wavelengths critical to the appearance of the colour viewed under one illuminant are missing in a second, they will not be present in the light reflected back to the observer. The reflectance spectrum of the pattern will then be deficient in these wavelengths and therefore the visual appearance of the colour will change in moving from one illuminant to another.

Although this *illuminant metamerism* is the most frequent in occurrence, other sources of discrepancy can arise from the slight differences that can exist in the colour vision of different observers (*observer metamerism*). Differences in appearance may also be a function of the angle of view (*geometric metamerism*) or of the changes in the area being viewed (*field size metamerism*). These are additional problems for the dyer who is formulating a recipe to provide the required match. They are also taken into consideration in matching through instrumental methods based on the CIE description of the position of a colour in colour space.

Colour match prediction

The significant success in the use of computer-aided colour matching is reflected by the confidence of the increasing number of dyers who plan to achieve 'first time' matches of the target shade. The systems used measure the reflectance of a pattern, convert the results into tristimulus values and synthesise a matched reflectance curve from stored reflectance data for the available dyes. As well as being influenced by the absorption properties of the dyes, the appearance of a woven fabric is also governed by the scatter of light from its surface. This in turn is controlled by other factors such as weave pattern, the fineness of the individual threads and their orientation with respect to the illuminating source.

The Kubelka–Munk equation

All these properties are embodied in the Kubelka–Munk analysis of the reflectance of a surface. The appropriate form of the equation for textile surfaces is given in Equation 7.6:

$$K/S = (1 - R)^2/2R \qquad (7.6)$$

where R is the reflectance of an infinitely thick layer of material illuminated with light of a known wavelength, K is the absorption coefficient and S is the scattering coefficient. The function K/S is directly proportional to the concentration of colorant in the substrate.

One of the properties of this relationship is that for a mixture of dyes the total value K/S may be calculated for any wavelength by summing the appropriate values for each dye. Thus for dyes of concentration c_1, c_2, and c_3, having absorption coefficients K_1, K_2 and K_3 respectively, the total K/S value is defined by Equation 7.7:

$$K/S = c_1(K_1/S_1) + c_2(K_2/S_2) + c_3(K_3/S_3) + K_s/S_s \qquad (7.7)$$

where the subscript s refers to the substrate.

The absorption characteristics for a range of dyes on a specified substrate over a range of visible wavelengths are measured. These data are stored in the computer memory for later use in calculating the proportion of each dye required to match the reflectance values of the pattern. Of course the ideal would be for the information to be made available for all wavelengths, but in fact the practical requirements may be adequately met by the use of 16 wavelengths spaced at 20 nm intervals throughout the visible spectrum.

Practical use of instrumental colour measurements

The X, Y and Z values of the shade required are used in the recipe prediction for matching shades. They can be fed into the computer together with reflectance information about the substrate. The stored absorption coefficients for the relevant dyes are called into play and the computer calculates the expected reflectance for each of the 16 wavelengths at given starting concentrations for the dyes used in the mixture. The result is converted into predicted X, Y and Z values; these are compared with the target values and the differences assessed. If the differences are too large, the program permits adjustment of the dye concentration for a further calculation. The process continues until the predicted X, Y and Z values are sufficiently close to the target values, at which stage the recipe is printed out.

Recipe correction

Although the ultimate aim is to provide a prediction that is 'right first time', it would be optimistic to expect any system to operate with consistent perfection. Colour matching is not an exact science, and there are many deviations from the theoretical concepts upon which instrumental colour matching are based. The systems used are in a perpetual state of development and refinement. Often unexpected variables may arise for which no account has been taken in the design of the operating program. It is easy to recognise contributory human errors in activities such as setting the operating parameters of the equipment or weighing the colour. These frequently have an easily identifiable cause, but the origin of other deviations can be more subtle and can call for careful refinement of operating procedures. For example, correction may be needed when the physical structure of the substrate is not identical to that used in the preliminary calculation. Furthermore, when applied at the calibration stage the dyes may behave differently from when they are applied in admixture, because of interaction with other dyes in the formulated recipe. Factors like these can give rise to differences between the actual and the computed results. Such differences may also occur when successful small-scale trials are scaled-up to full production, simply because of mechanical factors involved in dealing with a large bulk of material that cannot be foreseen from a small-scale trial.

Correcting bulk-scale dyeing is therefore another area in which computerised colour manipulation is of value. Instrumental measurements are able to provide values for the differences between the X, Y and Z values of the dyed and target patterns; these are then used to calculate a recipe suitable for making good the deficit.

Other applications

The information available within a commercial colour-matching system is not confined to the production of the final shade. It also enables the most economical route to the target to be established through sorting procedures, and similar principles are involved in predicting the likely degree of metamerism and colour constancy. Other relevant technical information may be stored for use in aiding the preliminary dye selection. Thus fastness properties, stability of the dye recipe, level-dyeing characteristics and the effect of pH and electrolyte may all be catalogued for easy reference and use at the appropriate stage of the operation. Relevant statistical information is also updated automatically, thus aiding inventory control and other management functions

Monitoring the quality of the colour of dyed fabric is a critical matter in clothing factories. It is not unusual for the dyed fabric to arrive from different sources, and even slight variations will become more obvious if they appear on adjacent panels of the assembled garment. Difficulties of this kind are therefore circumvented by grouping dye lots into closely matching batches through the application of colour-difference formulae. This is another area where the subjective nature of conventional visual inspection is being replaced. Colour-difference measurements have also become a valuable tool in pass/fail systems in which coloured articles are compared instrumentally against prescribed colour tolerances.

Whiteness and yellowness

Whiteness suggests cleanliness and freedom from contamination and as such it is taken as an indicator of quality. Nevertheless, objective measurement and meaningful numerical expression of the condition has proved technically complex. The CIE expression for a *whiteness index* has been available, in the form of Equation 7.8, only since 1982. It represents whiteness in terms of colorimetric values for the specimen and the chromaticity coordinates of the illuminant:

$$W = Y + 800(x_n - x) = 1700(y_n - y) \qquad (7.8)$$

where x, y and Y are the colorimetric values for the specimen under a specified form of illuminant D, and x_n and y_n are the chromaticity coordinates of the light source. A value for W of 100 represents a perfect reflecting diffuser.

Treatment with fluorescent brightening agents can lead to reflectance values of up to 150. Although the pattern appears to become whiter, the change in appearance is due to a change in chroma towards blue, and this fact is expressed in quantitative form as the 'tint factor'.

Allied to the appearance of the uncoloured fabric is the yellowness, which suggests scorching, or degradation by light or by gases. Various scales for yellowness have been devised in an attempt to establish a yardstick by which undyed fabric can be assessed for quality.

Clearly, colour measurement is becoming of even greater importance in defining the quality of the appearance of textiles. Computer-aided dye selection is just one area in which modern methods are aiding the rapid response of the manufacturer to the demands of the market.

References

1.   *Colour terms and definitions* (Bradford: SDC, 1988).
2.   *Munsell book of color* (Newburgh, NY: Munsell Colour Co.).
3.   *Colour physics for industry*, Ed. R McDonald, (Bradford, SDC, 1987) 211.
4.   K McLaren, *The colour science of dyes and pigments* (2nd Edn) (Bristol: Adam Hilger, 1986).

CHAPTER EIGHT

Practical notes

Coloration on the small scale

In practical dyeing, even on a small and experimental scale, patience is usually necessary to produce a satisfactory result. Simply dissolving the dye in the water and entering the goods is almost certain to result in disappointment, which may easily be avoided by taking a few simple precautions.

Wetting out the fabric

Whatever the scale of the operation, it is essential to ensure that there is an even distribution of dyebath auxiliaries in the fibre mass. For this reason it is generally best to allow the goods to soak in the bath with all the ingredients except the dye for about 5–10 minutes at 40–45 °C, before adding the dye. This procedure is referred to as *wetting out*.

The dye can then be added in portions with vigorous stirring. Better still, the goods can be removed whilst the dye is added and mixed into the liquor, and the goods are then re-entered. Dyeing can then begin.

Adequate movement of dye liquor

A steady flow of dye liquor through the goods during dyeing is essential for the production of a level dyeing. Exhaustion in localised areas leads to unlevel dyeing. A uniform distribution of dye is best obtained by ensuring that the liquor does not at any time become stagnant within or around the fabric. The bath should therefore be constantly stirred throughout the operation, or the fabric or yarn moved within the dyebath; the latter arrangement is adopted in most laboratory dyeing machines.

Where specially designed laboratory dyeing equipment for small-scale dyeings is not available, this movement of liquor between dye and fibre is best achieved by constantly moving the fabric up and down in the liquor. If there is sufficient fabric to form a closed loop, then a support can be provided over the top of the dyebath around which the fabric can be moved by lifting a section and allowing it to fall forward over the support and into the dye liquor. By repeating the process the liquor is kept circulating over the fabric.

A similar system may be adopted for dyeing yarn. For the purposes of craft dyeing, yarn is best dyed in hank form and a similar system for moving the hank may be adopted. Figure 8.1 shows the yarn looped over a bent glass rod, the latter being so positioned that the top of the hank is always just immersed in the liquid. The yarn may then be lifted and moved forward a few inches at a time over the support.

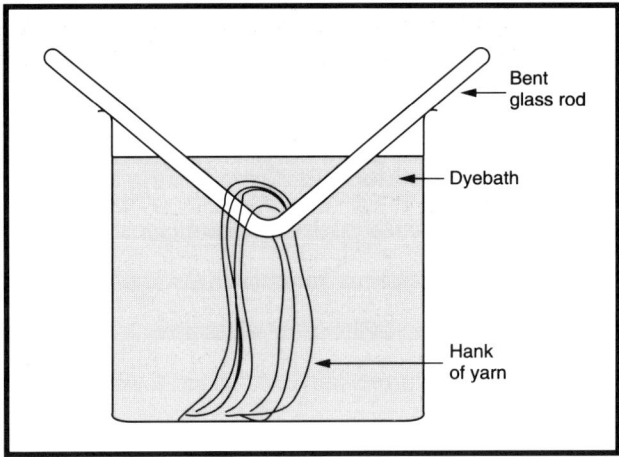

Figure 8.1 *Yarn dyeing on a small scale*

Liquor ratio

The intensity of the colour produced by a given mass of dye on a given mass of fabric is dependent upon the total volume of the dyebath used, that is, on the liquor ratio (see page 95). For the best reproducibility of the dyeing it is advisable to keep the volume of the dyebath constant, adding water occasionally to replace that lost through evaporation. The easiest way of keeping check on the volume is to put a mark on the side of the container with a water-resistant marker or wax pencil at the starting level of the liquid.

Depth of shade and dyebath composition

The depth of colour applied is expressed as a percentage on the dry weight of the fibre (o.w.f.) to be dyed. Care must be taken to avoid confusion between the percentage depth of shade and the percentage composition of the solution. The latter refers specifically to the concentration of the stock solution and not to the composition of the dyebath.

A recipe may indicate that a 1% shade is required and that 10% Glauber's salt should be added to the dyebath to promote exhaustion. These details mean that for every 100 g of fibre 1 g of dye and 10 g of Glauber's salt must be present in the dyebath, irrespective of the total volume of the dyebath. It does *not* mean that the fibres are to be dyed in a 1% solution of dye containing 10% of Glauber's salt.

The required total volume of the dyebath is calculated from the intended liquor ratio, which for craft purposes is likely to fall within the range of 30:1 to 100:1.

It is possible of course to weigh out the requisite amount of dye and dissolve it before starting the dyeing. For small-scale operations, however, the amounts required may be too small to weigh out accurately, making it difficult to repeat the procedure with any degree of precision. For example, a 0.5% shade for 5.0 g of fibre requires 0.025 g of dye.

In such cases stock solutions of dyes and other ingredients are prepared as described above and the required volumes measured out accurately into the dyebath. For example, 1 g of dye dissolved in 200 cm^3 of water gives a 0.5% stock solution. For each 1 g of fibre, 0.01 g of dye is required to provide a 1% shade (o.w.f.); 0.01 g of dye is contained in 2 cm^3 of stock solution. Therefore for every 1 g of fibre, 2 cm^3 of stock solution will be required to produce a 1% shade. The same reasoning applies to other additives; for example, the composition of 10% Glauber's salt, based on the mass of fibre, is calculated in the same way as a 10% shade of dye.

The general formula shown in Equation 8.1 may be used for representing the amount of stock dye solution required:

$$V = \frac{D \times W}{C} \tag{8.1}$$

where V is the volume of stock solution required (in cm^3), D is the percentage applied depth of dye or additive, W is the mass of fibre (in g) and C is the percentage composition of stock solution. Thus to produce a 3% shade of dye, on 4 g of yarn, the volume of a 0.5% stock solution of dye required is $(3 \times 4)/0.5 = 24$ cm^3.

In this way the required volumes of dye solution and other additives may be calculated, added together and subtracted from the total volume of dyebath to obtain the amount of water required.

Preparing stock solutions

The first step in the preparation of stock solutions is to dissolve the dye in the appropriate amount of water. With water-soluble dyes it is sensible to use warm water and sprinkle the dye powder slowly from a spatula or from the centre of a small piece of folded paper into the water, stirring meanwhile. This avoids the formation of sticky clumps of dye particles that are difficult to dissolve. All the water-soluble dyes, except reactive dyes, can be readily dissolved by bringing the dyebath to the boil for a few seconds and then allowing to cool. With reactive dyes such treatment may cause some premature hydrolysis, but in any case these dyes are generally quite soluble in water and boiling is unnecessary.

As we have seen, dyes form colloidal solutions. On standing for long periods these may become unstable and some dye may settle out at the bottom of the container. It is always advisable therefore to invert the bottle of dye solution several times or stir the solutions before taking a sample. With some dyes, including milling acid dyes and direct dyes, it may be necessary to heat up the solution again.

The situation with disperse and vat dyes is different. Dispersions of these dyes are best prepared by adding a little warm water to the powder and mixing thoroughly into a paste using a glass rod, before adding the rest of the water with constant stirring.

Labelling the samples

It is always advisable to label the goods to be dyed before starting a range of dyeing experiments. For yarn samples this is best done by threading a piece of string through the hank, tying a knot to form an open loop and then numbering the yarn sample by tying simple knots in the loose ends of the string according to the number of the hank. Counting the number of knots will then serve to identify the sample after it has been removed from the dyebath and washed.

Samples of fabric may be labelled by making a small fold at one end, folding again in the opposite direction and cutting the corner. This produces a small hole. The sample may therefore be labelled according to the number of holes cut in this way. Alternatively the fabric can be marked with an indelible marker. Such markers are often used in industrial laboratories [1].

Coloration experiments

Selectivity of dye adsorption

It is relatively easy to demonstrate the selective nature of the adsorption of dyes by specific fibres. If sets of fibres, including cotton, nylon, polyester and acetate, are carefully labelled and dyed together in each of three separate dyebaths containing a levelling acid dye, a direct and a disperse dye respectively, effects resulting from the different substantivity of each dye–fibre combination will become apparent. The results will indicate how special effects can be obtained when fibre blends are dyed, particularly if the different dye classes chosen are applied from the same bath.

Shirlastains

Shirlastains are used in the identification of unknown fibres [2], and as such they provide a good example of a practical application of the selective substantivity of dyes for fibres. The stains, which are used for undyed fibres only, contain appropriately selected dyes that will impart a characteristic colour to each different fibre type. There are four different Shirlastains, labelled A, C, D and E. As well as differentiating between different chemical types of fibre, some of the four stains are formulated to differentiate between fibres of the same chemical type but of different origins.

Shirlastain A serves to identify non-thermoplastic fibres – in practice, natural fibres and regenerated cellulosic fibres: for example, cotton gives a pale purple colour, viscose rayon (regenerated cellulose) pink and silk a dark brown. Shirlastain C provides a clearer distinction between the different types of cellulosic fibre. Shirlastain D is more specific, and distinguishes between cotton and spun viscoses. Shirlastain E provides distinctive colours for the various thermoplastic fibres.

Multifibre strip

The preparation of known fibres stained with the appropriate colorants is recommended to confirm the colours obtained with Shirlastains using the unknown sample. For this purpose a multifibre fabric strip is available [3], into which bands of all the common fibres have been woven in a defined sequence. It is therefore possible to produce the appropriate colours by dyeing a fresh sample of the strip in each of the stains. The multifibre strip is also a convenient and useful substrate for illustrating the differing substantivities of the different dye classes for different fibre types. Its incorporation into wet fastness tests as an 'adjacent fabric' will also indicate the likely level of staining of other fabrics. The strip contains secondary cellulose acetate (Dicel), bleached unmercerised cotton, nylon 6.6, polyester, acrylic (Courtelle) and wool worsted.

There is no difficulty in finding books dealing with the practical aspects of coloration on the craft scale. Theoretical concepts together with dyeing and related experiments are to be found elsewhere [4]. A further good example, intended specifically to meet the small-scale experimental needs of the DIY enthusiast, also deals clearly with the different application classes of dye used in industrial coloration [5]. This text indicates how to set about shade formulation and the production of specific effects. Since the same dyes and ingredients available to the coloration industry are used in the experiments described therein, the publication is particularly relevant to the commercial application methods described in Chapter 6. It also embodies detailed precautions for safe working when carrying out coloration on a small scale.

All the chemicals and dyes required may be obtained in suitable quantities for the small-scale worker from specialist suppliers, who package and supply commercial dyes, appropriate chemicals and technical information [6].

Colour physics systems

One development that stems from the application of colour physics to modern colour specification (Chapter 7) has appeared in a form useful to small-scale printing operations, such as the printing of designs for tee-shirts and sweatshirts. It is called the Pantone Colour Matching System. In essence nine basic colour standards have been chosen from a range of colorants, together with a suitable white and black. They are presented alongside a colour reference system that consists of coloured chips and formulations for almost 750 colours, which can be increased to 1000 by the use of additional pigments, thus saving the printer considerable time and effort in shade formulation.

In effect, the system is based on a colour space and is widely used for the selection, presentation, communication and matching control of colour. It is serviced by an international network of companies registered with the producers of the system.

Readily available condensed ranges of colorants capable of producing a broad colour gamut have also been devised for use by the small-scale worker. Whilst the representation of the possible colours are not specified using colour coordinates, there is a back-up colour-matching service for the user [7].

Examination of fabrics

It is not always easy to obtain fabric of known finishing history on which to carry out straightforward examinations into the quality of colour, but various textiles, and other goods incorporating textiles in their construction, can usually be tracked down for use in demonstrations. Various published articles, for example, on the use of textiles in footwear [8], furnishing fabrics [9–12] and motor car upholstery [13,14] provide background information concerning the consumer expectations from the appropriate materials.

Thus materials obtained from old seat covers, canvas shoes and discarded clothing can provide a useful indication of how well the colour and the fibres from various parts of the goods have stood up to wear and tear. Opening the seams of an old jacket or removing the lining will enable the unexposed side of the fabric to be compared with the outside, thus showing the extent to which the colours have faded.

Washing tests (see below) may also be carried out on the best preserved areas of the fabric, according to the recommendations given elsewhere [15], to provide an assessment of the different levels of fastness inherent in the coloured goods. Such experiments also enable the effects of aftercare conditions to be established, covering tests of varying severity that do and do not match those suggested by the aftercare labels on the goods.

Fastness to washing

The conditions of standard tests for the fastness of dyes to washing, and the procedures for assessing and presenting the results are published in the relevant standards [15] and briefly outlined in Chapter 1 (page 11).

Further information about the effects of fastness tests on other fabric properties may be readily obtained using separate pieces of fabric. For example, the effects of wet treatments on length and area shrinkage may be investigated by indelibly marking pieces of fabric [16].

Other wet fastness tests

A wide variety of other wet fastness tests can be carried out using simple equipment, such as water spotting, fastness to salt water, effect of acids (such as vinegar and battery acid), alkalis and so on. Relevant details are to be found elsewhere [15].

Fastness to light

Reliable testing of light fastness is a complex subject but the relative effects of the various regions of daylight spectrum that cause fading may be obtained by exposing samples of the same fabrics, side by side under identical conditions, at 45° to north daylight, behind appropriate filters. Filters are available from several suppliers [17], and relevant background information can be found in the *Journal of the Society of Dyers and Colourists* [18]. The experiments are usually carried out under conditions of known humidity, which for small samples can be controlled by including a saturated solution of the appropriate salt in the enclosed container alongside the pattern [19]. This will not of course control the temperature of the pattern, which will vary according to the intensity of the illumination, but it will show the effects of gross differences by exposure in a desiccated atmosphere and in one of high humidity.

Construction of textiles

Those with an interest in the construction of textile articles will also find assistance in the British Standards for stitch types [20] and seam construction [21]. Similar experiments may be extended to samples of carpet, for example, by studying the effects of water and shampoo used to remove stains such as coffee, tea, wine, etc.

References

1.   Dalo markers (Decon Laboratories, Hove, Sussex, UK).
2.   Shirlastains (Shirley Developments Ltd, Didsbury, Manchester, UK).
3.   Multifibre strip (SDC, Bradford, UK)
4.   D G Duff and R S Sinclair, *Giles's laboratory course in dyeing*, 4th Edn (Bradford: SDC, 1990).
5.   F Thompson and T Thompson, *Synthetic dyeing* (Newton Abbott, Devon: David and Charles, 1987).
6.   Dyestuffs (Hays Colours Ltd, London SE15, UK).
7.   Colour specification system (Brittons Printing Inks Ltd, Herne Bay, Kent, UK).
8.   *Text. Horizons*, (Dec 1985) 46.
9.   E Lowe, *Text. Horizons*, (June 1989) 61.
10.   E Lowe, *Text. Horizons*, (June 1985) 32.
11.   D Morley, *Textiles*, **17** (3) (1988) 75.
12.   *Text. Horizons*, (Aug 1985) 43.
13.   B Milligan, *Rev. Prog. Coloration*, **16** (1986) 1.
14.   K Czelny, *Text. Horizons*, (June 1985) 28.
15.   BS 1006 (Bradford: SDC, 1990).
16.   BS 4923, BS 1955, BS 4600, BS 4204, BS 4736.
17.   Colour filters (Philip Harris Ltd, Lichfield, Staffordshire; Nes Arnold Ltd, West Bridgford, Nottingham).
18.   K McLaren, *J.S.D.C.*, **72** (1956) 86.
19.   G W C Kaye and T H Laby, *Tables of physical and chemical constants* (14th Edn) (1973), 28
20.   BS 3870, Part 1 (ISO 4915).
21.   BS 3870, Part 2 (ISO 4916).

Some examples of commercial dyes

Acid dyes

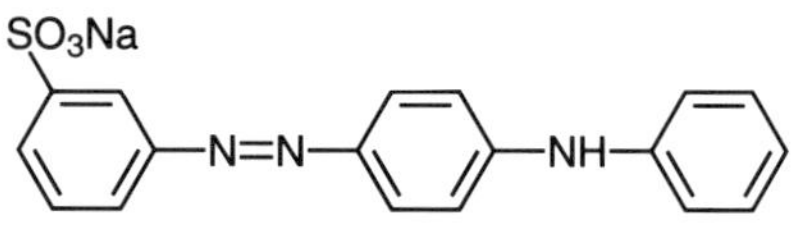

1   CI Acid Yellow 36

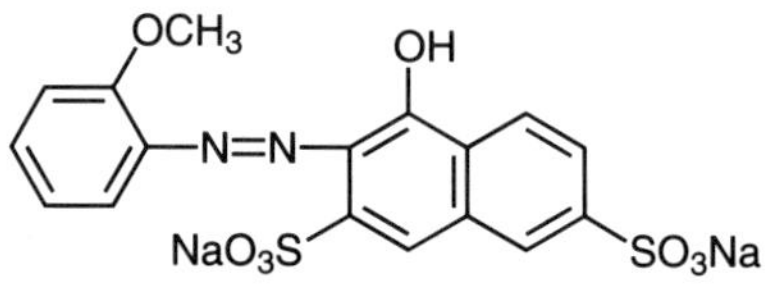

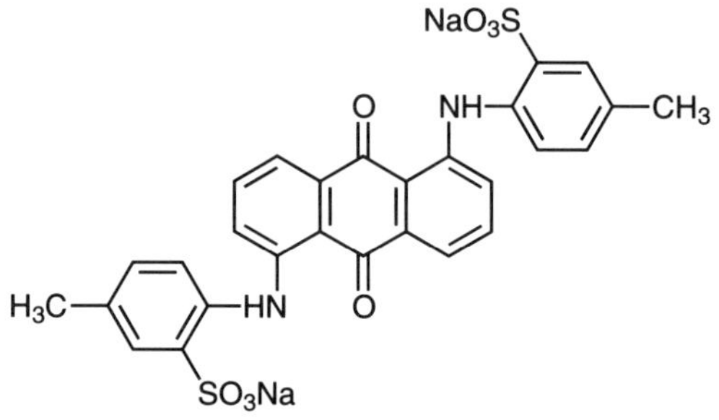

4   CI Acid Violet 34

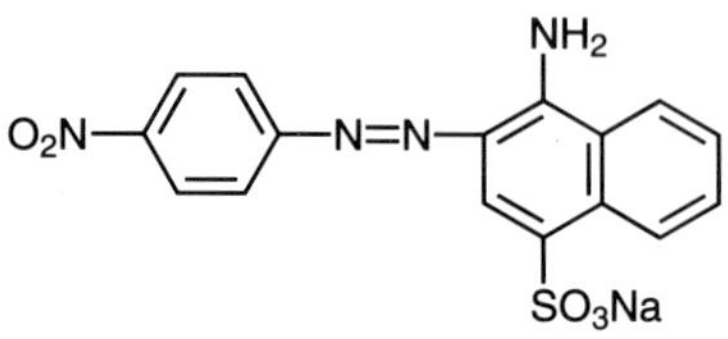

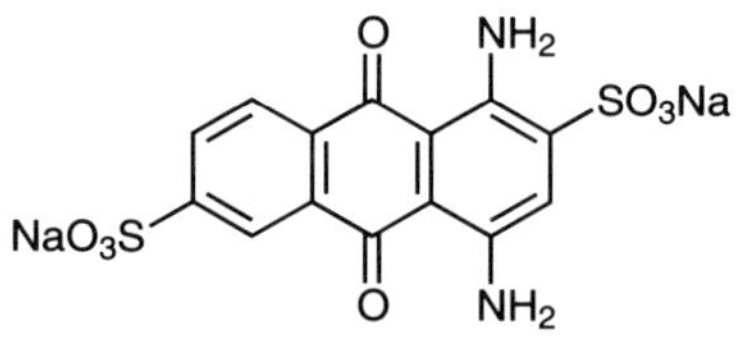

2   CI Acid Red 5

5   CI Acid Blue 56

3   CI Acid Red 74

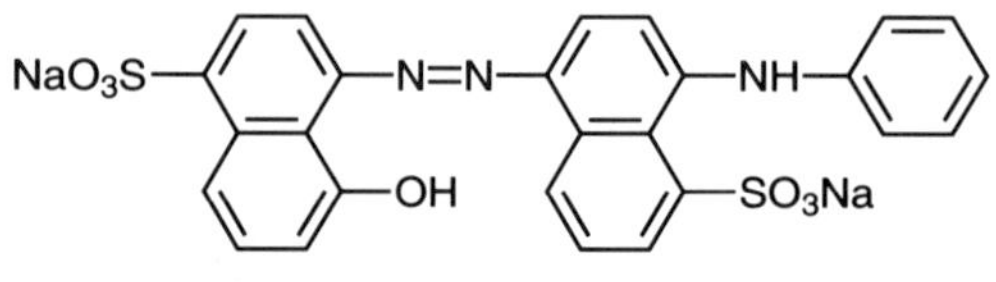

6   CI Acid Blue 135

Direct dyes

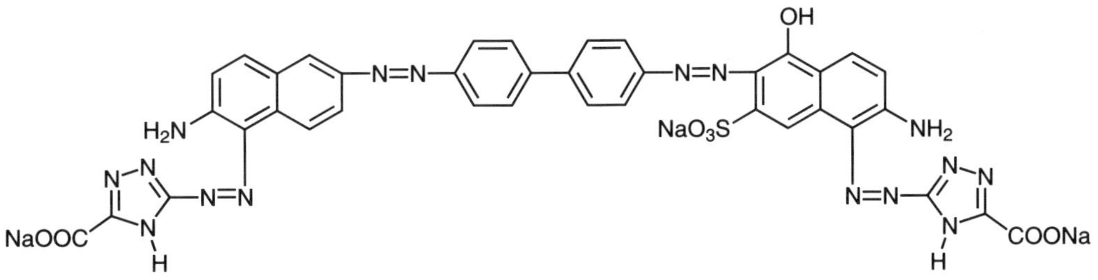

7 CI Direct Blue 150

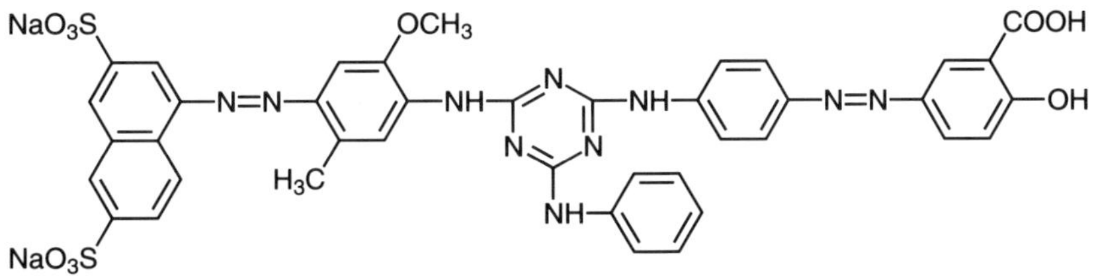

8 CI Direct Green 26

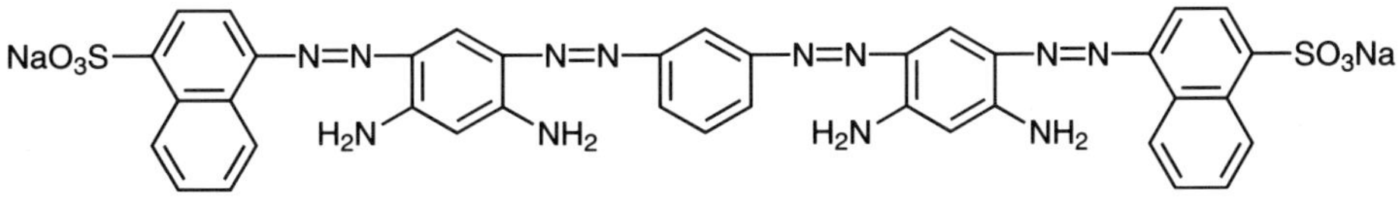

9 CI Direct Brown 44

Disperse dyes

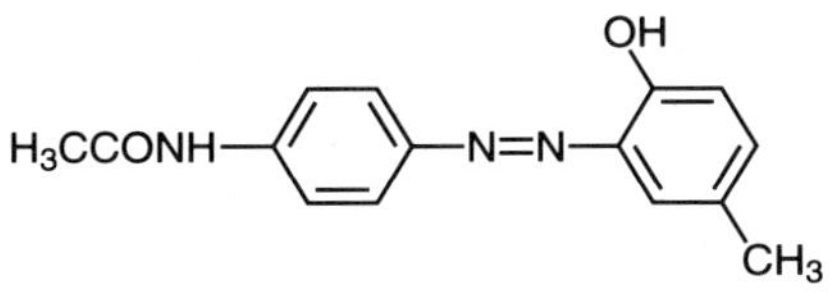

10 CI Disperse Yellow 3

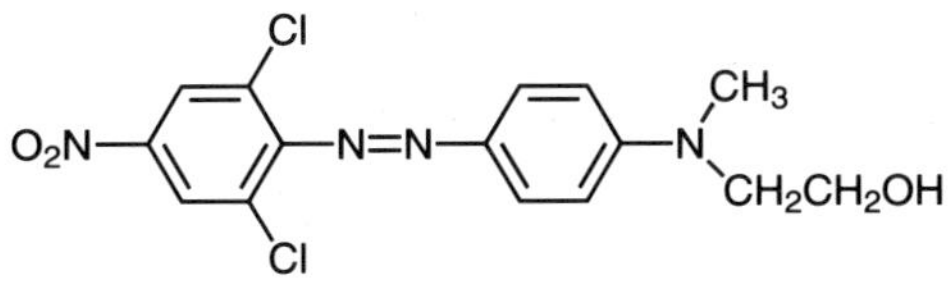

11 CI Disperse Orange 5

12   CI Disperse Orange 11

13   CI Disperse Blue 19

Vat dyes

14   CI Vat Yellow 3

16   CI Vat Red 48

15   CI Vat Orange 9

17   CI Vat Violet 15

Basic dyes

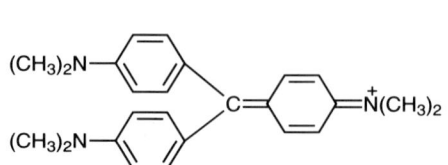

18   CI Basic Violet 2

19   CI Basic Violet 3

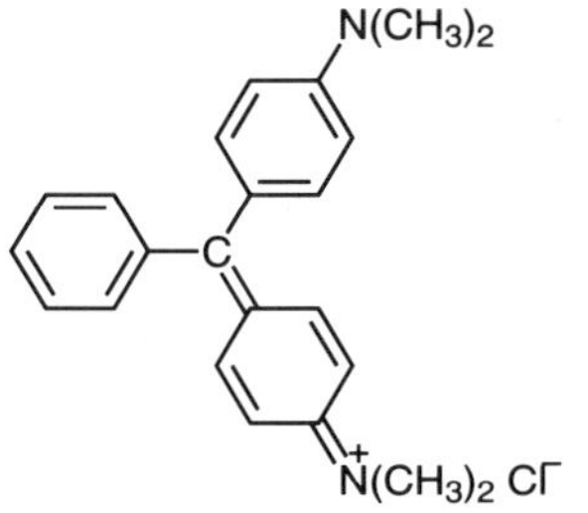

20   CI Basic Blue 1

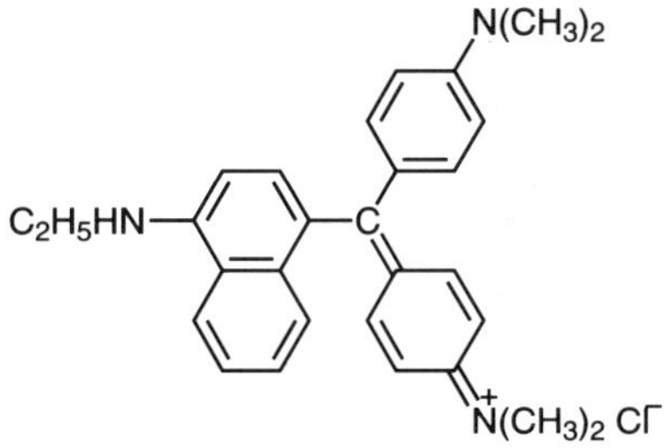

21   CI Basic Blue 11

Pigments

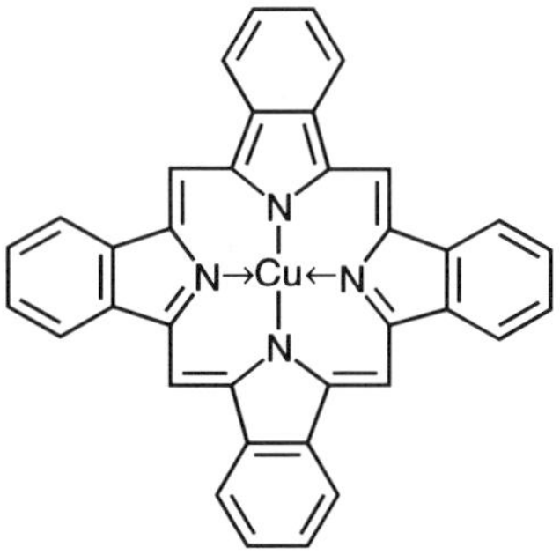

22   CI Pigment Blue 15
(copper phthalocyanine)

Azoic coupling components

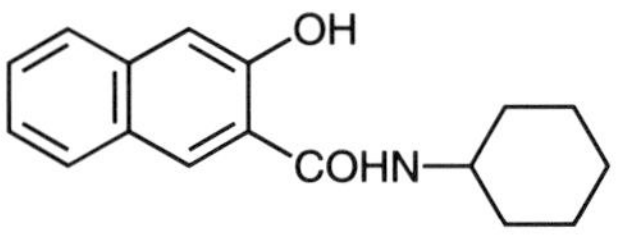

23   CI Azoic Coupling Component 2

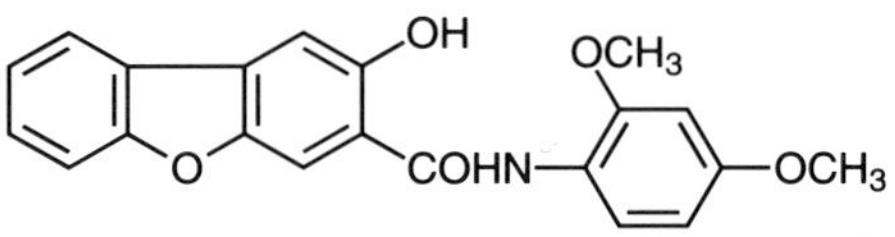

25   CI Azoic Coupling Component 16

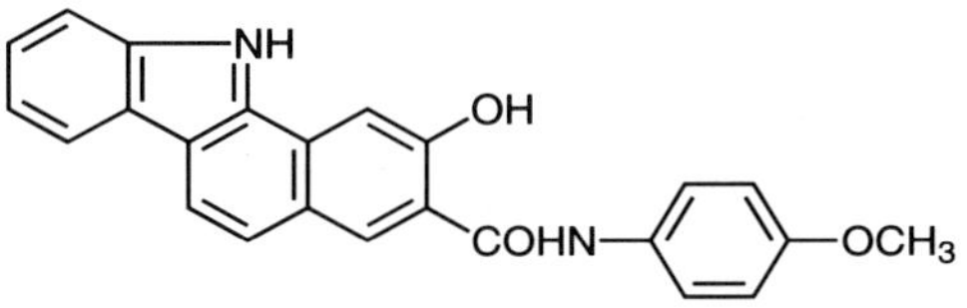

24   CI Azoic Coupling Component 13

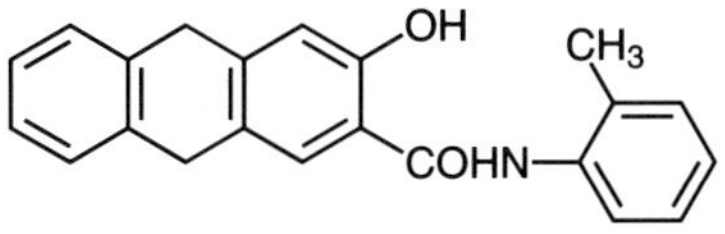

26   CI Azoic Coupling Component 36

Diazo components

27   CI Diazo Component 2

29   CI Diazo Component 5

28   CI Diazo Component 4

30   CI Diazo Component 36

Generic names of synthetic fibres

Generic name	Chemical constitution	Trade names	Country of origin
Acetate	Cellulose secondary ethanoate (between 74% and 92% cellulose hydroxyl groups ethanoylated)	Albene Celanese Dicel Estron	Germany UK UK USA
Triacetate	Cellulose triethanoate (at least 92% cellulosic hydroxyl groups ethanoylated)	Arnel Tricel Trilan	USA UK Canada
Acrylic	Poly(propenonitrile) (polyacrylonitrile) with small amounts of a comonomer	Courtelle Dralon Leacryl Nitron Orlon 42 (staple)	UK Germany Italy USSR USA
Modacrylic	Poly(propenonitrile) (polyacrylonitrile) containing < 85% but > 50% of propenonitrile by mass	BHS Creslan Lycra PAN Teklan	UK USA Germany UK
Cupro	Cellulose (regenerated from cellulose dissolved in cuprammonium hydroxide)	Bemberg Cuprama	 Germany
Modal	Cellulose (regenerated, made by high-wet-modulus process)	Vincel Hypolan	UK Japan
Viscose	Cellulose (regenerated by the viscose process)	Fibro Sarille Tenasco	UK UK UK

Generic name	Chemical constitution	Trade names	Country of origin
Nylon	Polyamide	Astron	USA
	Nylon 6.6 (stretch nylon)	Ban-Lon	USA
		BriNylon	UK
	Nylon 6	Akulon	Holland
		Amilen	Japan
		Carpolan	USA
		Enkalon	USA
		Grillon	Japan
		Perlon	Germany
	Nylon 11	Rislan	France
Polyester	Poly(ethylene terephthalate)	Crimplene	UK
		Dacron	USA
		Enkalen	Holland
		Lavsan	USSR
		Mylar (clear film)	USA
		Tergal	France
		Terlenka	Holland
		Terylene	UK
		Trevira	Germany
Polyethylene	Poly(ethene)	Boltathene	USA
		Courlene	UK
Polypropylene	Poly(propene)	Meraklon	Italy
		Monolene	Canada
		Polyfilene	USA
		Prolene	USA
		Ulstron	UK
Chlorofibre	At least 50% by mass of of poly(vinyl chloride) (poly(chloroethene)) or poly(vinylidene chloride) (poly(1,1-dichloroethene))	Rhovyl Saran Tygan	France USA UK

Index